SYSTEMS
OF
SOCIAL
REGULATION

THE AUTHOR

ELAINE CUMMING is Director of the Albany Mental Health Research Unit of the New York State Department of Mental Hygiene and Adjunct Professor of Sociology at the State University of New York at Albany. She received her B.A. and M.A. from the University of Saskatchewan and her Ph.D. from Harvard. Her research into varying aspects of social deviance and social control has been conducted with the Psychiatric Services Branch of the Saskatchewan Department of Health, with Cornell University under a joint appointment to the Department of Psychiatry and the Department of Sociology and Anthropology, and with the University of Chicago's Committee on Human Development.

Professor Cumming is a Fellow of both the American Sociological Association and the American Public Health Association, as well as a member of the American Psychological Association. With William E. Henry she is co-author of *Growing Old* and with John Cumming of *Closed Ranks: An Experiment in Mental Health Education* and *Ego and Milieu: The Theory and Practice of Environmental Therapy*. She has written extensively for professional journals and has served as a consultant to a variety of institutions.

ATHERTON PRESS • *New York* • 1968

SYSTEMS
OF
SOCIAL
REGULATION

Elaine Cumming

WITH THE ASSISTANCE OF
CLAIRE RUDOLPH AND
LAURA EDELL

In Memory of

KASPAR DAVID NAEGELE

Friend and Colleague

Address all inquiries to:
Atherton Press, Inc.
70 Fifth Avenue
New York 10011

Library of Congress Catalog Card Number 68-16406

FIRST EDITION

Manufactured in the United States of America
Designed by JoAnn Randel

PREFACE

The studies reported in this book were sponsored by the Mental Health Research Unit of the Department of Mental Hygiene of the State of New York, and they were supported in part by Grant Number MH 04735 from the National Institute of Mental Health.

A great number of people helped to carry out the research reported here, and they are acknowledged in the appropriate chapters; major contributions to data processing were made by Patricia Healy, Robert Porter, and Charles Eysaman. I am particularly grateful to my two assistants, Claire Rudolph and Laura Edell, who, between them, worked with me from the beginning to the end of what turned out to be a six-year process, but I alone am responsible for the contents of this report. A number of people read the manuscript or parts of it at various stages and provided important criticisms; these include James A. Davis, James Robb, Nils Christie, Douglas Bennett, Rhondda Cassetta, and the Reverend Charles J. Fahey. I am, as always, grateful to John Cumming for his unfailing help and encouragement.

The real heroes of this book are the staffs of the study agencies who so generously revealed their practices to our field workers. Although they are thanked individually in the appropriate chapters, I cannot overemphasize their contribution.

The production of the manuscript was a difficult and often irritating task because of the number and complexity of the tables; Beverley Galtieri, Mary Ellen Mathews, Jean Thornton, and Marjorie Johnston did the greatest portion of this work. Marcia David helped with all of the calculations in Part III and acted as production assistant in the final phases of the writing. I am particularly indebted to these people not only for the quality of their work but also for their unfailing cheerfulness.

Chapters 3, 8, and 14 contain material that has appeared in somewhat different forms in *Trans-Action, The American Journal of Sociology,* and *Social Problems.* A report based on the material in Part III appeared in the *Journal of the American Public Health Association.* I am grateful for permission from these journals to paraphrase these materials.

CONTENTS

II THE REGULATIVE SYSTEM

III THE POPULATION AND ITS PROBLEMS

I

The Regulative Agents

This study concerns the systematic regulation of social behavior. It reports a series of studies of the ways in which doctors, clergymen, policemen, welfare officers, psychiatrists, social workers, and other social agents divide the task of maintaining social order. Part I discusses the general problem of order, sets it in a theoretical perspective, and then describes, in terms of this perspective, a series of regulative agents and the encounters between them and the people approaching them. Part II discusses the regulative system taken as a whole and examines the relationships among its various elements, and Part III focuses upon the kinds of problems that the members of the regulative system must solve.

THE PROCESS OF SOCIAL
REGULATION

1

The General Problem of Order

Social order is defined here as that state of affairs in which it is possible to predict with reasonable accuracy what other people will do in routine situations. The nature of the order may change, but a range of behavior at once acceptable and predictable is imperative if any society, whether a large one like a nation, or small like a family, is to survive.

Social survival can be considered in terms of four standing problems that must continually be solved (Parsons, 1960). First, there is the problem of adapting to the environment, both physical and human—that is, food and shelter must be produced and danger fended off. Second, goals must be identified clearly enough to ensure some agreement about what the members should be doing day by day. Third, some method of inculcating in the young and reinforcing in the mature the values and moral codes that enlighten and control everyday behavior must be agreed upon; and fourth, the problem of coherence, or the integration of the different elements of a society, must be solved if the whole is to be more than the sum of the parts.

When social roles are specifically designed to forward society's goals by adaptation to the environment, they are called instrumental; when they are designed to regulate relationships among the members or to maintain acceptable standards of conduct, they are called socioemotional (Bales, 1953). It is on these latter roles, specifically designed to maintain the internal order of society, that this report is concentrated.

Informal versus Formal Social Regulation

INFORMAL REGULATION

Social order arises, in a sense, from a permanent running compromise between constraint and freedom, between the interest of the individual and the goals of society (Shils, 1956). This compromise takes place informally wherever people interact, and it is possible only because most people most of the time are willing to place themselves under one another's control and to submit to many kinds of correctives. Without this willingness, the problem of social integration could not be solved. It is assumed that although everyone learns to submit to the control of others, there remain, even among the most conforming, fleeting tendencies toward unpredictable or unacceptable behavior that arise from ignorance, error, incomplete learning of the rules, or circumstances beyond human control. Most illness, for example, is unintended, but it is in a sense unacceptable because it disrupts the orderly carrying out of social obligations. Mental illness, although still unintended, is even less acceptable because it raises possibilities of the unpredictable as well as the disruptive. Crime, unlike illness, appears to be willful, and therefore it is totally unacceptable because it is both disruptive and morally wrong. The criminal act, in other words, holds the moral order in contempt and symbolizes the possibility that society may lose its hold on its members.

In everyday life we monitor one another constantly, and this monitoring maintains predictability in face-to-face interactions. The very fact of being watched is a constraint against certain kinds of actions. A lifted eyebrow, a sharp word, an eloquent absence, a hovering presence—all these symbols control behavior.* Parsons' shorthand phrase for it is "ego's role expectations are alter's sanctions," which means that whenever two people (the smallest possible society) meet, the expectation each has of the other will exert a control over the other's behavior. Furthermore, the situation in itself is a source of control. As Naegele (1961) says, "Even a child knows that a church and a department store, a doctor's office and a wading pool, a home and a hotel stand for characteristically different courses of conduct." Whenever people care what others think of their actions they are under social control, even if, as often happens, those others are distant, either in time or place (Parsons, 1953).

Informal controls are most complex and binding in groupings like families whose members cannot escape from one another. They are simpler and less binding among strangers, who can choose to leave the group (Lemert, 1964). Even among strangers, however, informal controls are surprisingly potent; in a public waiting room, the newcomer scans those already there for clues about how to proceed, and even in a foreign country it is not too hard to take hints about what may not be done. In everyday life, furthermore, people whose jobs are not directly concerned with social regulation often engage in it; bartenders and beauticians get accustomed to supplying advice and counsel to some of their clients.

FORMAL REGULATION

Informal regulation alone cannot maintain order in soci-

* For the detailed exegesis of this point, see Parsons (1951); for a theory of how this sensitivity is learned, see Parsons *et al.* (1955).

eties complicated enough for groups to have conflicting goals and for individuals to become alienated from all or part of the social order, and hence unable or unwilling to abide by its norms. In such situations, informal controls are supplemented with formal ones; many implicit rules become codified, and relatively private sanctions are supplemented by relatively public ones. When large social groupings, rather than individuals or families, must have their interests reconciled and their activities brought into harmony, religious, political, and other regulatory and integrative institutions become involved. When individuals rather than groups escape from the informal control of their fellows, either because their disorders are refractory to everyday control or because special resources or skills are required to handle them, formal institutionalized controls can be brought to bear in the name of social order by doctors, social workers, policemen, and so on. All complex modern societies have a proliferation of agents and agencies charged with the social control of individuals; the response of these agents to those applying to them for service, the relationships among these agents, and the kinds of problems they must solve are the subjects of the studies reported here.

Support versus Control

GENERAL FRAME OF REFERENCE

Any act of social regulation, formal or informal, can be classified as relatively supportive or relatively controlling. In this view, support has the diffusely positive quality of encouragement or reward; it is offered to the individual to keep him performing acceptably, or, when necessary, to persuade him to return to conformity. Control always has at least the overtones of punishment; it is meant to suppress or isolate disruptive behavior or to enforce prescribed behavior in the interest of the common good.

It is difficult for anyone to offer both support and control simultaneously. In the world of informal sanctions, supportive and controlling acts tend to be strung out in time—the mother scolds the child, and *then* she forgives him and comforts him. When both support and control are offered at once, the recipient is said to be in a "bind," not knowing where he stands (Bateson *et al.,* 1956). Such contradictory messages are not infrequent in everyday interaction among people who know one another well, but they can be so frustrating that they tend to disrupt rather than regulate the flow of social events. In most social relationships, the expectations that act as controls tend to have their supporting side uppermost, with the potentiality of a more controlling sanction held latent. Everyday friendliness and responsiveness only turn to disapproval and coldness when expectations are badly upset.

While it is difficult to perform individual acts of support and control simultaneously, support without potential control is overprotection and invites passivity or manipulation, while control without potential support is tyranny and invites rebellion or despair. Furthermore, any society that tried to eliminate control would end in unpredictability and chaos, and one that tried to eliminate support would be decimated by the isolation or expulsion of its members. Both elements are essential to social regulation, the one affirming the individual; the other, the social order.

In the formal system, it is more difficult for the specialized agent to be at once overtly supportive and controlling because support and control require different skills. Furthermore, to be at once on the client's side and on the side of society can involve intolerable role strain (Davis, 1938; Goode, 1960). The difficulty of performing contradictory acts and adopting conflicting attitudes is one reason agents and agencies tend to become specialized in one or another aspect of the integrative process. Even a highly specialized agent, however, may be considered controlling when he is compared with some agents and supportive when compared with others. The probation officer, in his ordinary role, is more inclined to be on the client's side than is the policeman, but less so than the psychiatrist. Furthermore, an agent may consider himself supportive but be experienced as controlling, and vice versa; the prisoner remanded by the court for psychiatric treatment may experience his hospitalization as incarceration while a vagrant may be grateful, in midwinter, for a night in prison.

The balance of support and control within a role seems to shift not only when different roles are compared and when they are viewed from different perspectives, but also when the context in which the role is acted out changes, or when the target population is different. For example, the psychiatrist who spends part of his time in a public mental hospital and part with private patients can move in minutes from a controlling to a supportive role.

The balance of support and control can also vary throughout the time that the client is under the agency's care. Parsons (1955), for example, has suggested that psychotherapy progresses from support toward control. The patient is first accepted and encouraged, and then, as he achieves insight and competence, is persuaded to abandon his neurotic patterns through the use of interpersonal sanctions. A similar pattern probably holds for all overtly supportive services in which the client presents no major threat to any large sector of the society in which he lives. In contrast, in the most controlling agencies the balance probably moves in the opposite direction. The prisoner suffers maximum constraint at the beginning of his sentence; but as time goes by and if he keeps the rules, control is lessened until finally the supportive time off for good behavior is reached.

Undoubtedly an agency's choice of whether to specialize in one aspect of social regulation or to phase its activity between support and control is influenced not only by law, and by professional standards, but also by the over-all division of labor in the regulative system. In a finely divided system, there is room for specialization; in one in which there is duplication of services, both functions will have to be performed in each agency, perhaps by using different kinds of staff members for different phases.

While any single agent may specialize most of the time in either support or control, he must, nevertheless, have both in his repertoire in order that he neither tyrannize nor overindulge his clients. Both physicians and clergymen are generally supportive of people who come to them in pain or trouble; but they expect, in return, performances appropriate to the role of patient or parishioner. The support is a formal part of their interaction while the control is part of the informal structure of their relationship. Conversely, when the policeman arrests a suspect, a measure of support for going along quietly is usually forthcoming. In general, the agent's training and professional ethic are reflected in the skills needed for the overt part of his role, while the latent aspects are derived from and governed by the norms and values that characterize the informal controls of everyday interaction.

Whether support or control is manifest in any single interaction between client and agent will depend, obviously, upon the nature of the problem about which the client is complaining, the mandate of the agency, the agent's training, and a number of more idiosyncratic issues such as the client's characteristics. At times, in any regulative system, either support or control is used inappropriately, but this may be invisible at the time that it is happening. Throughout the studies reported here, it is assumed that both support and control are necessary elements in social regulation, and that a certain minimum of each is present in the activities of each agency, even when only one is singled out for special comment.

A final complicating feature of the balance between support and control is the long-term shift in the value placed on each element. Unquestionably, the first half of the twentieth century saw a value shift toward the individual and away from the social order at the same time that an over-all disciplinarian mood was giving way to a much more libertarian one (Russell, 1945). At the time that these studies were undertaken, the pendulum seemed to have swung to the point where a higher value was placed on the individual than ever before.

THE SPECIFIC FRAME OF REFERENCE

From the point of view of any particular regulative agent, the client is under adequate social control when he is meeting the agent's standards of acceptable behavior while he is under care, or can be expected to meet general social standards when he is released. The agent is supporting the client when he recognizes the requirements that the client expresses, or when he responds affirmatively to the behavior of the client's own choosing. The agent controls the client when he expects behavior that conforms to standards that the client does not understand or does not subscribe to, and can enforce his expectations with sanctions. From a psychological point of view, the client is being supported when his identity is affirmed, and controlled when it is being questioned.

The client's informal control of the agency is the mirror image of the agency's control of him, and if the agent modifies his activities in the light of the possible sanctions of the client, he is under the client's formal control. Obviously, informal controls between client and agent, as in all other interactions, are symmetrical. Equally obviously, formal controls are not symmetrical because the client is usually either seeking something scarce or being forced to accept something of general social value that he does not want. Less obviously, when the agency seeks the client, it places itself under his control; and, in such cases, the client supports or affirms the agency when he accepts its services and performs according to its standards.

An agency can be described in terms of the balance of control between itself and the client, in terms of the phase of the relationship when control is most overt, and in terms of the form in which the control expresses itself. Some evidence of an agency's pattern of control can be found in its regulations, its customs, and in the expectations that it conveys to its clients. Most of the studies reported here focused upon the activities at the boundary of agencies, and the patterns of interaction there were used to suggest the balance of support and control.

Almost all agents exert some overt control at the entrance to their service through eligibility criteria, sometimes financial, sometimes personal. During the course of care, control may increase, diminish, or continue unchanged. Sanctions are numerous, including the threat of expulsion. When a young girl who is illegitimately pregnant approaches a private agency, for example, she may have to agree beforehand to a program in which she attends casework interviews, pays for her confinement, and, after that, gives up her infant for adoption. If she fails to live up to any part of this regimen, she may be referred to another, perhaps public, agency that cannot legally refuse her. In extreme cases, control is maintained by force, rather than by rules, as, for example, when a client is brought to a hospital in restraint, kept there against his will, and finally transferred to a nursing home, still against his will.

Informal controls are, by definition, more subtle than formal ones. As an applicant enters the agency, his behavior can be controlled by a number of situations that set up expectations of certain kinds of behavior. If a patient must tell his affairs to a telephone operator, a receptionist, a bookkeeper, and a nurse and receive instructions from each of them before he sees the doctor, he is under more constraint than he would be if he could enter the doctor's office directly. If he must sit and wait for long periods for no visible reason, expectations of docility or passivity are implied. If, in contrast, he can go directly to the doctor without waiting, he is likely to feel that his own definition of his situation is being affirmed.

During the course of treatment, care, or custody, both latent and overt controls can be exerted in several ways: if the client is seen alone rather than in groups of people, he is under less need to control what he says; if he is seen in a private rather than a public room or a noisy cubicle, the same is true, although the greatest control is exerted when he is kept entirely alone in solitary confinement; finally, if the client knows that the agent is likely to exchange information about him with other agents, he is very likely to control quite closely the kinds of information that he reveals, and to behave, insofar as he is able, in ways he thinks acceptable to this and other agencies. Ironically, the greatest long-term control over the client is perhaps achieved in a supportive situation where the client is taken off guard and abandons his caution —the ruse of both brainwashing and psychotherapy. The great majority of agents, however, are concerned with immediate control of everyday behavior, not with long-term conversions.

The most effective single control available to both agent

and client is probably a common set of values and norms, and the more specific and numerous the norms, the greater the commitment the client and agent are likely to make to each other. This kind of normative control is part of the fabric of everyday interaction, but it becomes more compelling when there is a sharply defined subset of values to which both subscribe. When the agency is under religious auspices, for example, and the client is of the same faith, the specific norms are binding on both. Such control also occurs in certain military and quasi-military institutions: homes run by the armed services for the aged or for veterans—especially when the clients wear uniforms—or homes run by fraternal orders and lodges for their own members. Roth (1963) has described the processes by which the staff of a tuberculosis hospital developed norms that both exerted control over the patients' everyday behavior and at the same time discouraged them from going home prematurely.

The method of leaving a service reflects the agency's residual control over its client. The client who is free to collaborate upon the time and terms of his dismissal is under less control than the one who must accept the agent's dictum. If he is referred to another agent, and is constrained by regulation to go there, he remains under firm control; if he is referred to another agent but can choose to break his appointment, he is less controlled. If he is free to leave the regulative system altogether, he is completely freed from its control. If he is only steered to another agent, or given leave to re-enter the same agency if he wishes, he is essentially being offered support, for there has been a tacit agreement that he is able to conduct his own affairs.

The client's control over the agency is parallel to, but not equal to, the agency's control of the client. If the client is served by an agency to which he must pay a fee in order to continue in care, he is under control; but, by the same token, he has the reciprocal power to withhold payment. In all such agency-client contracts, the balance of control lies in the direction of scarcity. If the agency badly needs clients, it may be under more control than it can exert; if its services are scarce and in demand, the reverse may be true.

Specialization makes a difference to the balance between support and control. If agencies are highly specialized and participate in a finely divided labor, they will have more control over the client than when they replicate one another; the client cannot, in such a situation, exercise much choice among them. When an agency, like the Welfare Department, offers a number of specialized services that are vitally necessary to the client, and that is the only place where he can get them, its control over him is maximized.

Some relationships between clients and professionals are governed by legal regulations, and, in these cases, lawsuits for malpractice are possible. When this is so, the client has a strong latent control over the performance of the agent.

When an agency is constrained by law to accept certain classes of clients, it can exert control through strict eligibility and performance requirements, but the client in turn can threaten it with exposure if it withholds support. The most publicized and perhaps most common example of this tension is the giving of public financial relief. The relative balance of control between client and agent is, in this case, largely contingent upon the public mood. In libertarian times, the agent may give the client considerable support and the client may be able to achieve a fair degree of control over the agent; when the mood swings back to the disciplinarian, the agent is in strong control of the client. In this particular case, of course, the agent always holds the ultimate balance of control, for, in the last analysis, he can live without any particular client; the client may not be able to live without him.

Only when client and agent both subscribe to the same set of values with about the same level of enthusiasm, and when service is elective—that is, when the client's need for regulation is minimal—can social control approach symmetry. Perhaps treatment of a very rare, nonfatal medical condition by a famous specialist comes closest to this situation.

In the studies reported in Part I, the issues of support and control were examined from the point of view of the transactions between a series of agencies and the populations approaching them. The study agencies will be presented in common-sense groupings: medical services, counseling agencies, income maintenance services, residential institutions, and correctional agencies. The most supportive group of agencies will be presented first, the most controlling last. In Part II, the same data will be examined from the point of view of the relationships among the agencies, as they can be inferred from the movement of clients around the system. In Part III the problems presented to the agents by the clients will be scrutinized and the dimensions of the over-all regulative task estimated.

REFERENCES

Bales, Robert F., 1953. "The Equilibrium Problem in Small Groups," in Talcott Parsons, *et al., Working Papers in the Theory of Action,* New York, The Free Press.

Bateson, Gregory, D. D. Jackson, J. Haley, and J. Weakland, 1956. "Toward a Theory of Schizophrenia," *Behavioral Science,* Vol. 1, No. 4.

Davis, Kingsley, 1938. "Mental Hygiene and the Class Structure," *Psychiatry,* Vol. I, No. 1.

Goode, W. J., 1960. "A Theory of Role Strain," *American Sociological Review,* Vol. 25, No. 4.

Lemert, Edwin, 1964. "Social Structure, Social Control, and Deviation," in *Anomie and Deviant Behavior,* ed. Marshall B. Clinard, New York, The Free Press.

Naegele, K. D., 1961. In *Theories of Society,* eds. Talcott Parsons, E. Shils, K. D. Naegele, J. R. Pitts, New York, The Free Press.

Parsons, Talcott, 1951. *The Social System,* New York, The Free Press.

Parsons, Talcott, 1953. "The Theory of Symbolism in Relation to Action," in T. Parsons, *et al., Working Papers in the Theory of Action,* New York, The Free Press.

Parsons, Talcott, *et al.,* 1955. *Family Socialization and Interaction Process,* New York, The Free Press.

Parsons, Talcott, 1960. "Pattern Variables Revisited," *American Sociological Review,* Vol. 25, No. 4, August.

Roth, Julius A., 1963. *Timetables: Structuring the Passage of Time in Hospital Treatment and Other Careers,* Indianapolis, Bobbs-Merrill.

Russell, Bertrand, 1945. *A History of Western Philosophy,* New York, Simon and Schuster.

Shils, Edward A., 1956. *The Torment of Secrecy,* New York, The Free Press.

METHOD OF STUDY 2

A series of studies of clients approaching thirteen selected regulative agencies in Syracuse, New York, was conducted in the summer and fall of 1961 and the winter and spring of 1962. The specific purpose of the studies was threefold: first, to discover what happened to the clients who approached these agencies; second, to analyze the working of the regulative system from a study of the everyday contacts among its agencies; and third, to learn something about what kinds of problems people were taking to different members of the system. The general purpose of the study was to discover regularities in the system from which it might be possible to generalize.

The Study Community

The city of Syracuse, which was more or less co-extensive with the Syracuse urbanized area at the time of the studies, had an economic profile so similar to the nation's that new commercial products were often tried out there before being marketed generally. Whether the city's similarity to the nation in its instrumental activities signified a parallel similarity in integrative affairs is unknown; but, given regional differences, it seemed likely that, except for a certain political conservatism, Syracuse came as close to representing American cities of its size as any one city could. After the studies had been completed, an influx of money from the federal Office of Economic Opportunity exerted considerable pressure for change on many local agencies; the major findings of these studies, therefore, provide a baseline for the city and not a current picture. Indeed, some of the details of the various studies were out of date almost before they were completed. The studies were not conceived as topical, however, but were intended to suggest regularities given by the form and structure of American society. The major research questions were framed in terms of persistence rather than of change.

The Community's Integrative System

SPONSORSHIP

How much of the total energy of the city was given over to maintaining integration at the time of these studies was unknown and probably unknowable. Apart from the ubiquitous ongoing informal controls, formal regulative activities occurred, as they did in all cities, within both adaptive and socializing institutions. The factory had its personnel office, and the school its counselors, nurses, and visiting teachers. From such sources as these, a steady stream of service reached people by virtue of their memberships in central social institutions. When these services were left aside, however, there remained another, perhaps larger, group of agencies whose primary activity was social regulation of one sort or another.

Agencies that individuals can approach more or less directly can be classified as private services, locally sponsored public services, and services provided by the state and federal governments. Private services are provided by the whole array of agents who sell their services for a profit: doctors, dentists, proprietary hospitals, lawyers, psychiatrists, nurses, and even social workers. Social agencies funded by Community Chests* and sponsored by groups of citizens or by the three major religious faiths were also considered private. Such agencies often charged fees for their services, but were not expected to make a profit. Traditionally, these private agencies had received no public support; but at the time of the studies, multiple financing from overlapping jurisdictions was making it difficult to distinguish private agencies from those supported by public funds (Connery, 1967). Many services, such as public assistance, were jointly sponsored by local, state, and federal governments. Some services, in particular psychiatric facilities, were almost fully supported by the state but were moving toward local sponsorship, while others, such as those provided by the Veterans Administration, were fully supported by the federal government, somewhat removed from local affairs, and apparently stable.

REDUNDANCIES AND GAPS

It is obvious on the face of it that there was a possibility for both redundancy and gaps in such a spectrum of local services. There was one nonsectarian family casework agency, for example, as well as three others sponsored by religious groups. Attempts to combine two of these agencies under one particularly competent director were made during the course of the studies, but they met adamant resistance. In a similar fashion, the Veterans Administration system replicated many private and public services. Whether all these similar services were necessary was not usually questioned;

* The Syracuse Community Chest, like all others, was just barely a private charity. Pressure upon wage earners to contribute to it was often so great as to closely resemble a tax.

civic concern was expressed in terms of "unmet needs," not underused services.

Gaps in the system were harder to see than redundancies, both because those who lack services have little voice, and because those who initiate services tend to be well-to-do board members whose perspective is limited by their own position in the community. The division of labor among the many agencies that made up the system was only partly visible. While it was generally known that agencies served different classes of clients, it was not known quite where or how the sorting took place. One of the purposes of these studies was to throw some light upon this division of labor by studying part of the sorting, screening, and allocating process at the boundaries of a group of agencies.

General Research Strategy

The best method for studying the regulative system would probably be to conduct a prospective study of its potential applicants. In such a plan, a sample of this population would be asked at short intervals what contacts they had made, or attempted to make, among the community's regulative agents and agencies. This could not be done, however, because it was impossible to identify and judge the size and variability of the population from which the sample would be drawn. The characteristics of those who actually used the system are not necessarily a good index of the characteristics of the potential users. For example, it is known that the very young and the very old are more frequent users of medical care than the middle-aged (Anderson and Anderson, 1965), and that certain kinds of services are concentrated on a relatively few "hard-core" clients who tend to be poor and from minority groups (Buell, 1952); but it is not known whether these characteristics are representative of all potential clients. When so little is known to start with, a random sample is indicated; but a random sample that did not run the risk of losing some special groups would have to be prohibitively large.

For these reasons another approach was used. Various agencies and agents were selected and arrangements made to count attempts to use their services; various other less satisfactory methods supplemented this primary strategy. Two agencies were studied at more than one point in time, however, in order to provide some insight into the persistence of patterns of practice; and in two agencies some information was collected about clients already in care as well as clients applying for service.

That the study method had drawbacks will be evident as the report unfolds. Its most striking failures were in giving no picture of how many people looked for help and never found it, or even of how many of those eligible made use of the agents under study. Finally, there was no way to sample the agents themselves because there were too few within each class, and not enough was known about their functioning to classify them in any but traditional ways. The results of the study must be read with these limitations in mind.

Particular Strategy

STUDY AGENCIES

The complexity of Syracuse's formal regulative agencies could be seen in either the yellow pages of the telephone book or in a Social Service or "Red Feather" Directory put out by the Community Chest, which was, in its own words, "a descriptive index of the various health, welfare and leisure-time services provided in Syracuse and Onondaga County . . . including local agencies that are either privately financed or tax-supported as well as agencies and departments of the State and Federal Government which are located in Syracuse and which provide services within Onondaga County." Table 2-1 sorts the array of agents and agencies found in the telephone book, together with the list from the Social Service Directory, according to whether they were private, profit-making, or public in nature.

The agents and agencies are arranged in Table 2-1 roughly

Table 2-1. SERVICES IN SYRACUSE BY SPONSORSHIP AND SOURCE OF INFORMATION

Type of agent	Profit-making individuals and firms		Nonprofit agents and agencies[a]	
	Yellow pages	"Red Feather"	Yellow pages	"Red Feather"
Medical	1424	1	24	50
Physicians and psychiatrists	600[b]		8	34
Dentists	200			1
Quasi-medical[c]	120			
Nurses (RN and LPN)	380		3	3
Pharmacists	100	1		
Laboratories	7		1	
Physiotherapists	10			2
General hospitals	5		9	9
Clinics (special services)			3	1
Ambulances	2			
Counseling	678	1	282	21
Clergymen			275[d]	1
Lawyers and Legal Aid	675[b]	1		1
Individual and family counseling	3		7	16
Occupational rehabilitation and counseling				3
Total recreation	2		35	49
Organizations			21	18
Parks			14	6
Camps	2			25
Employment	18		3	2
Income maintenance			8	10
Public assistances			5	3
Private charities			2	4
Housing			1	3
Institutions	34	1	3	14
Nursing homes	34			4
Shelters and placement			2	8
Psychiatric hospitals		1		1
State school			1	1
Correction			23	13
Jails			2	1
Courts, judges, D.A., etc.			13	8
Probation and parole			4	3
Police			4	1

[a] These categories are not mutually exclusive.
[b] Probably two-thirds in at least part-time private practice.
[c] Osteopaths, optometrists, podiatrists, etc.
[d] In the 150 churches listed.

in order of their relative supportiveness, with the most overtly controlling agencies at the bottom of the table. It is plain that the private sector of the agency world was providing many more overtly supportive services, though not necessarily more individual agents, while, except for nursing homes, the public sector provided the agents of control.*

The universe of agents to be sampled consisted of these lists, while the knowledge of various professional staff members and consultants supplied the weights for the sampling process. An attempt was made to select agents who performed vital supporting and controlling functions for large numbers of people, while at the same time covering the whole range of special skills used by regulative agents. Children's agencies were excluded from direct study in order to keep the number manageable.

A group of eight agencies and two agents were finally chosen for primary study; they included both supporting and controlling agencies and were drawn from both the public and private sectors of the system; they included multifunction and highly specialized agencies, and they were known to serve large numbers of people. The three judged most vital to over-all social integration were: the Syracuse Dispensary, a group of outpatient clinics serving the medically indigent; the Onondaga County Department of Social Welfare; and the Syracuse Police Department. The first of these can be thought of as a relatively supportive agency, the second intermediate, and the third controlling.

Besides these three agencies, six others were chosen: the medical Social Service Department of the Syracuse Dispensary, Catholic Welfare, a family social agency, a nonsectarian family casework agency, the Planned Parenthood Center of Syracuse, and a home care nursing service run by the City of Syracuse Nursing Bureau. All of these latter six agencies can be considered more supportive than any of the first three. Two individual agents were chosen for study—clergymen and

---

* This concentration of nursing homes in the private, profit-making sector was a national condition; nine tenths of the 8000 nursing homes in the United States were still being operated for profit in 1964 (National Center for Health Statistics, 1965).

family doctors—both of whom were gatekeeper, or caretaker, agents approached by clients with many kinds of problems, and probably as supportive as any agents in the system.

Supplementary studies of other agencies were also undertaken. These included: studies of referral patterns in two psychiatric outpatient clinics, the operation of a men's shelter, and the statements of executives and professionals in 38 local agencies about what kinds of additional services they needed.

DATA COLLECTION

As far as possible, a standard method was adopted in the primary study agencies: a field worker sat at the boundary of the agency, usually the reception desk, and watched the clients approach. He made notes of what happened during their encounter with whoever received them, and at a later date the records of the agency were searched and the client's file abstracted. Sometimes it was possible to observe more than one stage of the entrance to the agency, but sometimes the situation did not permit continuous observation at the boundary. In the two psychiatric clinics, at Catholic Welfare, and in the Social Service Department of the Dispensary data were collected entirely from records, but in the latter two agencies some observation at the boundary was possible.

Sample members of Syracuse family doctors and clergymen were interviewed with respect to their activities, and an attempt was made to analyze the interviews so that the findings would be as comparable as possible with the other studies.

DATA ANALYSIS

Comparative Analysis of the Agents of Regulation. The major unit of analysis for comparing the "study agencies" was the fate of the client's application. Several variables were used to describe this fate. For each agency a standard table was constructed showing the source from which clients were referred to the study agency, the targets of out-referral chosen by the agency for the clients, the agencies with whom eligibility checks were made, those with whom information was exchanged, and finally, the agencies chosen for collaboration in the care of the clients. This standard table gave the profile of the agency's response to its applicants in terms of its relationships with the remainder of the regulative system.

The problems with which the client approached each agency were also set forth under standard categories. Three major types of problems, representing different relationships of the client to the environment, were recognized: transition states, role failures, and contingencies. Transition states were defined as those adjustment problems inherent in the life cycle that everyone can expect to encounter; they are part of the human condition. Transition states included developmental problems, marital misunderstandings, loneliness in old age, bereavement, and many transient, or self-resolving, maladjustments.

Role failure referred to failure in a central life role. The problems included in this category were assumed to lie primarily within individuals, although they may have had their genesis in the environment. Indeed, urban environments in the 1960's may have made it impossible for disproportionately large numbers of certain classes of people, such as male Negroes, to succeed in central life roles. The role failure category included such obvious deviance as criminal or quasi-criminal behavior, as well as unwed motherhood, marital breakdown, and chronic inability to get along with others or to hold a job.

Contingent problems were defined as primarily environmental; they included insufficient income for family size, medical indigence, temporary unemployment, and physical illness and disability. In general, such problems reflected defects and inadequacies of the environment rather than of the individual; many of the contingent problems could not have been ameliorated without concrete resources.

Contingencies and role failures can both be considered to be pathologies, one of the environment, the other of the person, and often causally related to each other, although the nature of the causal relationship is elusive. Transition states stand apart as normal life crises.

While the profile of interagency connections was comparable from agency to agency except for differences in reporting, the specific problem types were inherently not comparable because the nature of the service offered by the agency determined the kinds of information about problems that were in the record. Nevertheless, the grouping of the problems under the three major categories was roughly comparable from agency to agency.

For each study agency, a standard table reported the amount of service that the members of each problem type received. Each agency was examined in terms of its own core service plus any secondary services it offered. From the three standard tables describing each agency, and from the observations of the field workers, as well as from various published sources, a picture of each agency's position in the system, its level of specialization, and the degree of control exerted over the client, was built.

Analysis of the Regulative System. In this phase of the study, the agencies were reclassified into a less traditional and more analytic set of categories. The major unit of analysis was the interagency connection, and the interagency contacts that made up each agency's profile were treated as choices. Analyses were made of the bonds both among the study agencies and between them, and of the 302 agencies to which they were found to be connected through referrals, exchanges of information, eligibility checks, and interagency collaborations. Inferences about the everyday operation of the system, and particularly the division of labor within it, were made from these findings.

Some Dimensions of the Regulative Task. After the descriptions of the agencies and the analysis of the system *qua* system were completed, some selected characteristics of the applicants approaching each agency in a given period of time were studied. Three characteristics that were taken to be indices of trouble were also noted: first, the absence of young children from the family home for whatever reason was examined; second, the names of each client and the members of his immediate family were searched in the central files of the New York State Department of Mental Hygiene for evidence of hospitalizations for mental illness; and third, the name of each client was searched in the files of the Welfare Department. Using these three characteristics, together with the problem categories, the applicants approaching each agency in a given period of time were compared in terms of the seriousness of their social, personal, and economic problems.

REFERENCES

Anderson, Ronald, and Odin W. Anderson, 1965. "Family Life Cycle and Use of Health Services." Read before the Meetings of the American Sociological Association, Chicago, September 2, 1965.

Buell, Bradley, and Associates, 1952. *Community Planning for Human Services,* New York, Columbia.

Connery, Robert H., 1967. *The Politics of Mental Health—Organizing for Community Mental Health in Fragmented Metropolitan Areas,* New York, Columbia.

National Center for Health Statistics, 1965. "Characteristics of Residents in Institutions for the Aged and Chronically Ill," *Vital and Health Statistics Data from the National Health Survey,* Series 12, No. 2, U.S. Public Health Service, Department of Health, Education and Welfare.

THE FAMILY DOCTOR: *3*
PROTOTYPE OF MEDICAL
CARETAKER

The family doctor is the prototype of the supportive medical agent; for even when he exercises the most controlling aspect of his role and sends someone to a hospital, his supportive tone is almost always uppermost.

The supportive side of the family physician's role, in contrast to the technical side, involves him with the patient's family. As a Syracuse general practitioner expressed it, "I like the total picture of treating the entire family: seeing the

Isabel McCaffrey designed the sample for this study; Dr. Edward Taub conducted the interviews; Momoyo Ise and Charles Harrington assisted with the analysis; Dr. Herbert Notkin and Dr. Lionel Rudolph acted as consultants; and the Onondaga County Medical Association gave their approval to the project.

newborns and children, delivering the mothers as one phase, later taking care of all including the father. It is the attraction of an entire picture, that of medicine as a whole, rather than one part."

Some medical educators believe that the doctor's obligation to the patient and his family extends beyond medical care alone. In an influential statement, Richardson (1945) said, "[unless] all the ills of the family are concentrated in the individual who happens to come to a particular doctor for treatment . . . the family equilibrium needs to be taken into account . . . [with] a coordinated plan of treatment, using medical attention in combination with the resources for health and family welfare in hospital and community." Undoubtedly the family physicians practicing in Syracuse in 1961 had been told many times about their responsibility for the whole patient and his family. This investigation was aimed in part at discovering what use they made of the rest of the regulative system in meeting that responsibility.

Entering Medical Care

Most family doctors in Syracuse were reasonably accessible to their patients. Some practiced in local neighborhoods and were geographically close. Very few family doctors' offices had more than a receptionist or nurse to intercept the patient on his way to the doctor. Two controls, one formal, the other informal, were exercised, however: First, most family doctors refused to make house calls unless the patient was unable to come either to the office or to the hospital emergency room; and second, if the doctor was busy, the patients sometimes had to wait a long time to see him. Patients were free, of course, to change doctors, and this gave them considerable reciprocal control over the relationship.

Method of Study

There were 620 physicians listed in the Onondaga County section of the New York State Medical Directory in 1961, of whom 395 were either in fully specialized practice, or not in private practice at all. Of the remaining 225, 148 were general practitioners in full-time family practice and 77 were internists without a subspecialty. The latter were included in the universe to be sampled because internists, unless they are subspecialized, conduct what is essentially family practice among the higher socioeconomic groups (Backett, 1964). Thirty-one of the 148 general practitioners and 20 of the 77 internists were eliminated because their practices lay beyond the metropolitan area. Thirty of the remaining 117 general practitioners and 10 of the 57 internists were chosen to represent various age groups, places of training, and socioeconomic areas of practice.*

Of the 40 doctors in the sample, only 32 (27 general practitioners and 5 internists) were found, upon questioning, to be carrying on full-time family practices; and all of these were interviewed by a medical student who put himself in the position of asking for their advice because he was intending to enter general practice. Although this student did, in a sense, represent the medical school, he appeared to elicit very few of the "pious," or conforming, answers reported by Freidson (1964).

Each doctor was asked about his referring and consulting practices, his hospital preferences, the number of his patients with personal problems and his attitudes and practices regarding them, and, finally, about his knowledge, use of, and attitude toward selected community agencies—medical, psychiatric, and counseling.

Findings

REFERRAL SOURCE

The family practitioners in this study seldom asked their new patients who had sent them, but all assumed that most

* Area was judged as follows: Doctors practicing in downtown buildings housing other doctors were given the highest rating; doctors practicing in neighborhoods were scored according to their census tracts as rated by Willie and Wagenfeld (1960). Training was classified as: (1) local: graduated from the Upstate Medical Center, Syracuse, New York; (2) graduated from other American schools; and (3) graduated from a foreign medical school.

had come through the lay referral system—that is, that their own old patients had sent them. The five internists in the group did, however, receive some patients by referral from general practitioners. Examination of the referrals made by the eight primary agencies in the study series, however, showed that three of them—the Welfare Department, a psychiatric clinic, and the Planned Parenthood Center—had sent patients to family doctors during the study period. The fact that none of the remaining five agencies made such referrals during the period lends some credence to the doctors' contention that most of their patients had come through the lay referral system.

PROBLEMS PRESENTED

Although most patients first come to physicians with physical complaints, many of them eventually ask help with other kinds of problems. According to Gurin et al. (1960), for example, 29 per cent of Americans go first to a doctor for advice when they have a "personal problem."* This willingness to approach the physician for nonmedical reasons may be partly because there is no stigma attached to medical services and partly because of the support the doctor has provided during past illness. All 32 doctors in the study group said that their patients asked their help with many nonmedical problems.

SERVICES OFFERED

Medical Care. Twenty-seven of the family practitioners said that they gave medical care to anyone who sought their help either directly or through any other agent or agency. Of the remaining five, two had some reservations about accepting patients who could not pay from any source, one said that he simply refused to see indigent patients, and two referred them immediately to hospital outpatient clinics.

Medical Consultation and Referral. Six of the 32 doctors said that they resented both consultations with and referrals

---

* Figures are combined from Gurin's Tables 10.3 and 10.7.

to medical specialists because they resulted in loss of patients, and another 12 agreed somewhat grudgingly that they were sometimes necessary. The remainder replied that they were willing to refer their major surgical problems and also to consult with specialists about serious medical problems.* All these family physicians were, however, reluctant to consult psychiatrists unless driven to it by the acute condition of patients. Paradoxically, these doctors seemed to be referring difficult medical problems while treating the patients' diffuse personal problems.

Supportive Counseling. The family doctor can offer supportive counseling either on his own or in consultation or collaboration with other agents; 30 of the 32 family practitioners said they were willing to counsel with their patients about personal and emotional problems. There is some evidence that patients with such problems were a considerable proportion of these doctors' practices. Roth *et al.* (1959), studying a middle-class practice in a suburb of Syracuse, estimated that between 10 and 15 per cent of the patients were disordered enough to be given psychiatric diagnoses. Roth's figure is similar to the estimate of Shepherd *et al.* (1966) that in London nearly 14 per cent of all visits to general practitioners are for "minor mental illnesses." Of the 30 physicians who said that they counseled with such patients, 9 admitted that they could be a burden; but when they were asked about the circumstances under which they would refer them elsewhere, all but 3 said that they would never do so. Questioned about referring patients with definite psychiatric illnesses, 20 doctors replied, "I prefer to treat them myself." This response, reflecting a concern with the whole man, conforms with the findings of others (Rorie, 1963), and it also reflects a practice approved by many psychiatrists (Branch, 1965).

Interagency Collaboration. The doctors' attitudes toward collaboration with other regulative agents were in marked contrast with their willingness to offer support to patients

---

* In Syracuse hospitals, a general practitioner was required to have specialist consultation for patients with serious illnesses of certain types.

with nonmedical problems. Table 3-1 shows these physicians' responses to questions about their use of the clergy, the hospital outpatient clinic, the family casework agency, public health nursing services, the Veterans Administration medical services, and local psychiatric services. Only 2 doctors made more positive than negative or neutral comments about all of these agencies; 18 made mostly neutral comments; and 12 made predominantly negative ones. Of all of the agencies, only public health nursing escaped some negative comment.

Table 3-1. PER CENT OF 32 FAMILY DOCTORS WITH NEGATIVE ATTITUDES TOWARD SELECTED AGENCIES

Type of agency	No. of doctors Using	Not Using	% using	% negative attitudes Users	Non-users
Medical					
Dispensary	16	16	50.0	25.0	25.0
VA medical service	31	1	96.9	29.0	—
Public Health Nursing	25	7	78.1	0.0	0.0
Psychiatric hospital	15	17	46.9	60.0	23.5
Mental health clinic	20	12	62.5	50.0	33.3
Private psychiatrist	29	3	90.6	37.9	100.0
Counseling					
Clergy	14	18	43.8	28.6	33.3
Casework agency	11	21	34.4	18.2	0.0

The outpatient clinic was accused of having too much red tape, being unfeeling in its handling of the patients, and of not referring the patients back to the family doctor. The most common complaint against the VA system was that the patients were kept so long the family doctor lost control of the case.

Psychiatric services drew the highest rate of negative comment, which is concordant with the findings of others that family doctors are reluctant to make psychiatric referrals (Mills, 1962; Avnet, 1962). The local psychiatric hospital was particularly criticized for "picking and choosing" among patients, and for refusing acutely ill patients. The length of the waiting list maintained by the County Mental Health

Clinic was criticized by some doctors, while four of them complained about the clinic's general ineffectiveness. Major objections to private psychiatrists were their high fees and their refusal to discuss their patients with the referring doctor, although some praised them for arranging commitment to mental hospitals for difficult patients. The nearby State Hospital was also commended, in passing, because it accepted without question any patient that the doctor could no longer handle.

Unqualified approval for public health nursing services was given by all doctors, whether or not they ever called on them for help. Many doctors singled out specific services for praise, especially bedside care for postoperative cases, the chronically ill, and the old. The highest praise, however, was reserved for the nurses' faithfulness in reporting back to the doctor and thus helping him to keep control of his practice.

Nonmedical Referral. Referral is a form of service that requires the doctor to put aside his economic interest in the patient whenever the patient would be better served elsewhere. Most doctors denied referring patients to nonmedical agencies when they were asked a general question about their referral practice. Although half the doctors said that they sometimes recommended that patients see their clergymen, a quarter of these were unhappy about doing it. Skepticism was expressed in such phrases as, "I send some patients to their clergymen if they are religious—not that it does any good." Three doctors volunteered that they had in the past advised patients to go to lawyers for marital problems, two that they had used local services for alcoholics, and one mentioned, in passing, the Department of Social Welfare. Only four of the agencies listed in the Syracuse Red Feather Directory were mentioned by the 32 doctors during this open-ended questioning. In short, the family doctors in this study group, like their counterparts in other American cities, claimed to be virtually without knowledge of the community's regulative system (Knowles, 1965). Only 15 of the 32 recalled receiving a specially prepared directory of agencies that had been sent to them by the Council of Social Agencies, and only one had made use of it. Seventeen doctors said such vague things as, "Oh yes, I got it, but there is so much red tape in those places." No doctor acted as a consultant to a social agency, and none was an agency board member.

In spite of the doctors' disavowal of knowledge of local agencies, when they were questioned about their use of specific services they reported a much higher rate than their earlier answers had suggested (Table 3-1). Furthermore, during the study period, private physicians sent 100 patients to six of the eight primary study agencies, a large number compared to the six that were referred to physicians by these agencies. Over-all, a larger proportion of the study populations approaching the primary agencies had been sent by private doctors than by anybody else. As physicians probably care for more people than any other agent, it is hard to gauge the meaning of this finding. It seems clear, however, that these family doctors did not see themselves as part of a larger network of services.

The discrepancy between the physicians' expressed attitudes and their practices may have arisen because of their concept of the nature of a referral. Most doctors did not appear to understand the general question, "Do you ever refer patients to nonmedical agencies?" Of the nine who said "yes," eight explained that they sometimes *suggested* the use of an agency for some specific service like an adoption. As one doctor said, "How *could* you refer? Referrals are to other professionals." Besides not recognizing any legitimate target for referral except other physicians, these family doctors appeared to believe referral to another type of agent might antagonize the patient, and hence alienate him from the practice. All these doctors implied that they hated to lose patients, not only because it lowered their incomes but also because it lowered their self-esteem. The internists in the group differed from the general practitioners only in that they did not express this anxiety about losing patients.*

* Shepherd *et al.* (1966) found that English general practitioners referred almost none of their patients to social or welfare agencies although they recognized nonmedical problems among one half of them. Whether our interviewer and these investigators were all encountering an artifact, or whether the family doctors in our study were referring no one while *specialists* were making all the referrals to the study agencies cannot be determined.

A Specialized, Supportive, Conflicted Agent

In balance, the family doctor showed up as a highly supportive agent. He offered his patients diffuse support at times of illness and trouble under conditions that affirmed their right to consult him. Furthermore, because of the fee-for-service basis of private practice, such controls as existed tended to be reciprocal. Partly because of this symmetrical control, the family doctor's role appeared to involve conflicts: First, most of those in the study group were apprehensive about losing patients; that is, they felt that they did not have sufficient control over them; second, although their skills were highly specialized, these family doctors were approached by people with all kinds of problems, medical and nonmedical, and thus they were forced into a kind of gatekeeper or caretaker position. Nothing that any doctor said, however, suggested that he recognized any sorting or allocating obligation because of his gatekeeper position in the system. On the contrary, apparently because they feared the loss of patients, doctors seemed to be saying that to refer patients to nonmedical sources would not be a legitimate part of their role. Third, there was confusion among these practitioners about the relationship between being a family doctor and being in general practice. Twelve of the 27 general practitioners complained to the interviewer that they were treated as if they had a lower status than specialists, and that they were often forced against their own judgment to use specialist consultation in their hospital practices. Most declared, nevertheless, that their relationships with the patients and their families compensated for this. Their emphasis on "compensation" may contain a suggestion that the technical expertise of the specialist was, after all, a higher value for them. In a sense, the internist with a family practice had managed to get the best of two worlds, specialization and family practice, because, having higher status than the general practitioner, he could offer support and counsel to his patients while maintaining maximum control of their medical problems.

REFERENCES

Avnet, Helen H., 1962. *Psychiatric Insurance,* New York, Group Health Insurance.

Backett, E. Maurice, 1964. "The Family Physician—Extinction or Rebirth" in *The Family and the Doctor,* Washington, D.C., The United States Public Health Service.

Branch, Hardin, 1965. "Should the Medical Student be Trained to Refer or to Handle His Own Psychiatric Patients?" *American Journal of Psychiatry,* Vol. 121, No. 9, March.

Freidson, Eliot, 1964. "Physicians in Large Medical Groups," *Journal of Chronic Diseases,* Vol. 17, No. 9, September.

Gurin, Gerald, Joseph Veroff, and Sheila Feld, 1960. *Americans View Their Mental Health,* New York, Basic Books.

Knowles, John H., 1965. "The Role of the Hospital: The Ambulatory Clinic," *Bulletin of The New York Academy of Medicine,* Second Series, Vol. 41, No. 1.

Mills, Enid, 1962. *Living with Mental Illness,* London, Routledge.

Richardson, Henry B., 1945. *Patients Have Families,* New York, The Commonwealth Fund.

Rorie, Ronald A. B., 1963. "Psychiatry and General Practice in North America," *Canada's Mental Health Supplement,* No. 35, March.

Roth, V. E., J. L. Rury, and J. J. Downing, 1959. "Psychiatric Patients in a General Practice," *GP,* Vol. XX, No. 2.

Shepherd, M., B. Cooper, A. C. Brown and G. W. Walton, 1966. *Psychiatric Illness in General Practice,* London, Oxford University Press.

Willie, Charles V., and Morton O. Wagenfeld, 1960. *Socio-Economic and Ethnic Areas, Syracuse and Onondaga County, New York.* Syracuse Youth Development Center.

THE MEDICAL OUTPATIENT CLINIC

4

One-fifth of all money spent on personal health care in the United States in 1964 came from public expenditures (Muller, 1965). Most of the care paid for in this way was given through large, urban, outpatient clinics. These clinics arose partly because of a recognition that health was not entirely a private and optional matter, partly because the price structure in modern American society had left many people able

The Director of the Dispensary, Mr. Hans Tachau, kindly gave permission to conduct this study; Catherine Murphy and Margot Parsons gave invaluable help to the field workers, Charles Harrington, Giselle Harrington, Ernest Damianopoulos, and Erna Christensen. Patricia Healy, Robert Porter, and Joan Poltenson assisted with the analysis.

to attend to their everyday needs but not able to buy either health insurance or the services of a family doctor (Piore, 1965), and partly because of a belief that "public" patients were needed for training medical students.

In Syracuse at the time of these studies, much of the medical care for the poor was delivered through a system of 21 specialist clinics financed through grants from city, county, and state welfare payments, as well as from private funds and fees charged to patients. The clinics were called collectively by a misleading eighteenth-century name, "The Syracuse Free Dispensary." The Dispensary's services were provided by the medical staff and students of the Upstate Medical Center; although each clinic physician had complete medical autonomy, the administration of all the clinics was centrally organized, and the patients were admitted through a central intake office. There was an associated pharmacy and a Social Service Department to which any clinic physician could refer patients.*

Entrance to the Agency

The Dispensary's clinics were conducted in downtown Syracuse in a state-owned office building that also housed the Tax Department, the Bureau of Motor Vehicles, and other assorted public offices. Initial entrance to the Dispensary was both difficult and controlling. The new patient entered the agency from an elevator and was directed by a cashier-receptionist to the admitting office where, after a wait of anything from ten minutes to two hours, an admitting clerk, responsible for the flow of patients to various clinics, established a file. Although means-testing was generally known to be ineffec-

---

* After this research was completed, the Dispensary became the outpatient department of the State University of New York, Upstate Medical Center, with a new director and staff, although this administrative shift did not appear to have made much difference to its practices. At the time of the writing, however, Medicare was beginning to function and, in New York State, Medicaid, a bill to provide medical care to families with moderate incomes, had passed the legislature. It seemed possible that the "public" patient was about to pass into history in America as he had already done in the so-called welfare states of Western Europe.

tual as a method of restricting care to eligible populations (Lambert *et al.*, 1963), the admitting clerk's most important task was to determine financial eligibility and either to fix appropriate charges or to determine the Welfare Department's willingness to pay before assigning the patient to a clinic and leaving him to what might be another long wait. Before he saw a doctor, the average Dispensary patient had already seen a receptionist-cashier, an admitting clerk, and a nurse.

The admitting clerks were theoretically not to become involved with patients' problems without consulting their supervisor, a social worker; but, because of the great number of patients to be seen, they actually dealt with all kinds of issues concerned with patient care. For example, they decided upon patients' eligibility for free eyeglasses and advised them where to obtain drugs; they handled both emergency hospitalizations and the financial planning of routine hospital care, usually in consultation with the record-room clerks of the Department of Social Welfare; they arranged for taxicabs for people who could not pay for their own transportation; and they coped with the distress of patients who thought they were eligible for free medical care from the Welfare Department only to discover that they were not. In other words, they were the gatekeepers, traffic officers, and trouble shooters for the clinics.

Entrance to the Dispensary was complicated by its administrative interdependence not only with other agencies, particularly the Welfare Department, but also with the emergency rooms, public wards, social service departments, and clinics of various local hospitals.

Two-thirds of the patients who came to the Dispensary were either receiving public assistance at the time or had done so in the past, and the Welfare Department paid their Dispensary bills by the visit. Every time a patient requested treatment at the Dispensary, the admitting officer telephoned the Welfare file room to check his eligibility. At the end of the month, the Dispensary sent a list of patients to the Welfare Department record room whose clerks, in turn, sent one back for cross-checking.

Each hospitalization of a welfare client had to be cleared

by the Welfare Department. Medically indigent patients who were not receiving Welfare assistance had to apply for hospitalization at the Welfare Department's medical intake office, which was in another part of town. If the hospitalization was approved, the patient was sent back to the Dispensary.* A field note illustrates the effect of this administrative bottleneck when the patient is already a welfare client: "Five-year-old child—came through admitting because they need ambulance for emergency hospital; had to clear with Welfare before they could get ambulance—child has meningitis." Bad as such a situation was, it was worse when permission for both the hospitalization and the ambulance was needed.

The separation of the Dispensary both physically and administratively from a hospital created further problems. While patients needing emergency services had to go to a hospital emergency room, their follow-up care was given at the Dispensary. Many patients did not understand what they had been told by the hospital, and consequently the admitting clerks had to find out by telephone what they needed. Occasionally, as a result of misunderstandings, the patient was sent back and forth needlessly from place to place, and even "lost" in the shuffle. One field note describes a call from the aunt of a nineteen-year-old boy who had been sent to the Dispensary three days before and had not returned home since. He was finally located in a hospital ward, happy in the illusion that someone had informed his aunt that he had been dispatched there.

Such confusion at the boundary naturally inhibited people from using the Dispensary, no matter how good the medical care. Brightman and his co-workers (1958) compared the knowledge and use of medical facilities in Syracuse by poor families eligible for Dispensary care with that of families covered by health insurance under an industrial plan. They found that even though the poor families needed more medical care and knew that they were entitled to it, they sought it less often than the factory workers.

---

* New York State law requires Welfare Departments to take responsibility for the costs of hospitalization of the medically indigent.

Confusion at the boundary also had its effects on the admissions clerks. The constant, and often conflicting, requests of the medical staff, the Social Service Department, the Welfare record rooms and the various hospitals resulted in considerable role strain. All boundary roles are intrinsically subject to conflict (Snoek, 1966), but when the need to integrate diverse demands is compounded by inadequate communication systems and hampering administrative details, the conflict becomes much worse. Whyte (1946) explained outbursts of weeping among waitresses in terms of exactly this kind of cross-pressure; it is not surprising that some of these admissions clerks expressed their frustrations by a kind of retreatism in which the patients were ignored or dealt with peremptorily.

The Syracuse Dispensary was not alone in its problems. Somers and Somers (1961), Baumgartner and Dumpson (1962), Wilson (1963), Muller (1965), Knowles (1965), Yerby (1966), and many others had referred to the confusion and misunderstanding that marked attempts to provide services to the medically indigent within the framework of the large outpatient complex. In 1961 the Dispensary resembled many other similar facilities across the nation in providing a large amount of medical service under the supervision of the medical school, but under tangled administrative conditions.

Method of Study

The Dispensary made no appointments. All patients were expected to report at 9:30 A.M. or 1:00 P.M., and these periods of peak activity were attended by field observers who attached themselves to one of the three clerks who admitted the incoming patients for treatment. All patients were sent through the admitting office when they had a new illness, whether or not they had been Dispensary patients before. Observations were made from February 19 until March 6, 1962, a total of 11 working days. A total of 2244 visits were made to the Dispensary during this period, or an average of 204 a day, but of these, 1728 were made by patients who did not go through the admitting office because they were already in the course of treatment (Table 4-1). There were 516 visits to the admitting office, of which 452 were direct applications for medical care. Information was collected about 214, or 42 per cent of all visits to the admitting office, and patients' files were abstracted later.

Table 4-1. RELATIONSHIP OF 214 STUDY VISITS TO THE TOTAL ACTIVITY OF THE SYRACUSE DISPENSARY[a]

Type of activity	No.	In study No.	%
All visits	**2244**		
To clinic directly	*1728[b]*		
Visits to admitting	*516[c]*	*214*	*41.5*
Service applications	*452*	*214*	*47.3*
Direct to clinic	251	177	70.5
Re-rate procedures	58	17	29.3
Arranging charges	77	10	13.0
Arranging hospitalization	66	10	15.2
Other arrangements	*64[b]*		
Taxicabs	7		
Glasses voucher	57		

[a] Period of study in Tables 4-1 through 4-4 was February 19 to March 6, 1962.
[b] Excluded from study.
[c] All admitting office workers kept a tally of their activities for the study days.

The unit of analysis for this part of the study was the visit. In this particular study group, no patient appeared on different days, and, therefore, the number of visits was the same as the number of patients.

Findings

REFERRAL SOURCES

Table 4-2 presents a profile of the Dispensary's relationships with the remainder of the regulative system. Column 1 shows the agents from which the patients were referred into the agency. The largest single group of patients, 79 (or 37 per cent), came directly to the Dispensary themselves or through the informal referrals of friends and relatives.

The next largest group, 73 (or 34 per cent), came to the

Dispensary through a medical referral, five of them from public health nurses visiting in the home, one from a mental hospital aftercare clinic, and the rest in almost equal numbers from emergency rooms, public clinics, and private physicians.

Table 4-2. RELATIONSHIP OF THE SYRACUSE DISPENSARY WITH OTHER AGENCIES THROUGH REFERRAL SOURCES, INTERAGENCY CONTACTS AND REFERRAL TARGETS OF 214 PATIENTS

Agency	Type of relationship with other agencies				
	Referral		Arrangements	Information	Eligibility checks
	Source	Target[b]			
All patients	214	214	214	214	214
Without agency contact	79	182	207	200	81
With agency contact	135	32	7	14	133
Total contacts made[a]	*144*	*40*	*7*	*19*	*134*
Medical					
Private physician	22				
Outpatient clinics	22	1		1	
Emergency room	23	1			
Hospitals		20		13	
Public health nurses and VNA	5	1	2		
Psychiatric aftercare clinic	1				
Health Department clinic				1	
Temporal Bone Bank, Chicago				1	
Counseling					
Schools	16				
Personnel office	3				
Hospital social service	20				
Social Service, Dispensary	3	5			2
Income maintenance					
Welfare	23	11	3	1	131
Red Cross	1				
Workmen's Compensation		1			
Public housing					1
Social Security				1	
Rotary Club			1		
Institutions					
Men's shelters	3				
Mental hospital			1		
Nursing home				1	
Correction					
Police and parole	2				

[a] Number of contacts exceeds number of patients about whom contacts were made because some had double referrals and numerous interagency contacts.
[b] Referral target covers both referrals and "steers."

One-half of the family doctors had reported referring poor patients to the Dispensary (Table 3-1).

Twenty per cent came from counseling services, mostly hospital social service and schools, and 11 per cent from Welfare. Only six patients came from other sources. This referral pattern reflected the Dispensary's interdependence with the various hospital emergency services and social service departments, the public clinics, and the Department of Welfare. In all, 79 per cent of the patients came either through one of these agencies or on their own.*

PROBLEMS PRESENTED

All the patients approaching the Dispensary had both health and financial problems. Although one-third had never had Welfare assistance, all were medically indigent because they were either unskilled and therefore could command only low incomes or had been laid off long enough to have exhausted their unemployment benefits, or because they had such large families that even moderately good incomes were insufficient for paying medical bills. Some of the patients had additional complicating problems, and these have been grouped in Table 4-3 according to the information recorded in their files or presented at intake. Those with health problems only are classed as contingencies, and these are subdivided into health problems of children, adults, and the aged. Three-quarters of the applicants, as far as the records reveal, were simply medically indigent with no other complicating problems (Table 4-3).

SERVICES OFFERED

Medical Care. All but eight of the patients approaching the Dispensary met the eligibility requirements and received medical care either in one of the clinics or in a hospital. In

---

* The schools, which supplied 7 per cent of the Dispensary's patients, have an important caretaking role for children, and to some degree this extends to adults, although less so now than when an immigrant generation related themselves to an alien society through them. The schools are excluded from direct consideration here because services for adults were the focus of study.

Table 4-3.   PROBLEMS PRESENTED BY 214 MEDICALLY
INDIGENT PATIENTS ADMITTED TO THE
SYRACUSE DISPENSARY

Problem category	No.	%
All patients	214	100.0
Transition states	6	2.8
Temporary unemployment	3	1.4
Migration and removal	2	0.9
Marital adjustment	1	0.5
Role failure	44	20.5
Chronic economic inadequacy[a]	21	9.8
Inadequate wives and/or mothers[a]	12	5.6
Evidence of antisocial behavior	5	2.3
Homelessness	6	2.8
Contingencies (medical indigency only)	164	76.7
Children	83	38.8
Adults	43	20.1
Aged	38	17.8

[a] These two categories reflect failure in the central life roles of men and women. Typically, economic inadequacy is long-term inability to support a family for any reason except ill-health. Inadequate wives and mothers are women whose marriages break down, who have illegitimate children or multiple liaisons, or who have public notice taken of their neglect or abuse of children. Women who have been separated or divorced and do not have young children are classified as economically inadequate if they are permanent welfare recipients.

some of the cases served, there was reason to believe that the ailment was minor or could have been handled by a general practitioner, but the clinic doctor accepted the patients nevertheless. In other words, once past the controls at the boundary, the patient could expect relatively supportive care except for the level of informal control inherent in a large, busy, overcrowded clinic.

Interagency Contacts. One way in which an agency can both serve the patient and articulate itself with other parts of the regulative system is by collaborating with other agents in making arrangements on behalf of its patients. The Dispensary's ordinary routines included checking eligibility with Welfare and calling various medical supply companies and pharmacists to authorize payment for eyeglasses, prosthetics, and other medical aids. A search of the records showed that beyond these routine calls, an additional 34 contacts were made regarding 29 of the 214 patients (Table 4-2). Of these contacts, however, 27 were concerned either with extra eligibility checks* or the transfer of medical information, while only 7 were collaborations with other agencies in arranging for service. These 7 calls included such matters as the transfer of a cardiac patient to a ground-floor apartment. In 2 additional cases, arrangements were made with relatives of the patient.

Very little exchange of information took place in the course of care, indicating that most formal controls were concentrated on the issue of eligibility, a pattern no doubt more influenced by the public nature of the agency than by the nature of medical practice itself.

Referral Out. Referrals, like arrangements, both serve the patient and bind the agency to others in the system. There are two basically different ways of making a referral: it can be made actively, in which case the patient remains under some control, or it can be a simple suggestion intended to steer the patient to another source of help. The Dispensary referred or steered 32, or 15 per cent, of the 214 patients studied; of these, only 7 were actively referred, suggesting both that the doctors did not see much need for further control of the great majority of the patients and that most patients had selected an appropriate target when they came to this agency. It is not known, of course, whether some patients who were not on target were redirected between the front desk and the admitting office to other services.

Of the 32 patients steered and referred, 12 were sent to a hospital only, 8 to a hospital and another agency (5 to Welfare, 2 to the Social Service, Dispensary, and 1 to Workmen's Compensation). The remaining referrals or steers were 6 to Welfare only, 3 to Social Service, Dispensary only, and 1 each to an outpatient clinic, an emergency room, and a public health nursing service (Table 4-2). Because referrals to the Social Service, Dispensary were usually made by the clinic doctors at the end of a course of treatment, and because 70,

---

* Of the 131 eligibility checks with Welfare (Table 4-2), 126 were considered routine. There were 5 extra eligibility checks with the Welfare Department.

or one-third of the patients, were still under treatment and unreferred when the records were abstracted, another 2 or 3 referrals to this source and perhaps 5 or 6 to other sources might be expected to have occurred. The over-all pattern of referrals out of the agency resembled that of referrals in, the great majority being to the agencies with whom the Dispensary was administratively linked.

Summary of Services. Services were distributed evenly among the various problem categories, except that children whose illnesses tend to be less serious and to require fewer hospitalizations were significantly less often given multiple service (Table 4-4).

A Specialized Isolated Agency

The Dispensary's method of delivering medical care differed in several ways from the family doctors': first, its goal was at least as much to train medical students as to treat pa-

Table 4-4. SERVICE OFFERED TO 214 DISPENSARY
PATIENTS, BY PROBLEM TYPE

Services offered	Total No.	Total %	Transition states	Role failure	Contingencies Children	Contingencies Adults	Contingencies Aged
All patients	**214**	**100.0**	**6**	**44**	**83**	**43**	**38**
No service	2	0.9					2
One service	*180*	*84.1*	*5*	*36*	*78*	*33*	*28*
Medical care Arrangements	174	81.3	5	33	78[a]	32	26
Referral	6	2.8		3		1	2
Two services	*31*	*14.5*	*1*	*7*	*5*	*10*	*8*
Medical and referral	25	11.7	1	6	4	9	5
Medical and arrangements	6	2.8		1	1	1	3
Arrangements and referral							
Three services	*1*	*0.5*		*1*			

[a] More children from medically indigent families received a single service only than did patients in any other problem category. ($\chi^2 = 7.6$, d.f. = 1, P < .01.)

tients; second, it was intended to be a group of specialist services, scarcely able, because of the autonomy of its various clinics, to serve the whole man; third, it worked in greater isolation from the remainder of the regulative system than did the family doctors; and fourth, its control over its patients was much greater than the family doctors' and the patients' reciprocal control much less. The clinic doctors therefore faced none of the family doctors' conflicts about losing patients, but, from the patients' point of view, this method of delivering health care was hardly satisfactory. Indeed, by the time of this study the large outpatient clinic was beginning to be perceived as obsolete by the medical profession itself. Four years later a leading health care expert had this to say: "What [the ambulatory patient] needs is not short-term acute care but continued supportive care. He needs this near his home in a family and patient-centered clinic. Ambulatory care must be decentralized, brought near the home through branch clinics, store-front walk-ins, and easily available medical auxiliary services." (James, 1965)*

REFERENCES

Baumgartner, Leona, and J. R. Dumpson, 1962. "Health in Welfare: A Joint or a Divided Responsibility?" *American Journal of Public Health*, Vol. 52, No. 7, July.

Brightman, I. Jay, H. Notkin, W. A. Brumfield, S. M. Dorsey, and H. S. Solomon, 1958. "Knowledge and Utilization of Health Resources by Public Assistance Recipients," *American Journal of Public Health*, Vol. 48, No. 2, February.

James, George, 1965. "Medical Advances in the Next Ten Years: The Implications for the Organization and Economics of Medicine," *Bulletin of the New York Academy of Medicine*, Vol. 41, No. 1, January.

Knowles, John H., 1965. "The Role of the Hospital: The Ambulatory Clinic," *Bulletin of the New York Academy of Medicine*, Vol. 41, No. 1, January.

Lambert, Camille, H. E. Freeman, R. Morris, and L. J. Taubenhaus, 1963. "Public Clinic Care and Eligibility," *American Journal of Public Health*, Vol. 53, No. 8, August.

Muller, Charlotte, 1965. "Income and the Receipt of Medical Care," *American Journal of Public Health*, Vol. 55, No. 4, April.

---

* At the time of going to press, experimental family clinics in slum areas had been set up in Syracuse.

Piore, Nora K., 1965. "Metropolitan Medical Economics," *Scientific American,* Vol. 212, No. 1, January.
Snoek, Diedrich, 1966. "Role Strain in Diversified Role Sets," *American Journal of Sociology,* Vol. LXXI, No. 4, January.
Somers, Herman M., and Anne R. Somers, 1961. *Doctors, Patients, and Health Insurance,* Washington, Brookings.
Whyte, William F., 1946. "Where Workers and Customers Meet," in *Industry and Society,* ed. William F. Whyte, New York, McGraw-Hill.
Wilson, R. N., 1963. "Patient, Practitioner and Relationship," in *Handbook of Medical Sociology,* eds. H. E. Freeman, S. Levine, and G. Reeder, Englewood Cliffs, N.J., Prentice-Hall.
Yerby, Alonzo S., 1966. "The Disadvantaged and Health Care," *American Journal of Public Health,* Vol. 56, No. 1, January.

THE PLANNED PARENTHOOD CENTER: A SPECIALIZED MEDICAL SERVICE

5

For three related reasons, family planning agencies have always been at the center of controversy even though they offer a highly specialized medical service. First, in spite of being a medical agency, they have been viewed in moral terms by some religions, particularly the Roman Catholic, partly because of the opprobrium that has been attached to contra-

Dr. Philip Ferro, Medical Director, and the late Eleanor Zimmerman, Executive Director, gave kind permission to conduct this study, and the staff of the agency warmly cooperated under difficult conditions. Patricia Healy assisted with the field work and data analysis, and Steven Polgar read the manuscript and offered helpful criticisms.

ceptive methods other than abstinence. Second, their service, though personal, medical, and supportive, has had many social and economic implications when viewed in terms of population increases (Hauser, 1963). And third, they have served a population which has been largely medically indigent, at the same time that these agencies, having little access to public funds, have sought financial support from local sources. This, in turn, has drawn attention to their controversial characteristics.

Both those opposed to contraception on moral and religious grounds and those in support of it on social and economic grounds have had their zealots. In some states, such as Massachusetts, legislation has forbidden the sale of contraceptives; while in other states, such as California, laws allow the compulsory sterilization of various categories of the so-called unfit. The studies reported here were carried out during a time when a shift in the attitude of the Catholic Church had just become discernible. This change arose in part because in some places passage of sterilization laws designed to reduce the illegitimate birth rate among women dependent on public support was imminent, and this was considered much more objectionable than voluntary birth control (Thomas, 1964). Somewhat earlier, the American Public Health Association had declared its belief that birth control should be officially considered a health matter, and President Kennedy had expressed America's interest in the control of world population (Barrett, 1963; Polgar and Cowles, 1966; Jaffe, 1966).

In spite of these changes in the climate of opinion around family planning, as late as 1964 less than 10 per cent of medically indigent American women in the childbearing age were estimated to be receiving contraceptive service from either public or private sources (Polgar, 1964), and many individual agencies were still having trouble gaining acceptance in their communities.

The Planned Parenthood Center of Syracuse, like its sister agencies throughout the country, tended to stand apart from the rest of the regulative system. Its history had been stormy: two years before these studies were carried out, attempts to create a county-wide health council had been halted because the Catholic agencies refused to join if Planned Parenthood was to be a member. The agency had never been a member of the United Fund; and although it had a devoted staff, medical director and board, and an enthusiastic group of volunteers, its financial support derived from its own fund-raising efforts and the fees that it charged.

Some family planning agencies have tried to moderate the controversy they generate by publicly emphasizing their planning function; that is, by drawing attention away from birth control service and toward their counseling function and their cancer testing and fertility programs.* Although such efforts can protect the agency, particularly its medical staff, from public censure, some observers think that they result in the agency attracting the more affluent patient and disaffecting the poverty-stricken (Rein, 1963). Such a course would, of course, frustrate the most important agency goal, which is to reach those most in need of the service, and the Planned Parenthood Center of Syracuse had successfully avoided that course.

The agency was under the direction of a full-time social worker and a part-time medical director. Clinics were staffed by physicians practicing gynecology and obstetrics and members of the Medical Center faculty and staff. The Center's staff also included two nurses, a second social worker, and three clerks.

Entrance to the Agency

The Center was housed in an overcrowded, dilapidated building in an area of urban blight close to Syracuse University. Clinics were held three afternoons and two evenings a week. At other times, the office was open during the day for making appointments and for selling contraceptive supplies. Appointments could be made either in person, by telephone, or by referring agent.

Each incoming patient was interviewed, usually by a vol-

---

* Actually, these "secondary" services had never exceeded 1 per cent of total services, nationwide. (Steven Polgar, personal communication, 1966.)

unteer, whether or not she had ever attended the clinic before. If she was a new patient, she then received group instruction in the various methods of contraception, including, for those who wished it, the rhythm method. Girls or couples who came in for premarital counseling were seen by the clinic's social worker, or one of the nurses, and given a variety of literature. Sometimes group premarital sessions were conducted by the Medical Director. After the initial interview, and usually after a considerable wait, all patients were seen by a clinic doctor and a nurse.

The clinic's quarters were so inadequate that some interviews had to be conducted in makeshift, semipublic situations, and the waiting room was sometimes so crowded that not everyone could sit down. In spite of these uncomfortable physical conditions, however, there was a pleasant atmosphere in the agency because of the enthusiasm with which the patients were welcomed into the service. Of all the agencies studied, this was the only one that practiced active recruitment, mainly through talks given by the medical director before many kinds of gatherings. Part of this recruiting spirit undoubtedly sprang from the agency's belief in the value of its service, but part was probably a response to its controversial position in the community and its determination to reach its goals and thus prove its worth.

Control at the incoming boundary was slight; most of the eligibility requirements were a result of potential public pressure. All married or separated women and single women about to marry were eligible, but unmarried women were only accepted if they had already had an illegitimate child or if they were referred by an agent or an agency. This rule effectively prevented the college girls who lived nearby from using the clinic and thus bringing it into disrepute in the town.

The Planned Parenthood Center board and staff, along with those of many other agencies, believed that people who paid for health care "appreciated" it more than those who did not. For this reason, a sliding scale of charges for initial examination was made, and contraceptives were sold to the clients at roughly wholesale prices. Cancer tests were arranged at the usual cost. During the study period, the Welfare Department seldom used the agency except for serious medical reasons. Sometimes, therefore, Welfare clients paid for their contraceptives from their allotment, thus reducing the amount of money available for food and clothing. Failure to pay never resulted in refusal of further service, however, and the agency staff appeared to be making every effort to find reasons to eliminate as many charges as they could for these patients.

Two latent, and perhaps unintended, controls were exerted over the patients at the agency boundary, both of which must certainly have inhibited them from discussing personal problems: the public situation in which the intake interview and instruction were conducted and the use of middle-class volunteers as intake interviewers. Although the volunteers were expected to call a clinic nurse if the patient did want to discuss her problems during the intake process, the over-all situation probably reduced artificially the number of complicating problems reported.

Except for these inhibiting conditions, the patients entered the agency with a minimum of control. The staff's efforts to recruit patients must have conveyed to them the value placed upon them. Because of this high value, controls at the boundary of the agency approached symmetry.

Method of Study

One hundred and three patients entered the agency for the first time between January 2 and February 21, 1962, and these formed the study group. No patient re-entered during the period so that the number of applications was equal to the number of patients. A research worker acted as a volunteer in the agency for a period of two months at a later date in order to verify that the records, which were essentially medical in character, included all of the information that was acquired in the intake process.*

Because the agency was itself concerned about the success of its efforts to reach out to poor families and to hold them in care, it was agreed to extend the study to include three sep-

* This procedure was not as satisfactory as the direct observation carried out during the collection of the study groups at other primary agencies, but it assisted considerably in interpreting the findings.

Table 5-1. RELATIONSHIP OF PLANNED PARENTHOOD WITH
OTHER AGENCIES THROUGH REFERRAL SOURCES, INTER-
AGENCY CONTACTS AND REFERRAL TARGETS
OF 103 PATIENTS[a]

| | Type of relationship with other agencies | | | | |
Agency	*Referral* *Source*	*Referral* *Target*	*Arrange-* *ments*	*Infor-* *mation*	*Eligibility* *checks*
All patients	103	103	103	103	103
Without agency contact	55	100	103	102	102
With agency contact	48	3	0	1	1
Total contacts made	*53*	*3*	*0*	*1*	*1*
Medical					
Private physician	10	1			
Dispensary	1				
Hospital clinics	3				
Hospital doctors and					
nurses	3				
Public Health Nurse	2				
Health Department	1				
Planned Parenthood					
staff	3				
Planned Parenthood,					
out of town	3	1			
Counseling					
Clergy	6				
Social Service, Dis-					
pensary	1				
Hospital social service	13				
Private psychologist		1			
Income maintenance					
Welfare	6				1
Housing Authority	1			1	

[a] Period of study in Tables 5-1 through 5-4 was January 2–February 21, 1962.

arate groups of patients collected at different times. Appendix A will describe changes in agency activity between 1959
and 1965–66.

Results

REFERRAL SOURCE

The agency profile (Table 5-1) shows that more than
half of the patients were self-referred, were sent by friends

and relatives, or had heard of the Center through one of the educational activities of the staff. Of the 48 patients referred from 53 sources, all but 13 came from medical or medical social service agencies, suggesting that the Center was seen as a specialized medical agency by other agencies. Six patients were referred by clergymen, 6 by the Welfare Department, and 1 by a social worker in a housing project. Only 2 referrals were made by the Dispensary and its Social Service Department, although both agencies were serving the medically indigent.

PROBLEMS PRESENTED

Most of the patients approaching the agency were relatively poor, but there was considerable variation in their incomes, their family size, and their expectations for the future (Table 5-2). A small proportion of the patients were either the wives of college students or of white-collar workers who could be expected to enter private medical care, and probably to increase their families, as soon as their husbands were

Table 5-2. NUMBER OF CHILDREN, OCCUPATIONAL
STATUS, AND COLOR OF 103 APPLICANTS TO
PLANNED PARENTHOOD

Number of children and occupation	Total No.	Total %	Color Non-white	Color White
All patients	**103**	**100.0**	**19**	**84**
0–3 children	56	54.4	5[a]	51[a]
Students	5	4.9		5
White-collar	9	8.7		9
Blue-collar	36	35.0	3	33
Welfare recipient[b]	4	3.9	2	2
Armed forces	2	1.9		2
4 children or more	47	45.6	14[a]	33[a]
White-collar	2	1.9		2
Blue-collar	35	34.0	11	24
Welfare recipient[b]	9	8.7	3	6
Armed forces	1	1.0		1

[a] Proportionately more nonwhites than white clients have four or more children. ($\chi^2 = 6.06$, d.f. = 1, .02 > P > .01.)
[b] At the time of application, and for long periods of time prior to application.

established. The great majority, however, 71 of the 103, were the wives of blue-collar workers whose wages were at present sufficient to support their families but not to pay for medical care, and perhaps never would be. Thirteen women came from families that had been dependent on welfare assistance for a long time, two of them for reasons of health. Ten more patients had received welfare assistance in the past, or were temporarily unemployed at the time of the study, but they were classified with the blue-collar group.

Slightly less than half of the 103 families already had four children (Table 5-2). About one client in five was nonwhite, which was more than twice the proportion of nonwhites in the Syracuse population at the time.* Although proportionately more of the nonwhite group had families of four or more children, they did not differ from the remainder in occupational status.

Although the agency made no systematic exploration of complicating problems among its clients, financial setbacks were automatically recorded and some other complaints made spontaneously at intake were considered serious enough to record (Table 5-3). Nineteen women complained of problems serious enough to be classed as role failures; nine were married to men who were temporarily unemployed; and eight said that ill health among family members was a burden.

Because this agency, like the Syracuse Dispensary, was giving a specific health service to a medically indigent population, it is not surprising that the distribution of complicating problems presented in the two agencies was very similar (compare Tables 4-3 and 5-3).

SERVICES OFFERED

All the 103 women in the study group received the two core services of the agency: contraceptives and cancer-testing. Six of the 103 women received premarital counseling, but no patients were treated for infertility or referred to other services for this reason during the study period. The agency made

---

* Planned Parenthood collected this datum as a rough index of how well it was reaching deprived groups; it was the only agency in which it was possible to make this comparison.

Table 5-3. PROBLEMS PRESENTED BY 103 APPLICANTS
TO PLANNED PARENTHOOD

Problem category	No.	%
All patients	103	100.0
Transition states	9	8.7
Temporary unemployment	9	8.7
Role failure	20	19.5
Economic inadequacy	12	11.7
Marital conflict	8	7.8
Contingencies	74	71.8
Adult[a]	67	65.0
Health problems	6	5.8
Child	1	1.0

[a] Simple medical indigence.

arrangements for no patients and steered only three; at this rate, only one more referral of the 36 patients who were still in care four years after the study period could be expected. No other agency exerted so little control at both in and out boundaries.

The agency profile highlights vividly the isolation of the Planned Parenthood Center from the remainder of the regulative system (Table 5-1). No other agency studied had so few contacts of any kind for any purpose. This isolation was one reason for the low level of control exerted over the clients once they were in care, although great effort was made to keep them in care. In only one case was an eligibility check made, and in only one was information exchanged with another agency. Many of the patients seemed to be aware of the agency's isolation; several volunteered that either their doctor or their family had been opposed to their coming, but that they trusted the agency not to betray them. One forty-one-year-old woman, for example, did not want her married daughter, who had strong religious objections to contraception, to hear of her attendance at the clinic.

Because most patients needed to attend the clinic only once or twice a year, it was hard to determine when they had left the service and when they had skipped an appointment. Four years after the study period, however, one-third of the women were still in care (Table 5-4). Proportionately more non-white women, 13 of the 19, compared to only 24 of the 84 white women, remained in care, and this over-all difference was statistically significant. Although the high rate of separation among the occupational groups in which nonwhites did not appear accounts for some of the difference in the rates of leaving care, the 13 "chronic" welfare clients also contributed noticeably to the difference. In the blue-collar category, which made up the bulk of the study group, two-thirds of the white patients and only one-third of the non-

Table 5-4.   STATUS OF 103 PLANNED PARENTHOOD
PATIENTS FOUR YEARS AFTER INTAKE, BY
SPOUSES' OCCUPATION AND COLOR

Occupation	Total	Remaining open	
		No.	%
All patients	**103**	**37**	**35.9**
White patients	*84*	*24*	*28.6*
Students	5	0	0.0
White-collar	11	3	27.3
Blue-collar	57	19	33.3[a]
Welfare recipient	8	1	12.5[a]
Armed forces	3	1	33.3
Nonwhite patients	*19*	*13*	*68.4*
Blue-collar	14	9	64.3[a]
Welfare recipient	5	4	80.0[a]

[a] In the categories in which nonwhites are represented, significantly more whites than nonwhites leave care. ($x^2 = 7.2$, d.f. = 1, P < .01.)

whites left care. This difference taken alone is not, however, statistically significant. Neither age nor family size was significantly associated with leaving care, and within each age group and family size the excess of white over nonwhite patients persisted.

These findings suggest that the agency was, in part, reaching its goal of holding deprived groups, but it appeared to be more successful with nonwhite than with white clients of a comparable need for the service. No explanation of this finding is possible from the data collected in this study.

A Specific, Supportive, Patient's Agency

The benchmarks of the Planned Parenthood Center were its recruiting spirit, the specificity of its service, and the relative isolation in which it practiced. Of course, such a specialized, medical service offered to healthy women in an outpatient setting should not often require collaboration with other parts of the regulative system. Furthermore, when there may be constraints against collaboration because of the controversial character of the agency, pressure is exerted against the development of situations where collaboration or referral might become imperative. Complementing this agency's isolation, furthermore, was a spectrum of roles within its own structure, including doctors, nurses, and social workers, which suggested much less specialization. The agency's philosophy did, in fact, include the concern for the whole woman that its staffing pattern suggested, but its day-to-day activities stressed its specialized function.* Perhaps the presence of the three disciplines provided assurance to both staff and patients that secondary problems could be solved if they became too pressing. Isolation did seem to be allowing this agency to specialize in its birth control activities rather than fertility and counseling services, and hence to reach its own goals with no internal conflict and a minimum chance of conflict with other agencies. For whatever reason, the agency was able to provide service to a group of patients most of whom badly needed it and could not have found it anywhere else. In no other agency did the patients and the staff seem to need and like each other so sincerely, a situation, as Blau (1964) has pointed out, of almost perfectly symmetrical mutual support and control.

* The Syracuse agency seemed to have differed from other Planned Parenthood Centers in the concern it expressed for the nonmedical problems of the patients; it seemed to resemble them closely in its practice, nevertheless.

REFERENCES

Barrett, George, 1963. "Catholics and Birth Control: Growing Debate," *The New York Times,* August 5, page 1, column 3.

Blau, Peter, 1964. *Exchange and Power in Social Life,* New York, Wiley.

Hauser, Philip, 1963. *Cost of U.S. Population Growth,* Symposium, Annual Meeting Planned Parenthood World Population, New York, Planned Parenthood World Population.

Jaffe, Frederick S., 1967. "Family Planning, Public Policy and Intervention Strategy," *Journal of Social Issues,* Vol. 23, No. 4, October.

Polgar, Steven, 1964. "Social Science Research in Planned Parenthood Centers," *Advances in Planned Parenthood,* New York, Planned Parenthood World Population.

Polgar, Steven, and W. B. Cowles, eds., 1966. "Public Health Programs in Family Planning," *American Journal of Public Health,* Vol. 56, No. 1, January, Supplement (whole issue).

Rein, Martin, 1963. *An Organizational Analysis of a National Agency's Local Affiliates in Their Community Context,* New York, Planned Parenthood Federation of America.

Thomas, Rev. John L., S.J., 1964. "Problems of the Future: Sterilization, Abortion and Other Issues," in *The Problem of Population: Moral and Theological Considerations,* South Bend, University of Notre Dame.

THE HOME CARE NURSING   *6*
PROGRAM: AN EXTENSION
OF MEDICAL SERVICE

The public health nursing program chosen for study was one of the services provided through the Nursing Bureau of the Syracuse Public Health Department. It was fully supported by public funds. Public health nursing can be thought of as a versatile extension of the medical role; it includes a wide variety of services carried out in many kinds of public and private settings such as schools, clinics, factories, and hospitals,

Miss Isabel McCaffrey helped to design this study; Miss C. Riley, Director of the program, cooperated with the field workers. The 1962–63 students of the School of Public Health Nursing of the Upstate Medical Center interviewed the patients and searched the records; Louis Flohr also assisted with the field work. Patricia Healy, Robert Porter, and Joan Poltenson helped to analyze the data.

but always under the directorship, no matter how remote, of a medical doctor.

One of the traditional functions of public health nursing is to provide nursing care to patients in their homes. These nurses are popular with medical doctors because they extend their practice for them while still observing the traditional doctor-nurse relationship. This relationship provides nurses with the necessary authority for much of the care they give, but it can also hamper them in important ways. First, they are dependent for supervision upon someone who not only has different headquarters but is often inaccessible. Sometimes quite simple advice may be unavailable to patients because nurses cannot take responsibility for "medical decisions" and doctors cannot be interrupted for minor matters. For example, while a social worker and a public health nurse were visiting a young mother who had been in a mental hospital, the mother complained that her baby had been restless and crying since a recent visit to the clinic when its formula had been strengthened. The nurse said that she would check the formula with the clinic doctor, but the social worker, who was also the mother of three small children, said, "Why don't you try cutting down the formula for a couple of days?"

The traditional nurse-doctor relationship requires that the nurse must often carry out the doctor's orders without argument even when she thinks they are inappropriate in light of the patient's situation. This second disadvantage of the traditional relationship is at a maximum in the care of the chronically ill, because doctors seldom visit these patients and are, therefore, likely to be unaware of changes in home conditions that have a bearing on their health and comfort.

The Home Care Nursing Program studied was intended not only to give bedside care to the chronically ill but also to coordinate the efforts of the family to care for the patient with a variety of available community resources. The Nursing Bureau had located a nursing service in a housing project that catered for, but was not limited to, elderly persons living on small incomes or on Social Security pensions. This service was offered not only to the project residents but also to the people in the surrounding neighborhood. It was in this branch of the Nursing Bureau that the Home Care Program was developed. The service was designed to test the feasibility of maintaining in their homes patients who might otherwise find it necessary to go to hospitals, nursing homes, or other institutions for convalescent or long-term care. It was the philosophy of the program that everyone had a right to die in his own home if he wished, and if it were humanly possible to keep him there.

Like other programs of its kind, this one recognized that medical and nursing care for the aged and the chronically ill is always inadequate if it cannot be delivered to them in their homes (Furstenberg, 1965; Testoff and Levine, 1965). The concept of home care for the chronically ill usually includes a complete range of medical and social services as well as continuity of care. The program under study, however, required the patient to be under the medical supervision of a private physician or a clinic as a prerequisite for its care. Although the program nurses and the social worker made every effort to arrange for such supervision so that patients would not be refused admission for lack of medical attention, those who were supervised by the Dispensary or hospital clinics did not in any real sense have personal medical attention or continuity of medical care. Furthermore, patients who attended the Syracuse Dispensary had to be transported back and forth to the clinic, usually by volunteer drivers from local agencies. If the patient was not well enough to attend the clinic, the service could not achieve its goal of keeping him in his home. In general, the Home Care Program could be thought of as a good, well-staffed public health nursing service that enjoyed the services of a social worker but did not have the full range of resources that its name implied. In other words, the public health nurses' traditional attachment to private medical care, codified into the rules of the agency, was making it impossible for the service to use either the medical director or other available consultants when they were obviously needed.*

---

* Since this chapter was written, Medicare and Medicaid, the New York State program of medical care for middle-income families, have

The program's activities were under the immediate direction of a full-time public health nurse and a part-time medical director, who did not himself see patients, but who participated in staff conferences at which plans for care were made.

Method of Study

The study period covered the first seven months of operation of the Home Care Program, from August 15, 1962, through March 15, 1963. During this time, 50 family groups, including 66 patients, three-quarters of whom were sixty-five years or older, were referred for service. A total of 49 families, including 65 patients, actually received service. Thirty of the families (44 patients) were composed of married couples; 10 patients were living in the homes of relatives, 8 women and 1 man were living alone, 2 in rooming houses, and 1 man was living with a housekeeper.

Data were collected from the records of both the Home Care Program and the parent nursing agency, and an interview with every member of each family under care was attempted, although in seven families the attempt failed, usually because of the severity of the illness.

Entrance to the Agency

The nursing office in which the Home Care Program was housed was open five days a week, and applications for service could be made directly by patients and their families. All the families in the study group were already known to the basic nursing service, however, because a health survey of the housing project had been made by the agency at the time that it had been established.

When an application for care was received, one of the staff nurses and the program social worker made a home visit in order to assess the home situation, as well as the family's own

made it possible for many more patients to be under individual medical supervision.

resources for looking after its ill member. These assessments, together with the written orders and recommendations of the patient's physician, were then presented at a staff conference and a plan of care was made if it was decided to admit the patient to the program. Changes of plan and the decisions to discharge the patient from care were also made in staff conference.

Interviews with the patients seemed to suggest that they took the program for granted as part of the supportive complex of health services and other conveniences supplied through the Health Center in the housing project. As one spry seventy-five-year-old said, "If anyone finds fault, they're crazy." Nevertheless, most patients had only a vague idea of what the service was and how they had got into its care.

The only eligibility requirement set by the agency other than medical supervision was that the patient be able to manage at home with the help that could be mobilized either by the service or by his relatives. Two families left the service immediately after being accepted; one was too confused to remain at home and was referred to a hospital, and the other had a private physician who would not cooperate with the plan. One patient died within a week of being admitted to care.

Findings

REFERRAL SOURCE

As the agency profile shows (Table 6-1), two-thirds of the patients entered care upon a recommendation from the parent agency, indicating that all the 50 families involved had either been using the nursing service before their condition warranted placing them under special home care or had already been found by the health survey team. The remaining one-third were referred by health agencies, usually private physicians.

PROBLEM PRESENTED

According to the problem categories used in the core agencies, 14 of the Home Care Program patients were suffer-

Table 6-1. RELATIONSHIP OF HOME CARE SERVICE WITH OTHER
AGENCIES THROUGH REFERRAL SOURCES, INTERAGENCY
CONTACTS AND REFERRAL TARGETS OF 50 FAMILIES[a]

Agency contact	Type of relationship with other agencies				
	Referrals		*Arrange-ments*	*Infor-mation*	*Eligi-bility*
	Source	*Target*			
All patients	66	66	66		
Without agency contact	0	55	0		
With agency contact	66	11	66		
Total contacts made	*70*	*11*	*135*		
Medical					
Private physician	12		19	6	12
Hospital		1	7	7	
Dispensary	4		8	7	6
Special clinics	4		15		
Other PHN	46	10	1		
Medical-Commercial					
Druggists			13		
Hearing aid service			3		
Laboratory service			6		
Optometrist			2		
Podiatrist			3		
Recreational					
Agency unspecified			1		
Counseling					
Clergy			3		
Family agency			1		
Lawyer or Legal Aid			3		
School services			2		
VA Contact Office			1		
Friendly Visitors			3		
Hospital social service	3				
Employment					
Employment agencies			1		
Sheltered workshop			1		
Vocational rehabilitation			1		
Lighthouse			1		
Income Maintenance					
Welfare	1		9	9	
Housing or landlord			8		
Surplus food			4		
Christmas Bureau			2		
Loan Closet			5		
Meals on Wheels			4		
Red Cross			1		
Railroad retirement board			1		
Institutions					
Nursing homes			2		
Marcy Hospital			1		
Other: nonagency					
fire chief; funeral home			**3**		

[a] Period of study in Tables 6-1 and 6-2 was August 15, 1962, to March 15, 1963.

ing from disorders contingent upon being aged, and 50 were chronically ill. The seriousness of the patients' illnesses ranged from acute illnesses from which full recovery could be expected, through chronic illnesses in which an optimal level of functioning was maintained, to terminal illness.

In six families the patients complained of economic deprivation as well as illness. In one of these poor families there had been a long history of indebtedness and economic inadequacy, and one family was having difficulty with relatives; both were classed as role failure. The only man living alone complained of loneliness. In five families in which only one member was in care, other family members had poor health. Considering that the patients had very real health problems, however, and especially that one-third of them were suffering from terminal illnesses, the patients interviewed appeared to be in good spirits and pleased with the service they were receiving. One old lady living alone was particularly grateful because she would not have to go to a nursing home and give up her dog and cat.

SERVICES OFFERED

Nursing Care. The agency gave two core services: nursing care and the arranging of other services. Nursing care itself varied according to illness. In a family in which a patient had arthritis or had suffered a cerebral accident, a visit once a week during the rehabilitation period was sufficient. In some cases of terminal illness, daily nursing care was necessary. Sometimes all members of the family were served even though they were not enrolled in the program; if, for example, the wife of a program patient developed an acute illness, she would receive the necessary nursing care under supervision of her own doctor at the same time that the patient was receiving regular care. Furthermore, the nurse and the social worker routinely offered support and encouragement to all members of the family, ill and well. This aspect of care seemed to be most appreciated by the patients. One man who had just returned from hospital said, "The nurses in the hospitals were like executives; these are *real* nurses—so patient."

Arrangements. Mobilization of resources for the patients

was at least as important in this program as the bedside care. Chronic illness, with its disabling effects, requires many services if function is to be maintained. In all, 32 different agents and agencies were involved in the program's care of its 50 families (Table 6-1). The program staff not only made arrangements with these regulative agents, however; they also made contact with undertakers, druggists, grocery stores, telephone companies, and numerous other places that the patients were unable to reach. Although it was not clear from the records which contacts were arrangements and which were eligibility checks or exchange of information, the nature of the agencies contacted as well as the nature of the service itself suggests that most were arrangements. It is probable, nevertheless, that some of the 18 contacts with the Welfare Department involved patients' eligibility for medical care under the Welfare program of medical aid to the aged and that many of the contacts with physicians and the Dispensary represented exchanges of information. No other agency, however, made one-third as many total interagency contacts as this one.

In spite of these efforts, some patients seemed to lack fairly simple services: several said that they would have liked more visitors, and two complained that they never got outside and would have liked help in getting to church or in running errands. Whether these were particularly complaining patients, or whether the nurses lacked time or the community sufficient volunteer services for visiting and transportation, was not clear.

Undoubtedly the intense activity of the nurses, which in its way wove a web of control around the patient, arose from the great variety of needs and the general dependency of the aged ill. The program's latent control over the patients was further heightened by the knowledge that although they could leave its care, if they did, they would have little alternative to entering the overtly controlling care of a nursing home.

Referral Out. Only 10 patients were actually returned to the public health nursing service during the study period, and perhaps another 6 or so of the 37 still in care would be before their cases were closed. Because the Home Care Program and the parent nursing service had the same staff, none of the patients realized that they had been transferred. Again, the tight control of the patient latent in such continuity of care arises from the nature of the geriatric illness.

Summary of Services. Table 6-2 summarizes the major types of care being given to the 50 families in the study, and at the same time reflects the major medical problems. Where more than one patient was in care, the one requiring the

Table 6-2.   MAJOR SERVICE PROVIDED TO 50 FAMILIES BY HOME CARE SERVICE

Major service	Families receiving	
	No.	*%*
All families	*50*	*100.0*
None	1	2.0
Health maintenance	16	32.0
Physical rehabilitation	11	22.0
Care of progressive terminal illnesses		
Early stages	7	14.0
Late stages	13	26.0
Social rehabilitation	2	4.0

most care was used to characterize the family. All families who were accepted received both of the core services, but the emphasis depended upon the nature of the most critical problem. In one family, for example, a diabetic woman was having her insulin dosage supervised at the same time that her dying husband was given daily nursing care, and the whole family, including visiting relatives, were receiving emotional support from the nurse. Other families, in which patients were recovering from accidents or paralytic strokes, needed transportation, equipment, or Friendly Visitors rather than bedside nursing care. As Table 6-2 shows, about one-third of the patients were receiving intensive care for terminal chronic illnesses; another third were chronically ill and receiving health maintenance care; while the remainder were being treated for disorders from which at least partial recovery was expected.

A General Supportive Service to a Special Population

Although the Home Care Program was obviously finding
solutions for a variety of serious problems, it was handi-
capped in not having a full range of services at its own dis-
posal. Emphasis upon coordination of services tended to dis-
guise the fact that certain core services, like medical care,
are much more efficient when freely available at the point
where plans are made (Walker, 1965). As one patient said,
"You can't get along without doctors, but don't get sick on
Thursdays or Sundays!" Furthermore, some nonmedical services either did not exist in a form appropriate for geriatric
illness or were inaccessible for other reasons. Private duty
nursing and housekeeping services* were nonexistent in Syracuse at the time of the study and the program had no mandate to try to develop them. One aged woman whose husband
had recently died in hospital said, "He couldn't talk . . .
never send anyone to hospital who can't talk. . . . I would
have taken care of him but I couldn't manage any longer
. . . and they sent me home the night he died although I
wanted to stay with him." Similarly, while Meals on Wheels
was available to bring in food to disabled patients, many of
the families interviewed referred to it in derogatory tones,
either because the cost was prohibitive, or because it was not
available on weekends. Because not all vital services were
available, the goals of the program could not always be met.
If, for example, a woman was too disabled to care for herself
and to perform light housekeeping tasks, or if a man did not
have a wife to provide these services for him, they were almost certain to be sent to a nursing home in spite of the zeal
of the program workers.

The agency's tight control over the patients was necessary
because of their illnesses and vulnerability, but, in spite of its
many contacts with other agencies, it did not have a tight

* After the study period, a Home Aide program was successfully
introduced in Syracuse.

enough control over medical resources to give the full-scale service that its clients needed if their desire to grow old and die in their own homes was to be fulfilled.

REFERENCES

Furstenberg, F. F., 1965. "Comprehensive Care for the Aging in the Outpatient Department," *Bulletin of the New York Academy of Medicine,* Vol. 41, No. 1.
Testoff, A., and E. Levine, 1965, "Nursing Care Supplied to Older People in Their Homes," *American Journal of Public Health,* Vol. 55, No. 4, April.
Walker, James E. C., 1965. "Concepts of Patient Care for the 1960's," *Bulletin of the New York Academy of Medicine,* Vol. 41, No. 1.

PSYCHIATRISTS

Of all the medical specialties, psychiatry is the most diverse, both in its content and its conditions of practice. Some psychiatrists, much like other medical specialists, conduct private practices in offices and hospitals, treating a variety of illnesses with a number of different techniques; some, like public health officers, spend much of their time in planning and policy making. A majority of American psychiatrists, at the

A. C. Brown, M.D., and Elizabeth Tucker, M.D., kindly contributed the data from their study of private practitioners; Ralph Cooper and Roxane Cohen contributed the data from the first clinic; Gerhart Saenger, with the kind permission of Francis Durgin, M.D., contributed the data from the second clinic. All data were collected under the sponsorship of the Mental Health Research Unit.

time of these studies, were taking responsibility for the care of patients in the wards of large hospitals; some of these were developing new techniques for treating groups of patients (Cumming and Cumming, 1962; Kraft, 1966), but most were mainly occupied with day-to-day administration. Finally, some psychiatrists were limiting their practices to psychotherapy and were acting in roles difficult to distinguish from those of any other kind of counselor. Despite this wide diversity, however, most American psychiatrists were conducting part-time private practices and using a variety of skills (Blain, 1959; Avnet, 1962).

This chapter concentrates on private practitioners and upon psychiatric practice in outpatient clinics. In the studies reported, there was some overlap between these two groups because almost all clinic psychiatrists had private practices. The reverse was not necessarily true (Brown, 1965).

Most of the data reported here were reanalyzed from other studies. Mental hospitals were omitted from study because there was a substantial descriptive literature about them, and their position in the regulative system was fairly well understood; ironically, this omission tended to present a conservative picture of psychiatric practices.

Sources of Data

Data were available from a one-in-three sample of the private practitioners of New York State in 1964. Of the 592 psychiatrists in this group who spend at least part of their time in private practice, ten were practicing in Syracuse (Brown, 1965). No statistically significant differences appeared in any analyses reported here between the ten Syracuse psychiatrists and the remainder of this New York State sample, and figures for the whole sample will be used.

Data from two Syracuse outpatient clinics were made available. Both of these clinics were financed by the State and Onondaga County, and both charged fees to their patients; one had some voluntary financial support and was attached to a hospital. In the first clinic, information was available for a group of 107 patients characterized as dropouts because they had left care against medical advice before the fifth interview session, and in the second for a cohort of 100 consecutively admitted patients.* Observations were made in the waiting room of the first clinic.

Entrance to Service

Most private psychiatrists are careful to provide a supportive atmosphere for their patients, with provision for privacy and even anonymity. Offices are seldom overcrowded and many do not have receptionists. If there is a receptionist, she is usually very tactful, and the general air of the office assures the patient that his confidences will be kept. There are, however, two overt, stringent controls at the boundary of private psychiatric practice: one is the large fee that the patient undertakes to pay, and the other, the psychiatrist's refusal to treat certain types of patients. Little is known about control during the course of private psychiatric treatment; but it has been suggested that although it achieves regulation through support, it becomes more controlling as the patient recovers and can be expected to meet more rigorous role demands (Parsons *et al.*, 1953).

In contrast to entering a private practitioner's office, there were obvious formal and informal controls at the in-boundaries of mental health clinics. There were often stringent eligibility requirements, long waiting lists, and long delays in the waiting room, perhaps because of a belief that patients would respond better to psychiatric treatment if it was difficult to acquire, and because the high fees of private practice cannot be used for this purpose.

Observations in the first clinic revealed that the patient was expected to make his own appointment so that his motivation to attend would be demonstrated, even when he had been referred by some other agent. Once the patient entered the clinic waiting room, he had the frustrating task of filling out

---

* Half of the 107 dropouts had had as many as four sessions before leaving care, while 29 of the patients from the second clinic had had four sessions or fewer. There was, therefore, considerable overlap between the two groups although they were not truly comparable.

a complex questionnaire, in inadequate light, balancing the questionnaire on his knee. After these formalities were completed, the patient was seen by a social worker, and then perhaps by a psychiatrist. Eventually his name was put on a waiting list, or, alternatively, he was assigned to group therapy while he awaited his turn for individual treatment.*

The waiting list was used as a powerful control; patients were not chosen from it in temporal order but when a staff psychiatrist decided to accept them for his own reasons. For some kinds of patients, the wait was short, for others long. The waiting list itself was never in reality very long, but the clinic preferred other agents to believe that it was, because the vision of a long list discouraged referral of certain kinds of patients, particularly those in need of emergency care.† In this practice, the clinic was following an accepted method of training other agencies to screen patients for them. Robinson *et al.* (1960), for example, report of one child guidance clinic:

> The waiting list here was not as long as at most clinics. One reason for this, however, was the fact that the community agencies protected the clinic. They told us how careful they were in screening cases before referral. The child welfare services were trying to make arrangements for psychiatric services outside of the clinic, because so few children under their care could receive diagnosis—and even fewer, treatment. The courts, too, held back in order not to swamp the clinic, but they hoped rather wistfully that some day someone would

* A total of 451 new patients approached the clinic in this manner between October 1, 1959, and December 31, 1960. Sixty per cent of these patients either dropped out before five interview sessions or terminated treatment against medical advice. Of the 150 patients who dropped out, 107 were followed up and interviewed. These 107 were used in this comparison.

† No observations were made at the second clinic but it was described by the patients at the follow-up interview as having "a long intake process" and a "long waiting list." There is no reason to believe that either clinic departed much from the standard practice of the time.

Table 7-1. PER CENT OF 592 PSYCHIATRISTS REPORTING
PATIENTS REFERRED FROM VARIOUS AGENCIES[a] AND
PER CENT OF THOSE NOT REPORTING WHO
WOULD ACCEPT OR REFUSE THEM, 1964

Referral source of patients	% Reporting		% Not reporting who would	
	Many	*Some*	*Accept*	*Refuse*
Informal				
Self	12.8	52.6	17.6	5.9
Other patients	32.6	59.5	3.4	2.4
Medical agencies				
Other psychiatrists	50.5	41.5	4.7	0.3
Psychiatric clinics	7.8	46.3	34.6	4.1
Medical practitioners	42.1	49.8	6.2	0.0
Counseling services				
Psychologists	8.8	52.5	32.8	0.8
School services	5.4	27.5	49.3	8.8
Social workers (private)	4.6	40.7	46.4	0.8
Clergymen	3.5	33.1	54.4	1.4
Lawyers	2.4	36.7	45.6	7.8
Income maintenance				
Social service agencies	3.4	38.8	44.1	5.6
Institutions				
Mental hospitals	2.2	31.8	46.0	11.8
Correction				
Courts	1.0	19.8	44.8	25.0

[a] The psychiatrists were asked to check how often they received patients from each source. If they checked "never," they were asked whether they would accept patients from that source. The third and fourth columns above represent the proportions of the 592 psychiatrists who would and would not accept patients from each source were they to receive such referrals. The rows do not add to 100 per cent because of nonresponses.

give attention to their needs for at least diagnostic psychiatric services.

Results

REFERRAL SOURCE

The private practitioners were asked only to check on a mailed interview schedule whether they received "some," "many," or "no" patients by referral from each of several selected sources (Table 7-1). The majority of the 592 practitioners reported that at least some patients were sent to them by the informal referral network, and almost all of them reported receiving patients from medical practitioners and other psychiatrists. Slightly more than half reported receiving some patients from psychiatric clinics, and slightly less than half reported receiving them from social workers and psychologists in private practice. In general, the proportion of these psychiatrists reporting referrals from any given agency decreased as the character of the agency became more controlling.

Table 7-2 compares the referral source of the 107 patients who had dropped out of the first clinic with the cohort of 100 patients from the second clinic.

Although in general the private practitioners and both clinics were receiving their patients from the supportive end of the spectrum, the dropout group included significantly more informal referrals and fewer from both medical sources and the more controlling nonmedical agencies. As a number of studies of referral to all forms of psychiatric treatment (Kadushin, 1960; Cumming, 1962) have found that the longer the path toward treatment, the more public and controlling the agents encountered on the way, the dropout group may have been at an earlier stage of their search for treatment than the intake cohort.

PROBLEMS PRESENTED

Over 90 per cent of private practitioners reported seeing, although not necessarily treating, psychoneurotic patients and patients with personality disorders; these were the most popular of all diagnostic categories (Table 7-3). About four-fifths of the psychiatrists reported seeing "sex deviants" as well as patients complaining of various kinds of transitional problems; between two-thirds and three-quarters reported alcoholics and sociopaths; between one-third and one-half reported both disturbed children and patients whose problems were classed under the general category of contingencies. In this agency, the latter are patients suffering from various organic problems, most of them beyond the control of either the individual or his environment.

Of the 100 patients in the second clinic, 46 were diagnosed as psychoneurotic, 23 as psychotic, 21 as personality disorders, 5 as transient situational disorders, 1 as a brain syndrome; 4

Table 7-2.   RELATIONSHIP OF FIRST AND SECOND CLINICS WITH OTHER AGENCIES THROUGH REFERRAL SOURCES AND TARGETS

Agency	Referral source		Referral target	
	First clinic (dropouts) 1959–60	*Second clinic (intake) 1963–64*	*First clinic (intake) 1959–60*	*Second clinic (intake) 1963–64*
All patients	107	100	451	100
Without agency referral	39[a]	20[a]	404	94
With agency referral	68	80	47	6
Total referrals	68	80	47	6
Medical	49	54	36	6
Private physician	15	22	3	1
Syracuse Dispensary	8		5	
Other medical clinic	5	3		
Hospitals	12	8	4	
Private psychiatrist	6	17	5	
Psychiatric hospital	3	4	16	4
Psychiatric clinic			3	1
Counseling	14	21	7	0
Clergymen	3	4		
Family agency	1	1	4	
VA Contact Office	1			
School services	6	6		
Medical social service	2	5		
Psychiatric social service	0	3	1	
Employer and personnel office	1	2		
Vocational rehabilitation			2	
Income maintenance	5	1	0	0
Welfare	2	1		
Social Security	2			
Housing Authority	1			
Institutions	0	0	4	0
State hospital			4	
Correction	0	4	0	0
Family Court		3		
Probation		1		

[a] Proportionately more patients came to first clinic without an agency referral. ($\chi^2 = 6.1$; d.f. = 1; $.02 > P > .01$.)

Table 7-3. PER CENT OF 592 NEW YORK STATE PRIVATELY
PRACTICING PSYCHIATRISTS REPORTING THAT THEY
SEE AND TREAT PATIENTS IN VARIOUS
PROBLEM CATEGORIES, 1964

Problem category	% Reporting	% Treating
Transition states		
Marital problems	94.6	79.6
Transient situational disorders	90.7	81.4
Adolescent disorders	85.5	67.2
Role failure		
Psychoneurotic disorders	97.3	93.6
Personality disorders	94.3	87.5
Borderline psychotic	94.3	74.5
Psychotic disorders	93.4	60.5
Sex deviants	87.8	73.8
Acutely disturbed	84.6	32.6
Alcoholics	75.2	38.7
Adult sociopaths	67.9	37.7
Childhood neurosis	54.6	30.2
Addicts	51.7	19.1
Delinquent children	49.2	23.1
Contingencies		
Brain syndromes[a]	56.3	20.1
Convulsive disorders	43.2	17.1
Mentally retarded	39.4	7.6

[a] This compendious category of patients includes some alcoholics who should be classed as role failures, but the majority are probably suffering from diseases of the senium and other contingent problems.

were undiagnosed. Although these data are not commensurate with those from the private practitioners, the general ordering of the categories is similar.

Diagnoses were not available for the dropout group from the first clinic because diagnostic labels were often not applied until after discharge from care, but as patients from both clinics were followed up and interviewed regarding the kinds of problems that had caused them to seek treatment in the first place, these can be compared. The patients' presenting symptoms were tentatively grouped under the three major problem categories, although it was only possible to guess at which symptoms belonged in which category. In Table 7-4, patients from the second clinic group who had left care be-

Table 7-4. PER CENT OF 107 PATIENTS FROM FIRST CLINIC AND
84 FROM SECOND CLINIC REPORTING AT FOLLOW-UP THAT THEY
HAD COMPLAINED AT INTAKE OF VARIOUS SYMPTOMS

Symptoms	Total	% First clinic	% Second clinic Dropout	% Second clinic Treated
All patients	**191**	**100.0**	**100.0**	**100.0**
Possible transition states	*46*	*33.6*	*19.1*	*9.5*
Marital problems	29	19.6	14.3	7.9
Parent-child problems	9	6.5	4.8	1.6
Work or school problems	8	7.5	0.0	0.0
Possible role failure	*130*	*55.1*	*81.1*	*90.5*
Nervous, anxious, tense	27	16.8	4.8	12.7
Depressed, crying, despondent	48	17.8	33.3	34.9
Phobias, confusion, obsessions, and panic	18	10.3	14.3	6.3
Hallucinations, delusions	6	0.0	0.0	9.5
"Nervous breakdown"	9	3.7	4.8	6.3
Follow-up from mental hospital	3	0.9	4.8	1.6
Attempted suicide	8	0.9	14.3	6.3
Sex deviance	4	0.9	0.0	4.8
Alcoholism	7	3.7	4.8	3.2
Possible contingencies				
Physical complaints	13	9.3	0.0	4.8
Don't know; won't discuss	2	1.9	0.0	0.0

fore the fifth interview, and were therefore comparable with
the first clinic group, are considered separately from those
who remained in care.

Although the second clinic group reported more serious-
sounding symptoms than the first, the majority of patients in
both clinics reported symptoms of either depression or neu-
rosis.

SERVICES OFFERED

The core service of most private practitioners of psychiatry and of the staff psychiatrists in the study was counseling,
which, when performed by psychiatrists, is called psychotherapy; it is the most supportive of the psychiatric skills.* Drugs

---

* Counseling is taken to mean, here and hereafter, the art of de-were also widely used by both practitioners and clinic staffs.

Because the psychotherapeutic relationship requires that the patient have suitable characteristics, one of which is an appropriate level of eagerness for treatment, patients had to be carefully selected for this core service. Besides their high fees, the private practitioners' major screening device appeared to lie in refusing referrals from certain sources. As Table 7-1 shows, for example, although one-fifth of the private practitioners reported seeing some patients referred by the courts, one-quarter said that they would not accept such referrals even if they were made. It is obvious from Table 7-3, furthermore, that diagnosis as well as referral source was related to the psychiatrists' selection of patients for treatment. Although the proportions of doctors reporting that they treated each diagnostic category was of roughly the same order as the proportions reporting that they saw them, the preferences for patients with neuroses and personality disorders appears sharper when treatment alone is considered.

Generally speaking, the more responsive the illness to the core service, psychotherapy, and the less likely the necessity of a more controlling, biological type of treatment, the more likely the patient was to be accepted.

These data do not, of course, show the actual distribution of patients in the practices of these physicians, but their general order is roughly similar to the distributions reported in Avnet's New York study (1962) and Bahn *et al.*'s national study of private practice (1965 *a*), both of which suggest that roughly 40 to 50 per cent of the patients in private psychiatric practices were being diagnosed as psychoneurotic, another 20 to 25 per cent as personality disorders, between 15 and 25 per cent as psychotic, the remainder being divided among various types of transition states and contingencies. These proportions are not only consonant with the order of preference expressed by the private practitioners in this study, but are almost the same as the distribution of diagnosis in the second clinic.

---

ciding what a patient's problems are, deciding how they might be solved, deciding how to communicate these decisions to the patient, and then doing so.

One of the consequences of psychiatrists' careful selection of patients for their core service is a high attrition rate among applicants for service. In the first clinic, for example, only 9 per cent of 451 consecutive applicants were either given the core service or wait-listed for it. Another 3 per cent were treated with group therapy. Eleven per cent of the applicants were ineligible for service because their incomes were too high, another 11 per cent were referred elsewhere at intake, and 4 per cent had moved away before treatment could be started. In the second clinic, the attrition rate was lower: 71 per cent of the patients receiving five or more interviews; 22 per cent, one to four interviews; and 7 per cent, no service. In the first clinic, in contrast, the largest proportion of patients, 62 per cent of the whole group, dropped out of treatment before the sixth session, more than half of them during the intake process itself. There was evidence from the records and from the follow-up interviews that many of these patients felt that the clinic was discouraging their attendance.* In other words, besides the more overt selection mechanisms, informal processes also resulted in the high loss rate. Such processes are well recognized and have been variously described as resulting from the psychiatrist's preoccupation with his own interpretations rather than the patient's statement of his problem (Frank, 1961), emphasis on the psychotherapeutic process itself rather than the patient's progress (Astin, 1961), and disjunction between the values and norms of the psychiatrist and the average patient approaching him (Kadushin, 1962).

In general, both the private practitioners and the clinic psychiatrists appeared to have been selecting for treatment a special segment of the population approaching them by

---

* One subgroup of 21 patients said, for example, that they had been told not to return to the clinic, even though their files indicated that they had been expected to continue. In a small substudy these cases were combined with a random 21 from the remaining dropout group and read blind by a social worker instructed to sort them into those who had received an encouraging versus a neutral or discouraging reception. Those who claimed that they had been told not to come back were significantly more often sorted into the discouraging group than the others.

means of various techniques, probably most of them informal. Evidence of collaboration with other agencies is lacking, but observers believed it to be minimal.*

REFERRALS OUT

Any agent with highly selective intake practices might be expected to refer those patients not considered suitable for service. The private psychiatrist's referral practices were unknown, but both clinics had a low rate of out-referral at the point of intake and, as far as could be learned from the records, referrals in the course of care were not made.

Referral targets were similar for both clinics, most of those who were referred being sent to other psychiatric or medical services. The first clinic did send seven patients to counseling agencies while the second clinic sent none, but this difference was not statistically significant. At follow-up, it was found that a large proportion of the dropout group had probably been in need of referral service, because one-quarter of them had found other psychiatric care by themselves, another quarter had been under the care of a family doctor, and an additional 10 per cent had been in touch with both a medical doctor and a clergyman. One-quarter had seen a wide variety of supporting and controlling agents. Only 15 per cent of this group had had no contact with any regulative agency.

In general, the clinic staff, and probably the private practitioners, exerted maximum control at the in-boundary—demanding at least appropriate expressions of motivation and providing a supportive treatment service to those they accepted—and had little interest in continuing to control patients at the out-boundary.

A Specialized, Supportive, Agent's Agency

Although the psychiatrist is technically a highly specialized medical doctor, the practice of psychotherapy effectively removes him from that category and at the same time creates

---

* Social workers, who would normally make arrangements with other agents, were at this time members of "the clinic team," usually acting as therapists for both patients and relatives.

confusion in the minds of other physicians. Problems that can be treated by psychotherapy are the same ones, by and large, that the family doctors had stated they themselves preferred to treat. At the same time, these doctors believed that many acute psychiatric illnesses, as well as biologically based psychiatric conditions, were beyond their skill, and therefore should be referred to psychiatrists. It seems clear that most of the private psychiatrists in this study, as well as those in the clinic, were accepting for treatment the same kinds of patients the family doctors were treating, while at the same time refusing those they were trying to refer. It was this pattern of practice that led to the family physicians' complaints about psychiatrists.

The narrow area of overlap between the kind of patients that the private psychiatrist treated and those that the family physician would have liked him to treat echoes findings from an earlier Syracuse study (Rudolph and Cumming, 1962) in which it was found that scocial agencies of every kind would have liked more psychiatric services for their severely disordered clients than were then available to them. Workers in all agencies thought, for example, that treatment for alcoholics, the acutely disturbed, and the brain-damaged required a level of skill possessed only by psychiatrists, while psychiatrists characteristically thought that these agencies should learn to make better referrals. There is evidence, furthermore, that not only family doctors, but also other medical specialists were treating, or at least not referring, their psychiatrically ill patients. Locke *et al.* (1966) reported that the internists, pediatricians, allergists, and dermatologists in a group health plan diagnosed 15 per cent of their patients as having psychiatric problems, but, when treatment was made available, referred only 1 per cent of their patients to it.

There appears to have been a major two-way misunderstanding between the remainder of the regulative system and the practice of psychiatry, at least in its private and outpatient clinic forms. Such a disjunction ought to have led to role-strain, and there is some evidence that the move toward "community psychiatry" that followed shortly after these studies was at least in part a response to the frustrations and complaints of members of the rest of the system. At the time of these studies, however, the clinics and the private practitioners were a relatively isolated medical speciality receiving most of their patients from other medical agents and referring very few to other agents of any kind.

For the private practitioner, the outpatient clinic may have offered a situation in which he was able to treat patients who could not afford private care but who still met his criteria of desirability for psychotherapy. For young psychiatrists, this advantage may have been doubly appealing because they were unlikely to have been able to afford to screen patients in this way in their private practice. In other words, in the clinic the psychiatrist could belong to a colleague group and, at the same time, round out his practice with selected patients of a kind not easily accessible to him in his private practice.

In summary, the psychiatrist in private and clinic practice appeared to be a specialist who would have liked to be more specialized than other agencies wanted him to be, but specialized in a different kind of task. Although these psychiatrists were qualified to care for a wide variety of patients, a concentration on a single skill led many of them to take responsibility for only a narrow segment of disorders, a practice that created a strain between them and other members of the regulative system. The psychiatric outpatient clinics may have been reducing this strain by deflecting onto themselves the hostility generated by the waiting list. Perhaps the protective function was the reason the number of psychiatrists practicing in clinics was increasing year by year (Bahn *et al.,* 1965 *b*), but even at that time the outpatient clinic, as it is described here, seemed to be moving toward obsolescence.

REFERENCES

Astin, Alexander, W., 1961. "The Functional Autonomy of Psychotherapy," *American Psychologist,* Vol. 16, No. 2.

Avnet, Helen H., 1962. *Psychiatric Insurance,* New York, Group Health Insurance.

Bahn, Anita, *et al.,* 1965 *a.* "Survey of Private Psychiatric Practice," *Archives of General Psychiatry,* Vol. 12, March.

Bahn, Anita, *et al.*, 1965 *b*. "Current Services and Trends in Out-patient Psychiatric Clinics, 1963," *Psychiatric Studies and Projects*, Mental Hospital Service of the American Psychiatric Association, Vol. 3, No. 7, October.

Blain, Daniel, 1959. "The Organization of Psychiatry in the United States," in *American Handbook of Psychiatry*, Vol. 2, ed. Silvano Arieti, New York, Basic Books.

Brown, A. C., 1965. "Psychiatrists' Interest in Community Mental Health Centers," *Community Mental Health Journal*, Vol. I, No. 3.

Cumming, Elaine, 1962. "Phase Movement in the Support and Control of the Psychiatric Patient," *Journal of Health and Human Behavior*, Vol. 3, No. 4.

Cumming, John, and Elaine Cumming, 1962. *Ego and Milieu*, New York, Atherton Press.

Frank, J., 1961. *Persuasion and Healing*, Baltimore, Johns Hopkins Press.

Kadushin, C., 1960. *Steps on the Way to a Psychiatric Clinic*, New York, Bureau of Applied Social Research, Columbia University.

Kadushin, C., 1962. "Social Distance between Client and Professional," *American Journal of Sociology*, Vol. LXVII, No. 5, March.

Kraft, Alan, 1966. "The Chronic Patient in the Community Mental Health Center," paper read before International Research Seminar on Evaluation of Community Mental Health Programs, May 17–20, 1966, Airlie House, Warrenton, Virginia.

Locke, Ben Z., G. Krantz, and M. Kramer, 1966. "Psychiatric Need and Demand in a Prepaid Group Practice Program," *American Journal of Public Health*, Vol. 56, No. 6, June.

Parsons, Talcott, Robert F. Bales, and Edward Shils, 1953. "Phase Movement in Relation to Motivation," in T. Parsons, *et al.*, *Working Papers in the Theory of Action*, New York, The Free Press.

Robinson, Reginald, *et al.*, 1960. *Community Resources in Mental Health*, New York, Basic Books.

Rudolph, Claire, and John Cumming, 1962. "Where are Additional Psychiatric Services Most Needed?" *Social Work*, Vol. 7, No. 3, July.

THE CLERGYMAN: PROTOTYPE 8
OF COUNSELOR

All religions are concerned with social regulation inasmuch
as one of their goals is to keep the individual integrated with
society through his attachment to a set of values expressed
both ritually and collectively (Eister, 1957; Bellah, 1958).
The clergyman, in his pastoral role, was once the keystone of
the regulative system and he is still a centrally important
member of it.

The clergyman's sacred functions are usually considered
the core of his role. The more supportive counseling function

Ernest Damianopoulos helped to design the sample for this study.
Charles Harrington conducted the interviews and carried out most of
the analysis. Much of the material presented here has appeared in
Cumming and Harrington (1963).

is, in this view, an instrument through which the individual is helped to achieve his human potential and hence to receive the greatest benefit from religion. In practice, many clergymen spend much of their time in pastoral counseling. Gurin *et al.* (1960) report that 40 per cent of Americans say that they would turn first to clergymen with personal problems, whereas 29 per cent say they would go to family doctors.* There are probably many reasons why the clergy stand at the threshold of the regulative structure. First, religion emphasizes the inevitability of trouble and the redemptive role of the church; Christianity especially emphasizes Jesus' concern for sinners. Second, many people look upon their clergymen as friends rather than professionals; there is a tendency to choose *a* doctor but *the* particular clergyman (Kadushin, 1962). Third, as Eaton *et al.* (1961) say, "Clergy are close to many people during crucial periods of the life cycle. . . . For those who know they need help, the clergy is accessible without a waiting list or an intake worker to screen applicants. And going to a clergyman does not require a self admission of helplessness on the part of the client."

Social workers and social scientists sometimes consider the clergyman "too judgmental" to be a successful counselor, but their objection seems ill-founded. Judging one another's behavior by standards of right and wrong is part of all informal social regulation; the clergyman differs only in symbolizing these standards; for most people, he is approachable because he cares about the over-all well being of those who appeal to him for help.

As an agent of social regulation in a complex modern society, the clergyman has the unique characteristic of being a member of the very group he controls (Campbell and Pettigrew, 1964). This membership can be expected to enhance and to stabilize his relationship with his parishioners because he will share with them "common expectations and optimum cathexis" (Kadushin, 1962). His membership in his own congregation will also influence his articulation with the rest of the system, both because others will perceive him in terms

---

* Figures combined from Gurin's Tables 10.3 and 10.8.

of it and because the congregation's values and norms will influence some of his ideas about secular matters (Braude, 1961). Because of this difference from other agents, a special feature of the study reported here was the prediction that the relationship maintained by the clergyman with the rest of the regulative system would be associated with the characteristics of his congregation.

Entrance to Service

Clergymen, on the whole, are the most approachable of all regulative agents. They are available without intermediaries or fees, and most will go to the homes of those who need them. There are very few formal or informal controls exerted over approaching clients, with the important exception of a body of shared norms and values. Because the clergyman symbolizes these values, the control is not symmetrical, except perhaps when the client is also an influential member of the congregation.

Method of Study

A stratified random sample of Syracuse's 150 churches was drawn up;* it was composed of 61 churches, including 10 Roman Catholic, 6 Episcopal, 3 Lutheran, 3 Eastern Orthodox, 8 Methodist, 7 Presbyterian, 5 Baptist, 7 Fundamentalist

* Church names and addresses were taken from the City Directory; local church officials contributed further details. Size was classified as follows: small, up to 150 total members; medium, 150–500; large, 500–1,000; and very large, over 1,000. The neighborhoods were classified as upper-, middle-, lower-status and mixed-metropolitan (Willie and Wagenfeld, 1960). Empty cells appeared in the stratification plan because of the absence of small Roman Catholic churches and large Fundamentalist churches. Some "store-front" churches had disappeared by the time of research, and were replaced by further random choices from the cells from which they had been chosen. The final sample included 45 per cent of Syracuse's Roman Catholic churches, 40 per cent of the other liturgical churches, 48 per cent of the Fundamentalists, 47 per cent of the remaining Protestant denominations, and 37 per cent of the Jewish temples. The sample represents neither the clergymen of Syracuse nor the people of the various faiths, but the churches themselves.

or Evangelical, 3 Jewish, and 6 of other Protestant denominations. One clergyman from each of 59 churches was interviewed as a representative of that church. Two Fundamentalist clergymen refused to be interviewed although eight different attempts were made in each case.

The characteristics of each congregation were discovered by asking the clergyman questions about its size and about the average age, income, and occupation of its members. With this information, and with the interviewer's knowledge of the neighborhoods, 31 of the 59 churches were classified as predominantly white-collar and 28 as predominantly blue-collar.

Findings

REFERRAL SOURCE

All the clergymen said that they counseled with any member of their own congregation who approached them; 49 of the 59 counseled with and offered help to nonmembers equally readily. A total of 20 clergymen reported receiving referrals from one or more of 12 outside sources (Table 8-1), but all of them said that such referrals were infrequent and that most clients reached them through their own efforts. Examination of the out-referrals from other agencies in the study group suggests that this was indeed the case; one agency, Catholic Welfare, referred a total of three clients to clergymen during the study period.

PROBLEMS REPORTED

Each clergyman was asked to describe the problems brought to him for counseling and the extent of his counseling activities; 41 more or less different problems were distinguished from the descriptions, and these were grouped into the three major problem categories: transition states, role failures, and contingent problems. Forty-nine, or 83 per cent, of the clergymen reported seeing transitional problems; and 42, or 71 per cent, described various contingencies, such as illness, legal problems, and temporary unemployment, which

Table 8-1. NUMBER OF CLERGYMEN REPORTING RELATION-
SHIPS WITH OTHER AGENCIES THROUGH REFERRAL
SOURCES AND TARGETS[a]

Agencies related to	Referral	
	Source	*Target*
Without agency contact	39	6
With agency contact	20[b]	53
Medical		
Private physicians	7	33
Hospitals	4	9
Outpatient clinics		4
Planned Parenthood Center		19
Public health nursing	1	2
Psychiatrists	1	26
Mental health clinics		19
Counseling		
Casework agencies		27
Alcoholic services		25
Council of Churches		14
Lawyers and Legal Aid	1	18
School services	5	8
Other clergy		8
Recreation		
Neighborhood Houses	2	3
Youth Clubs		3
Golden Age Clubs		4
Employment		
N.Y.S. Employment Service		1
Income maintenance		
Welfare		19
Catholic Charities		4
Meals on Wheels		5
Red Cross		4
Public housing		1
Travelers Aid		1
Institutions		
Mental hospitals		22
Men's shelters	1	14
Homes for aged		9
Children's placements		2
Maternity homes		6
Correction		
Children's Court	1	4
Judge and D.A.	1	2
Probation	3	3
Police	2	3

[a] Data in Tables 8-1 through 8-3 based on interviews of 59 clergymen in the summer of 1960.
[b] An additional four clergymen reported that they received agency referrals, but did not specify the agency.

people brought to them for help. Forty-five, or 83 per cent of the whole group, said they were approached with such serious difficulties as unwed motherhood, alcoholism, mental disturbance, family breakdown, and poverty. Even though these data are subject to errors of memory, they suggest that people were bringing a wide array of difficult problems to clergymen.

SERVICES OFFERED

The core of the pastoral role is counseling, encouragement, and support. These clergymen claimed to be offering this service to people with problems ranging from mild and transitional to severe and irreversible; they were also providing temporary financial assistance from church funds, helping people to apply to the Welfare Department, and making arrangements with the Public Housing Authority, hospitals, nursing homes, and clinics. Like the clergymen studied by Eaton *et al.* (1961), these men spent between one-third and one-half of their time in these generally supportive activities; their range of service was wide, and their interest in the whole man was usually manifest, although one or two were strangely indifferent. Several clergymen said they could do much more for their parishioners if they could afford to hire social workers.

REFERRALS OUT

Fifty-three of the 59 clergymen reported referring clients to other agents, the median number of referral targets being 4.5, with a range from 0 to 25. The majority of clergymen referred clients who had difficult role failure problems and problems that required specialized expertise, such as illness or unwed motherhood. The most popular target services were medical, followed by counseling and income maintenance services, especially the Welfare Department (Table 8-1).

The marked asymmetry between referrals in and out reported by these clergymen was confirmed by an examination of the patterns of referral in the other study agencies. During the period studied, clergymen made 46 referrals to five of the eight primary agencies, compared to the three they received from one agency, a ratio identical with that experienced by doctors. In an earlier study, Robinson (1960) and his co-workers reported a similar referral asymmetry for clergymen in widely separated parts of the country.

When they were asked what additional services were needed in the community, 27, or almost half, of the 59 clergymen compared to 3, or 10 per cent, of the family doctors saw no need for any; the remaining 32 proposed 28 different types of additional service, compared to the 5 types suggested by 29 doctors. This difference between the two gatekeeper agencies reflected a different level of interest in and involvement with both the regulative system and the client's entire range of problems. Services requested by the clergymen included mental health clinic facilities, more nursing homes for old people, religious and secular recreational services for youth, emergency services, and day-care centers. There was a sprinkling of requests for counseling services for families, special help for large, poor families, or for "impossible marital problems." One clergyman wanted more and better public housing; one said, "We need a financial service for the aged that does not have the indignity of welfare." One aberrant clergyman requested "sterilization for juvenile delinquents and other deviants," and another said, "We have too many services already; it is socialism."

On the whole, these clergymen seemed to have a clearer picture of the over-all regulative system and their own place in it than did the doctors. When they were asked their reasons for making referrals, 40 of them gave answers that suggested a clear-cut division of labor: either their own repertoire of skills was limited or there was an indefinable "appropriateness" about some kinds of pastoral counseling and not about others.

Only four of the clergymen expressed attitudes toward social agencies in general that were more positive than negative, and these were all men who reported referring clients to more than four agencies. Of the remainder, 30 were neutral and 25 were unfavorable; most complained of the uncooperativeness of social workers. One clergyman said, "Agencies like to leave you out . . . you can just mind your marbles because they know how to do it." The complementary attitude showed up in one study agency when one social worker commented to another, "The Reverend Brown called about Mrs. Smith, but, of course, I didn't tell him anything."

In spite of their negative feelings toward social workers, the clergymen did not express the apprehension about losing clients that the doctors had about losing patients; although 2 of the 53 making referrals said that nobody who was referred to another agency ever returned to him, 20 said that they themselves made an effort to follow up all of their own parishioners, a practice that would verge on the unethical for doctors. One clergyman said, "See, you don't just dump them over completely because they still need another dimension to their relationship. They want to know you're concerned. . . ."

SPECIAL PREDICTION

A "boundary activity score" indicating the amount of interaction the clergyman had with the regulative system was constructed in order to test the hypothesis that the level of interaction would be more closely associated with the characteristics of the congregation than with denomination or with certain personal characteristics of the clergyman. One point was assigned for each of five signs of articulation with the larger system: the receipt of either referrals or information about clients from sources outside the congregation; at least one referral to an outside agency in the month prior to the interview; actively referring most clients rather than steering them; referring to more than the median number of target agencies; and spontaneously naming any agent from whom referrals were sometimes received. These five items formed a Guttman-type scale with a reproducibility of 90.3 per cent.

As Table 8-2 shows, boundary activity scores were significantly lower among the eight Fundamentalists than among the remainder of the group. Only one has a score higher than 0 and none has a score as high as 2. The Fundamentalists also differed significantly from the other Protestant clergymen taken alone. For most of the clergymen in our sample, however, the boundary characteristics of the counseling role

Table 8-2. NUMBER OF CLERGYMEN BY DENOMINATION AND
BOUNDARY ACTIVITY SCORE

Denomination	Total	Boundary score						Mean score
		0	1	2	3	4	5	
All clergymen	*59*	*12*	*10*	*10*	*7*	*12*	*8*	
Roman Catholic	10	0	0	4	3	2	1	3.00
Liturgical Protestant	12	2	3	1	1	4	1	2.42
Other Protestant	26	3	6	4	2	5	6	2.69
Fundamentalist[a]	8	7	1	0	0	0	0	0.12
Jewish	3	0	0	1	1	1	0	3.00

[a] Fundamentalists have a significantly higher proportion of 0–1 scores than all other clergymen (P = .00014 by Fisher's Exact Test), and they have a significantly higher proportion than do all other Protestants (P = .0012 by Fisher's Exact Test).

appeared to be dependent on factors other than denomination.

The size and socioeconomic class of his congregation have both been linked to the clergyman's practices and attitudes (Fichter, 1954). In this study group, clergymen of the large white-collar churches had the highest boundary scores, and those of the smaller blue-collar churches had the lowest, no matter what their denominations.* When church size and collar color were both controlled, furthermore, no significant differences between boundary score and denomination appeared. So far as articulation with the rest of the regulative system was concerned, therefore, the Fundamentalists were not so much qualitatively different sects as representatives of the smallest, poorest congregations.

Differences in boundary score were not found to be associated with the ages of the clergymen, but when the group was divided into two groups according to whether or not they had been educated at a college other than a theological or Bible school, education was found to be associated with boundary

* The 20 small, blue-collar churches included seven of the eight Fundamentalists, the remaining 13 small, poorer churches being distributed among all the remaining denominations except Roman Catholic.

activity.* A still closer association was found between boundary activity and the "fit" or concordance between the clergyman's education and the collar color of his congregation.
Table 8-3 shows that 28 of the 31 better educated clergymen

Table 8-3. NUMBER OF CLERGYMEN BY CHARACTERISTICS OF
CONGREGATIONS AND THEIR CONCORDANCE WITH CLERGY-
MEN'S EDUCATION AND BY BOUNDARY ACTIVITY SCORE

Types of congregation and education of clergy	Total	Boundary score						Mean score
		0	1	2	3	4	5	
All churches	59	12	10	10	7	12	8	
White-Collar Congregations *College-educated clergy*	31	0	3	5	5	10	8	
Congregation size								
Over 1000	16	0	1	3	4	4	4	3.44
Under 1000	15	0	2	2	1	6	4	3.53
Blue-Collar Congregations *College-educated clergy*	15	2	4	5	2	2	0	
Congregation size								
Over 1000	7ᵃ	0	0	4	1	2	0	2.71
Under 1000	8	2	4	1	1	0	0	1.13
Blue-Collar Congregations *Clergy without college education*	13	10	3	0	0	0	0	
Congregation size								
Over 1000	1	1	0	0	0	0	0	0.00
Under 1000	12	9	3	0	0	0	0	0.25

ᵃ Clergymen in these large, blue-collar "discordant" congregations have significantly
higher boundary activity scores than those in the smaller, blue-collar "discordant"
congregations ($P = .00559$ by Fisher's Exact Test).

in white-collar churches had scores of 2 or more, compared
to only 9 of the 15 in blue-collar congregations. Ten of the 13
less well-educated clergy in blue-collar congregations had
scores of 0; the other 3 had scores of 1. These differences are
statistically significant.

The effect of the size of the congregation appeared (Table
8-3) to be limited to those churches in which there was a

* Details of each clergyman's training in pastoral counseling were
unfortunately not collected.

discordance between the clergymen and his congregation.*
Here, all of the clergymen in congregations of more than a
thousand members had high scores compared to only two out
of the eight in congregations of fewer than a thousand; this
difference is statistically significant.

Although the special hypothesis was upheld regarding the
size and collar color of the congregations, the relationship
was not a simple one. While concordance between education
and collar color successfully predicted the level of relationship, congregation size was needed in order to make a prediction about the discordant cases.

The reasons for the differential effect of congregation size
were probably themselves complex. In large, white-collar
congregations there were usually professional members whom
the clergyman could use as bridges to the agency world. In
the blue-collar churches, fewer of these bridges were available. In some small churches there were none, and if the
clergyman himself had no personal acquaintanceship among
professionals, he was cut off from informal contacts that
could be used to help his congregation. The importance of
these informal bridges is emphasized by the many studies that
have shown professionals to have a marked preference for the
"better type" of client (Saenger, 1957; Rudolph and Cumming, 1962; Community Research Associates, 1963; Gordon,
1965).

A Diffuse, Supportive, Gatekeeping Agent

From his front-line position in the regulative system, the
clergyman offered a diffuse, supportive service (Kalif, 1950),
but not without suffering from strains inherent in his role. In
the first place, he was in a screening and allocating position,
but other agencies were not always happy about either accepting his clients or cooperating with him in their care. Furthermore, while the clergyman's need for specific services for
his clients, such as medical care, was palpable, the other

---

* No comparison is, of course, possible between blue-collar, concordant and discordant churches, as there are none of the latter.

agents' need for the allocating role he performed was less so, and this discrepancy contributed to his sense of being unappreciated.

A second strain for the clergyman arose from the ambiguities of the counseling function. Although it was questionable whether pastoral counseling could be easily distinguished from casework, or casework, in turn, from psychotherapy (Klausner, 1964), considerable importance was attached to these distinctions, usually on the basis of the training required for each. As pastoral counseling required the least training and psychotherapy the most, the psychiatrist tended to regard both the social worker and the clergyman as amateurs, while the social worker, in turn, considered the clergyman as poorly qualified (Robb, 1958). Because their client populations overlapped, moreover, the clergymen and the social agency were often in competition, and this led to a strain between the two groups that was exacerbated by the tendency of social workers either to exhort clergymen about how to counsel or to exhort them not to counsel at all (Kelley, 1964; Robinson *et al.*, 1960). Perhaps it was for these reasons that the clergymen, although firmly tied to the regulative system, complained more about it than any other agent in the study.

REFERENCES

Bellah, Robert N., 1958. "The Place of Religion in Human Action," *The Review of Religion,* Vol. XXII, No. 3–4, March.

Braude, Lee, 1961. "Professional Autonomy and the Role of the Layman," *Social Forces,* Vol. 39, May.

Campbell, Ernest, and Thomas F. Pettigrew, 1964. "Racial and Moral Crisis: The Role of Little Rock Ministers," in *Religion, Culture and Society,* ed. Louis Schneider, New York, Wiley.

Community Research Associates, 1963. *Foundations for the Prevention and Rehabilitation of Mental Illness and Social Disorders.* New York.

Cumming, Elaine, and Charles Harrington, 1963. "Clergyman as Counselor," *American Journal of Sociology,* Vol. LXIX, No. 3, November.

Eaton, Joseph W., *et al.,* 1961. *Pastoral Counseling in a Metropolitan Suburb,* Pittsburgh, Pennsylvania, Southeastern Community Guidance Association.

Eister, Allan W., 1957. "Religious Institutions in Complex Societies: Difficulties in the Theoretic Specifications of Functions," *American Sociological Review,* Vol. 22, No. 4, August.

Fichter, Joseph H., S. J., 1954. *Social Relations in the Urban Parish,* Chicago, University of Chicago Press.

Gordon, Sol, 1965. "Are We Seeing the Right Patients?" *American Journal of Orthopsychiatry,* Vol. XXXV, No. 1, January.

Gurin, Gerald, Joseph Veroff, and Sheila Feld, 1960. *Americans View Their Mental Health,* New York, Basic Books.

Kadushin, C., 1962. "Social Distance between Client and Professional," *American Journal of Sociology,* Vol. LXVII, No. 5, March.

Kalif, George Todd, 1950. "Pastoral Use of Community Resources," *Pastoral Psychology,* Vol. 1, No. 9, November.

Kelley, J. L., 1964. "The Modern Minister—A View from the Furnace," *Clergy and Family Service Collaboration,* Washington, D.C., National Institute of Mental Health.

Klausner, Samuel Z., 1964. *Psychiatry and Religion,* New York, The Free Press.

Robb, Philip H., 1958. "Professional Relationships between Social Workers and Clergymen," Master's Thesis, Washington, D.C., Howard University School of Social Work.

Robinson, Reginald, *et al.,* 1960. *Community Resources in Mental Health,* New York, Basic Books.

Rudolph, Claire, and John Cumming, 1962. "Where are Additional Psychiatric Services Most Needed?" *Social Work,* Vol. 7, No. 3, July.

Saenger, Gerhart, 1957. *The Adjustment of Severely Retarded Adults in the Community,* Albany, New York, NYS Interdepartmental Health Resources Boards.

Willie, Charles V., and Morton O. Wagenfeld, 1960. *Socio-Economic and Ethnic Areas, Syracuse and Onondaga County, N.Y.,* Syracuse University Youth Development Center.

THE CATHOLIC WELFARE AGENCY

The Catholic Welfare Agency chosen for study was a member agency of Catholic Charities, a large complex of health, recreation, educational, and welfare services of the type sponsored by many Roman Catholic dioceses. In Syracuse Catholic Welfare offered emergency financial assistance and social services, including adoptions, child placement and case-

The Right Reverend Monsignor Daniel E. Lawler, at that time Director of Diocesan Charities and Welfare, kindly gave permission for this study; the Reverend Father Charles Fahey, who became Director in 1966, was kind enough to review the manuscript. Miss Marian Donovan, Administrative Supervisor, and her staff cooperated with the field workers, Charles Harrington and Ernest Damianopoulos. Patricia Healy and Robert Porter assisted in analyzing the data.

work, as well as allocating clients to other services in the complex. The agency was supported by Diocesan funds and money from churches and the United Council, and had an open, nonsectarian admission policy.

Method of Study

The social workers at Catholic Welfare routinely kept a list of people applying for help with financial or personal problems, and from this list, the names of 172 clients approaching the agency in October and November, 1961, were selected.* One name was discarded because no information about the client's request or its disposition was available. One hundred and two of the applicants requested only financial assistance, while the remaining 69 requested various social services, sometimes in addition to financial aid. These two groups of applicants were considered separately in order that the two aspects of the agency function— immediate relief of hardship and longer-term mitigation of underlying problems—could be compared with those of other agencies offering similar services. Three months later, the records were abstracted. Some of the records were sparse; for example, some contained only an account of a transient asking for a meal ticket. Five of the 171 clients were discovered to have approached the agency twice during the study period, four of them for financial assistance only. Because the unit of analysis in these chapters is the application rather than the applicant, all approaches to the agency are treated as if they were independent.

Entrance to the Agency

Entrance to any one of the various services of Catholic Charities could be direct, or it could be through the Welfare Agency, which acted as a referral service for the remainder.

* These were considered by the agency to be moderately busy months, surpassed only by Christmas and the opening of school in September.

All telephone calls were received by an operator at a central switchboard, and those concerning family problems were directed to the casework supervisor. Catholic Welfare did not require that the client call the agency personally or make an appointment before coming, and as its office was centrally located and clearly marked, many of the clients walked in unannounced. There was no receptionist except for the switchboard operator, and clients followed signs leading to a rather dark waiting room where they were seen by a social worker, in the order in which they had come in. There was no centralized intake procedure, the agency's social workers assuming responsibility for the incoming clients in rotation. This open-door policy reflected the agency's religious and charitable orientation as expressed in its brochure: "As long as you did it for one of these, the least of my Brethren, you did it for Me."

As a result of its open-door philosophy, the agency had many applications for help from transient men, many of whom were already familiar with this agency or with others like it. As a matter of policy, most transients were given meal tickets and clothing vouchers, which could be redeemed at selected restaurants and at a clothing store run by the Society of St. Vincent de Paul. If the applicants were known by the agency to have worked in the area before, they were given meal tickets and at the same time referred to the New York State Employment Service, the Welfare Department, or some other appropriate agency. Sums of money were sometimes supplied to parents of small children and to families who were in financial crises. Assistance was withheld if the applicant was drunk, if he was known never to have made any effort to help himself in the past, or if he was considered to have enough resources of his own.

Direct referrals either from priests or from other social agencies were handled by the casework supervisor, who sometimes assigned a worker directly to the client without his being seen, and sometimes suggested that he come to the agency where he would be seen by the day's intake worker.

At its in-boundary, Catholic Welfare was among the least controlling agencies in the study series. The waiting room, with its inevitable informal control, was all that stood between the client and the agent. There was no formal intake process during which the agency could exert informal control over the way in which the client formulated his problems, and there were no forms to fill in. Eligibility was almost never checked (Tables 9-1 and 9-2).

Findings

REFERRAL SOURCE

Most of the clients applying to Catholic Welfare for either financial help or social services were self-referred, as the agency profiles show (Tables 9-1 and 9-2). Over 90 per cent of those asking for money came on their own, the remaining few being sent either by priests or the Welfare Department. Half of those approaching the social work service also came on their own, with the remainder being referred from 11 different sources. Priests referred two-thirds of these, however, while 10 different agencies contributed the remaining one-third.

The casework supervisor herself handled all referrals from parish priests because she said it gave her an opportunity to interpret the agency's program, about which clients were not always clear. The social service agency appeared to be backstopping the clergyman's counseling function, while the charitable agency was itself acting as a gatekeeper agency for clients requiring immediate financial help.

PROBLEMS PRESENTED

More than half of the clients applying for financial assistance complained of problems serious enough to be classed either as failures in central life roles or as seriously deviant behavior; among these applicants homelessness was the modal problem (Table 9-3). The complaints of one-third of these clients were classed as transitional problems and the remainder as problems that appeared to be caused by contingencies beyond the client's control. One-half of the clients applying for social service complained of serious role failure problems,

Table 9-1. RELATIONSHIP OF CATHOLIC WELFARE WITH OTHER AGENCIES THROUGH REFERRAL SOURCES, INTERAGENCY CONTACTS, AND REFERRAL TARGETS OF 69 SOCIAL-SERVICE APPLICATIONS[a]

Agency	Type of relationship with other agencies				
	Referral Source	Target	Arrangements	Information	Eligibility checks
All welfare clients	69	69	69	69	69
Without agency contact	35	40	61	62	67
With agency contact	34	29	8	7	2
Total contacts made	*35*	*30*	*13*	*7*	*2*
Medical					
Private physician	3			1	
Public health nurses		1			
Private psychiatrist		1			
Syracuse Psychiatric Hospital	1	1	1		
Health Department			1		
Hospital			2		
Counseling					
Clergymen	21	2		1	
Hospital social service	1				
School services	2	1	1		
Legal Aid or lawyer	1	1		1	
Alcoholics Anonymous			1		
Community Chest			1	1	
Employment					
Employer	2			1	
Employment agency		6			
Income maintenance					
Welfare	1	12	3	1	1
Red Cross	1		1		
Unemployment Insurance Benefits		1			
Housing		1			
Institutions					
House of Providence		1			
VA Psychiatric Hospital	1		1		
Correction					
Children's Court	1	1			
Probation		1	1		
Other, nonagency					
Bank and finance company				1	1

[a] Period of study in Tables 9-1 through 9-5 was October–November 1961.

the majority of marital breakdown. Almost one-third of the remainder had contingent problems, most of them associated with low incomes and large families, and the remainder were

Table 9-2. RELATIONSHIP OF CATHOLIC WELFARE WITH OTHER AGENCIES THROUGH REFERRAL SOURCES, INTERAGENCY CONTACTS, AND REFERRAL TARGETS OF 102 CHARITY APPLICATIONS

Agency	Type of relationship with other agencies				
	Referral Source	*Target*	*Arrangements*	*Information*	*Eligibility checks*
All charity clients	102	102	102	102	102
Without agency contact	94	45	98	98	88
With agency contact	8	57	4	4	14
Total contacts made	*8*	*60*	*4*	*5*	*15*
Medical					
Private physician		1			
Dispensary		1			
Hospitals		1			1
Health Department		1			
Outpatient clinic		1			
Counseling					
Clergymen	5	1		1	
School services					1
Family agency elsewhere				1	
Alcoholics Anonymous		1			
Recreation					
YMCA		1	1		
Employment					
Employer		1			2
N.Y.S. Employment Service		12		1	
Income maintenance					
Housing (or landlord)			1	1	1
Welfare	3	29			8
St. Vincent de Paul Society			1		
Unemployment Insurance Benefits		1			1
Travelers Aid		7			
Institutions					
Willard State Hospital				1	
House of Providence			1		
Correction					
Court					1
Police		1			
Immigration		1			

in what appeared to be temporary financial distress. The wide variety of problems discussed by clients of both services of the agency during the study period suggests that it was perceived as less specialized in function and perhaps more supportive than any other regulative agent except the clergy themselves (Table 9-3).

Table 9-3. PROBLEMS PRESENTED BY 69 APPLICANTS FOR SOCIAL SERVICE AND BY 98 APPLICANTS IN 102 APPLICATIONS FOR CHARITABLE SERVICE, CATHOLIC WELFARE

| | Clients applying for | | | |
| | Charitable service only | | Other services | |
Problem category[a]	No.	%	No.	%
All applications	**102**	**100.0**	**69**	**100.0**
Transition states	*34*	*33.3*	*11*	*15.9*
Temporary unemployment	10		3	
Migration	23		1	
Marital maladjustment	1		4	
Maladjustment of children	0		2	
Adult maladjustment	0		1	
Role failure	*56*	*54.9*	*38*	*55.1*
Economic inadequacy	14		4	
Emotionally disturbed children	0		7	
Marital breakdown	2		21	
Inadequate parents	3		1	
Evidence of crime	7		3	
Homelessness	30		2	
Contingencies	*12*	*11.8*	*20*	*29.0*
Children	1		6	
Adults	8		5	
Aged	3		9	

[a] Of the five applicants who applied twice during the study period, two had recently migrated to the area, one was temporarily unemployed, one was economically inadequate, and one was an adult with a contingent problem. Each had received the same designation at each application.

SERVICES OFFERED

The Catholic Welfare Agency offered four services to its clients: financial assistance, counseling, arrangements for service with other agencies, and referrals to other sources of care (Tables 9-4 and 9-5). The core services were counseling and

Table 9-4. SERVICE OFFERED TO 69 CLIENTS APPLYING FOR SOCIAL SERVICE, CATHOLIC WELFARE

| | Total | | Problem category | | | | |
| | | | | | Contingencies | | |
Service offered	No.	%	Transition states	Role failure	Children	Adults	Aged
All applications	69	100.0	10	39	6	5	9
One Service							
Counseling	34	49.3	5	24	2	1	2
Arrangements	1	1.4		1			
Referral (or steer)	22	31.9	3	9	3	1	6
Two services							
Counseling and arrangement	5	7.2	1	2		2	
Counseling and referral	2	2.9	1		1		
Arrange and refer	2	2.9				1	1
Three services							
Counsel, arrange, refer	2	2.9		2			
Counsel, refer, charity	1	1.4		1			

financial assistance. Fourteen applicants for financial help were refused outright: two were thought to have sufficient resources of their own, five to have a history of financial irresponsibility that suggested they could not be helped to a better level of management by temporary help, and seven were drunk and automatically ineligible for help. All applicants for social service received some service.

Financial Assistance. Financial assistance was offered to 1 of the 69 clients asking for social work assistance, and to 54 of the 102 asking for money only. Meal tickets and clothing vouchers were issued to 51 of these applicants and sums of money for rent payment or for children's clothing were given to the remaining 3.

Counseling. Counseling was offered to 44 of the 69 clients asking for more than financial help and to none of those requesting financial help only. Most counseling was kept brief as a matter of policy because the agency was concerned not to develop undue dependency. Because records were not kept in great detail, it was not possible to discover the number of visits to the agency, but 20 of the 44 clients offered counseling were still under care three months later. This group was drawn evenly from the three major problem categories, and resembled the whole group in containing a majority of couples complaining of severe marital problems.

Arrangements. The workers in Catholic Welfare made arrangements with 10 different agencies on behalf of 8 of the 69 social-service clients and 4 of the 102 applicants for financial assistance (Tables 9-1 and 9-2).

Referral Targets. It is clear from the agency profile shown in Tables 9-1 and 9-2 that Catholic Welfare was performing a sorting and screening function. Twenty-nine of the 69 social-service clients were sent to 13 different agencies, 5 by active referral. Twelve clients were sent to the Welfare Department, and another 6 to employment agencies; another 3 or 4 of the 9 clients still in care at the end of the study could also expect to be referred. Only 2 of the clients were sent to their parish priests, in contrast with the 21 who were referred in to the agency by priests. This finding highlights the position of this agency as a second-line service, standing be-

Table 9-5. SERVICE OFFERED TO 98 CLIENTS MAKING 102 APPLICATIONS FOR CHARITABLE SERVICE, CATHOLIC WELFARE

Service offered	Total No.	%	Transition states	Role failure	Contingencies Children	Adults	Aged
All applications	*102*	*100.0*	*34*	*56*	*1*	*8*	*3*
No service	14	13.7	4	9			1
One Service							
Charity	29	28.4	10	12		7	
Arrangements							
Referral	34	33.3	12	22			
Two services							
Charity and arrangement	2	2.0	1		1		
Charity and referral	21	20.6	7	12		1	1
Arrangements and referral							
Three services	2	2.0		1			1

yond the primary gatekeepers. Of the 102 clients applying for financial help, 52 were steered and 4 referred to 15 different agencies, half to the Welfare Department and most of the remainder to employment services. Seven stranded travelers were referred to the Travelers Aid Society for assistance. In spite of this extensive allocating activity, however, only 3 each of the social-service clients and clients applying for financial assistance were actively referred. The agency appeared to be relinquishing control of the client at the out-boundary.

SUMMARY OF SERVICE

Tables 9-4 and 9-5 summarize the services offered to the clients in the different problem categories. Most of the 69 social-service clients were offered only one service; half of them the core service, counseling. Twenty-two clients, or one-third of the group, received no service beyond a referral, and of these, 19 were steered to what the agency considered to be more appropriate targets; for the remaining three, active referrals were made. Twelve of the 69 social-service clients received more than one service.

Slightly more than half of the applicants for financial assistance received it, and half of these were also steered to other agencies, usually employment services. Five clients were actively referred to other resources. About one-third of the group received no service beyond being steered to other sources of help. Clients in all problem categories received proportionately the same amount of service.

The agency's services were given under conditions at once supportive and controlling, and the clients may therefore have felt themselves to be in a bind. Records were not kept in any great detail, confidentiality was strict, and little information was exchanged with other agencies (Table 9-2), all of which were conditions designed to protect the client. Furthermore, the religious aegis under which the agency operated demanded a respect for the individual, no matter what his need, and militated against the tendency shown by the psychiatrists to select clients on the basis of their ability to profit from a particular form of care. On the other hand, religious sponsorship was the visible sign of the agency's espousal of a well-known body of norms and values, and even clients who did not share its faith were probably reasonably aware of them and willing to accommodate to them. Such a pervasive normative control exerted on workers as well as clients probably produced a level of social control that had no counterpart in nonsectarian agencies.*

An Unspecialized, Supportive Agency With Strong Normative Control

The religious sponsorship of Catholic Welware distinguished it from the other formal agencies in the study series. The difference was especially noticeable in boundary conditions. Catholic Welfare was fully accessible to its clients, offering a wider, less specialized, and in some ways a less controlling, service than most of the study agencies. In profile, Catholic Welfare appeared to be both a sorting and a serving agency, perhaps somewhere between casework agencies and the clergymen themselves in function.

Although the social workers in Catholic Welfare were trained in casework, the open-door philosophy of the agency left them with little time to use this skill. For social workers identified with a casework speciality, some role strain might be expected to arise from time to time in such an agency, just because of a dual attachment to both goals and skills; the only evidence of strain apparent during this study, however, was the workers' suggestion that the referrals made by priests did not always reflect a complete understanding of the agency's function. On the whole, attachment to the values and goals of the sponsoring church, and especially that of stable family life, appeared to override attachment to any particular method of reaching them.

---

* Clients sometimes go to an agency sponsored by a different faith in order to avoid normative sanction. This is said to be especially true of unmarried mothers.

THE FAMILY AGENCY   *10*

The social service function of the Family Agency overlapped that of Catholic Welfare, but because it had no funds for providing financial relief, it had a more specialized regulative role. Like Catholic Welfare, this agency had a mandate to arrange adoptions and to place children, but it specialized in casework service to individuals and families almost to the exclusion of these arrangements.

Casework is one of the three specialties taught in social

Mr. Robert Hill, Executive Director of the agency, kindly gave permission for this study, and all of his staff cooperated with the time-consuming field work. Joan Poltenson, Patricia Healy, and Robert Porter assisted with the analysis of the data.

work schools, the others being group work and community organization. In 1922, Mary Richmond defined "differential casework" as "those processes which develop personality through adjustments consciously effected, individual by individual, between men and their social environment" (Richmond, 1922). Later, psychiatric theory affected casework practice, but, as Perlman's (1957) definition showed, the goal remained utopian, the method vague: "Casework is a process used by certain human welfare agencies to help individuals cope more effectively with their problems in social functioning." Between these two definitions, myriads of similar ones have been offered as social caseworkers have continued to define the goals and content of their discipline (Flexner, 1915; Comments on Currents, 1964).

For many caseworkers, the diffuseness of their discipline is unimportant because they work in agencies whose primary goals are both given and clear: religious charities, hospitals, clinics, recreation centers, welfare departments, employment offices, public housing units, and schools. In such settings, the caseworker has tangible signs of success: the reconciled family, improved health, new social skills, successful work patterns, better household management, or greater progress at school. Although the individual worker might attach more importance to the client's adjustment than to these outward signs of conformity to social expectation, they indicate successful intervention and are, therefore, a source of gratification. In contrast, the practitioner in the family casework agency strives for the more diffuse goal of better personal and social adjustment for his clients, often without any outside criterion of what constitutes progress. Perhaps because of this vagueness, success is often gauged by the way in which the client participates in the casework process, and this process tends to become an end in itself.

Like many such "freestanding" casework agencies, the one chosen for study had a well-qualified staff, was responsible to a high-status, rather conservative Board of Directors, and was supported both by the United Council and by fees charged to most of its clients. The agency operated under the usual supervision method; the clients were first seen by an intake worker and then assigned to a caseworker who subsequently reported each client's progress to a supervisor. The supervisor, herself an experienced caseworker, was expected to help the worker to understand his own role in the casework process. In all, the agency had positions for an executive director and for 13 trained workers; 10 positions were filled at the time of the study.

Method of Study

In the Family Agency, thanks to the patience of the staff, the process by which the clients entered the service could be studied in greater detail than was possible in any of the other study agencies. A field worker made a series of observations at the boundary of the agency between June 20 and August 18, 1961, first listening to 150 incoming telephone calls and noting their disposition, then collecting 74 consecutive intake calls, and at the end of each day interviewing the intake worker about their content. During this time, the fate of clients who walked into the agency without appointments was noted. Finally, the intake worker was interviewed regarding the problems presented by the new clients after they came to the agency. The study group itself consisted of 54 clients, numbered consecutively by the agency, who entered or re-entered care between July 17 and August 18, 1961.* Files were abstracted six months later.

Entrance to the Agency

The Family Agency was located in a pleasant house on a shady street in a neighborhood of expensive apartment houses and commercial offices. Apart from the fact that poorer clients might hesitate to come into such a neighborhood, the physical situation was supportive: the waiting room was quiet and pleasant and the atmosphere was friendly.

* Of the 54 clients, 36 entered via an intake telephone call, 8 walked in, 2 received appointments through other agents, and 8 were first seen during the period of observation but had arranged appointments before the observation started.

The majority of the Family Agency's clients telephoned for an appointment before presenting themselves, however, and thus spoke first with the telephone operator. Switchboard operators, like receptionists and admitting clerks, are agency gatekeepers who can either help or hinder a client in his attempt to find service. It is usually understood that they should not exercise control over who enters and who does not; but, in reality, they often determine priorities, and even make the ultimate selection among applicants. Deutscher (1967), for example, found that the clerk who handled applications to the Syracuse Public Housing Authority categorized them into those who were possible tenants and those who were not, with the result that the professionals who made the actual selections had access only to those applications that the receptionist had determined through experience to be most likely to be acceptable to them. In this way, the receptionist effectively removed from the agency the opportunity of changing its selection policy.

Findings

SWITCHBOARD

The telephone operator in the Family Agency was under instruction to transfer all calls as they came in, or, if that was not possible, to take a message, name, or number. Calls from clients applying to the agency were to be transferred immediately to the intake telephone, covered by a worker at all times. The operator followed these rules with remarkable closeness, even though when she did fail to route a call to the appropriate worker, for whatever reason, it was always a call from a client and never from another professional person. Calls from 8 of 98 old clients and 4 of 14 new applicants were terminated at the switchboard, while all 26 calls from agents were transferred. These differences are not statistically significant, however, and the switchboard operator was controlling the entrance to the agency of only a small fraction of the incoming group of clients.

INTAKE PHONE CALLS

Clients calling for first appointments in the agency were interviewed over the telephone by an intake worker who decided whether they should be seen or steered elsewhere. Between July 17 and August 18, 74 intake calls were collected; of these, 2 were requests for information, which was given by telephone, and 3 were requests for employment involving the agency as foster parents. Seven applications for service were discarded from the study because their assigned appointments fell outside the study period. Of the remaining 62 applicants, 10 were immediately steered to other resources, 4 of them to the Welfare Department's adoption service* (Table 10-1). Of the remaining 52 callers, 36 came to the agency for at

Table 10-1.   FATE OF CLIENTS AT VARIOUS STAGES OF ENTRY TO THE FAMILY AGENCY[a]

Application type	Number applying	Proceeding to next stage	Referred elsewhere or postponed	Terminated, failed or withdrew No.	%
Switchboard	18	14	2	2	11.1
Intake calls	62	36	20	6	9.7
Walk-in	12	8	1	3	25.0

[a] Period of study in Tables 10-1 through 10-4 was June 20–August 18, 1961.

least one interview and became part of the study group, 6 were given appointments but failed to keep them, and 10 either postponed their own appointments or were promised service at some future date by the agency.

WALK-INS

Although the agency liked clients to telephone to make

* The Welfare Department's requirements regarding the age of the parents and the number of other children in the family were not so strict as the Family Agency's; for example, they would give an older couple a child or allow a third child to be adopted, which the Family Agency would not.

appointments, they also welcomed those who walked in un-announced, thus displaying an initiative in seeking service that they believed to augur well for success in casework treatment. During the period of observation, 14 clients walked in, and 2 were given appointments for a time outside the observation period. Of the remaining 12, 1, a grandfather seeking placement for a grandchild, was steered to the Welfare Department and 1 couple who had adopted a child through private channels and had then discovered it to be blind was refused service because the worker felt that the agency could do nothing about the problem. Ten of the 14 clients who walked in were given appointments within the observation period, and 8 kept them.

INTAKE INTERVIEW

The last step before being accepted for service in the agency was an evaluation of the client and his problems by an intake worker who subsequently assigned him to a caseworker or directed him elsewhere. Of the 54 clients in the study group who took this last step across the agency boundary, 32, or 59 per cent, returned to the agency for casework treatment.

The rate of attrition of applicants, estimated from the rates of loss at the various stages, appears to have been around 70 per cent by the end of the intake interview, a rate that approximated that of patients approaching psychiatric clinics. In other words, about 30 per cent of all those initially calling the switchboard appeared to end up receiving casework, the core service of the agency.

Such a high attrition rate suggests strong controls at the agency boundary, but in this agency, controls were mostly latent and subtle. As in the psychiatric clinic, however, the client was required to make application on his own, and to appear motivated for the kind of service offered. If, in the intake interview, his orientation was found to be unsuitable for casework service, he might be advised, in the words of one worker, "he was not ready for the service of the agency," or he might just be steered to another source of help.

REFERRAL SOURCE

The profile of the Family Agency's contacts with the rest of the regulative system shows that a few more than one-third of the clients in the study group came on their own, another third were referred by the primary gatekeepers, doctors, and clergymen, for whom, like Catholic Welfare, the agency appeared to be acting as a second line of defense, and the remainder were sent by eight different agencies (Table 10-2).

PROBLEMS PRESENTED

All 54 of the clients approaching the Family Agency complained of interpersonal difficulties or personal problems, and 37 of them had problems serious enough to be classified as role failure or deviant behavior (Table 10-3). The majority of these 37 clients reported severe family conflict or total marital breakdown.

One-quarter of the clients complained of transitional maladjustments and these included children, adolescents, and adults. Only three clients had difficulties that could be thought of as purely environmental contingencies; one of these had temporary financial problems following an illness, and the other two needed placement services for children for reasons beyond their own control.

SERVICES OFFERED

Casework. Forty of the 54 clients were offered the core service, casework, and of these, 19 returned for at least four interviews; six months later, 8, or 15 per cent of the starting group, were still in casework care at the agency.

Adoptions and Child Placement. Child placement and adoptions were part of the agency's mandate, but no client in the study group received these services during the observation period.

Referral Targets. The Family Agency sent 17 clients to a total of 22 referral targets ranging over 10 agencies in all sectors of the regulative system, and 2 of the 6 unreferred clients who were still in care could have expected ultimate referral. Nine referrals were made to psychiatric facilities that could

Table 10-2. RELATIONSHIP OF THE FAMILY AGENCY WITH
OTHER AGENCIES THROUGH REFERRAL SOURCES, INTER-
AGENCY CONTACTS, AND REFERRAL TARGETS
OF 54 CLIENTS

	Type of relationship with other agencies				
Agency	Referral Source	Referral Target	Arrangements	Information	Eligibility check
All clients	**54**	**54**	**54**	**54**	**54**
Without agency contact	21	37	48	48	54
With agency contact	33	17	6	6	0
Total contacts made	*34*	*22*	*6*	*10*	*0*
Medical					
Private physician	11				
Private psychiatrist				1	
Psychiatric clinic	1	5	1	1	
Child Guidance Clinic	1	4			
Counseling					
Clergyman	8				
Family agency elsewhere				1	
Legal Aid	3	1	1		
School services	1	1	1	3	
Hospital social service	3	3		1	
Adoption agency		1			
Alcoholics Anonymous	1				
Private psychologist				1	
Employment					
Employment offices		1			
Employer	1				
Income maintenance					
Welfare departments	4	2			
Housing Authority	1				
Institutions					
Maternity homes and shelters		3	2	1	
St. Christian's School				1	
Correction					
Children's Court			1		

be looked upon as similar in character to the Family Agency
but more specialized and perhaps more controlling. Within
each group of agencies, the referral targets used by the agency
tended to be more controlling than the source from which the
clients came, suggesting that the agency was a way station between the primary gatekeepers and other more controlling

Table 10-3. PROBLEMS PRESENTED BY 54 CLIENTS
TO THE FAMILY AGENCY

Problem category	No.	%
All clients	54	100.0
Transition states	*14*	*25.9*
Child behavior	2	
Adolescent behavior	6	
Adult maladjustment	1	
Marital maladjustment	5	
Role failure	37	68.5
Unwed mothers	8	
Economic inadequacy	3	
Inadequate wives and mothers	4	
Emotionally disturbed children	4	
Evidence of criminal behavior	2	
Marital breakdown	16	
Contingencies	*3*	*5.6*
Insufficient income	1	
Child placement	2	

agencies in the system. All but 2 referrals were actively made
by the workers, further suggesting a continuation of control
over the client as he left the service and a concern on the
part of the agency that he not slip out of the network of regulative agencies.

SUMMARY OF SERVICES

Most of the clients in the study group were offered a
single service, either counseling or referral. The services were
not evenly spread over the problem types, however, as Table
10-4 shows. Clients with the milder transitional and developmental problems were more likely to be counseled or have arrangements made for them than were the other two groups
who were more often referred or refused service. Multiple
services were distributed over all problem categories, and the
rapid attrition of clients in the early phases of treatment occurred in all problem categories. The over-all high loss rate
in this agency has been commented on by Garcea and Irwin
(1962), who pointed out that similar rates were being experienced at the time by many casework agencies as well as
by outpatient clinics. A pilot study in this series of an earlier
cohort of clients from the Family Agency had suggested that

Table 10-4. SERVICES OFFERED TO 54 CLIENTS OF THE FAMILY AGENCY, BY PROBLEM PRESENTED

Services offered	Total No.	%	Problem category		Contingencies		
			Transition states	Role failure	Children	Adults	Aged
All clients	**54**	**100.0**	**14**	**37**	**2**	**1**	**0**
No service	2	3.7		1[a]	1[a]		
One service	42	77.8	12	29			
Counseling	33	61.1	11	22	1		
Arrangements	1	1.9	1				
Referral	8	14.8		7[a]	1[a]		
Two services	9	16.7	2	6		1	
Counseling and arrangements	1	1.9		1			
Counseling and referral	5	9.3		4		1	
Arrangements and referral	3	5.6	2	1			
Three services	1	1.9		1			

[a] All 14 clients complaining of transitional disorders received counseling or arrangements, while ten of the remaining 40 clients received a referral elsewhere or no service (P = .048, Fisher's Exact Test).

the agency's views of the client's problem often did not reflect the client's views, and that only those clients who came to accept the agency's views remained in care for long.

Although the agency was controlling at both its in- and out-boundary, the service itself was probably perceived as supportive; evidence for this comes from the high proportion of clients (9 of 17) persisting in care for more than ten sessions after the initial stages were passed.

A Specialized, Relatively Supportive Agent's Agency

In a sense, the Family Agency could be viewed as a professional's rather than a client's agency, because, like other casework agencies, it practiced fine mesh screening in order to produce a population suitable for the skilled treatment in which it specialized (Lindenberg, 1958; Goodman, 1960; Leichter, 1961). In general the agency received clients with difficult problems and tended to refer the most disordered to more controlling agents. In its selectiveness, as well as in its relation to the rest of the regulative system, the Family Agency was similar to the mental health clinics. Like the clinics, and to some degree like family doctors, the agency was a sorting, screening, allocating agency, apparently passing clients along a path from relatively supportive to more controlling agents, conducting its own core casework service without collaboration with outside agencies. Probably because the agency was willing to take difficult clients from gatekeeper agents and allocate them to more controlling services, it was fairly well knit into the over-all regulative system. This process, in turn, freed it to offer its highly specialized skill to the small proportion of suitable clients, which, in turn, allowed it to hold a highly trained staff. Because of its selective practices, this agency was viewed with mixed feelings by its clients as well as by the agents in the regulative system.

REFERENCES

Comments on Currents, 1964. "Social Work's Concern: Problem or Method?" *Social Work,* Vol. 9, No. 2, April.

Deutscher, Irwin, 1968. "The Gatekeeper in Public Housing," in *Among the Poor, Encounters with the People,* eds. I. Deutscher and E. Thompson, New York, Basic Books.

Flexner, Abraham, 1915. "Is Social Work a Profession?" *Proceedings of the National Conference of Charities and Corrections.*

Garcea, Ralph, and Olive Irwin, 1962. "A Family Agency Deals with the Problem of Dropouts," *Social Casework,* Vol. 43, No. 2, February.

Goodman, Nathaniel, 1960. "Are There Differences Between Fee and Non-Fee Cases?" *Social Work,* Vol. 5, No. 4.

Leichter, Hope J., 1961. "Kinship Values and Casework Intervention," *Casework Papers,* New York, Family Service Association of America.

Lindenberg, Ruth Ellen, 1958. "Hard to Reach: Client or Casework Agency?" *Social Work,* Vol. 3, No. 4.

Perlman, Helen, 1957. *Social Casework; a Problem-Solving Process,* Chicago, University of Chicago Press.

Richmond, Mary, 1922. *What is Social Casework?* New York, Russell Sage Foundation.

THE MEDICAL SOCIAL SERVICE DEPARTMENT

11

Medical social work is the oldest speciality of the profession, social service departments first appearing in hospitals and clinics in the early years of this century (Lubove, 1965). These social services were designed for the specific purpose of helping patients to solve those nonmedical problems that interfered with their recovery from illnesses. In the course of performing this function, medical social workers forged a link between medical services and the rest of the regulative system.

Miss Pauline Hagen, Casework Supervisor, kindly arranged for the field work for this study, and the agency social workers cooperated more than fully with the field team.

The Syracuse Dispensary's Social Service Department was staffed by four social workers and a supervisor, and it provided four basic services: arrangements, coordination, referral, and casework. The workers also supplemented the activity of the admitting office by solving particularly difficult administrative or eligibility problems.

Because the agency had no discretionary funds, arrangements for payment from public and private sources for such things as hospitalizations, eyeglasses, and orthodontia were made on a case-by-case basis. Numerous sources, both public and private, were tapped on behalf of patients whose marginal incomes left them unable to afford these adjuncts to medical care but who were at the same time ineligible for public assistance.

The agency social workers served as a communication and coordination center within the Dispensary and between it and the rest of the regulative system; they supplied the clinic doctors with the social histories of the patients and outside agencies with medical information needed for decisions about general welfare. If a tenant in public housing, for example, asked to be moved to a larger apartment because of a sick child's need for a room of his own, the authorities could ask the Dispensary's Social Service Department whether there was sufficient medical reason for the change. More commonly, when a teacher had a problem with a school child, she could inquire as to whether his medical or psychiatric condition warranted special consideration in the classroom. The agency social workers also provided a wide variety of information about local services to the clients themselves.

Much of the staff's time was spent in the routines of making financial arrangements with various charities, service clubs, and formal agencies whose services the clients might never have reached in any other way. Coordination of resources, arrangement of services, and, at times, the development of individual resources was undoubtedly the agency's core activity. At the same time, the typical arrangement required the worker to call on a service club to request eyeglasses for a particular child. This process appeared to absorb the time of a trained social worker to gratify the voluntaristic impulses of the service clubs as much as to serve the child.

All the agency's social workers maintained some clients in casework, and because they considered this their most valuable skill, they would have used it more if they had had time to do so.

Method of Study

The five social workers in the agency kept a log detailing all their contacts with both clients and other agencies during the period from February 15 to March 16, 1962. These logs were then abstracted, and the appropriate Dispensary files searched.* A total of 136 names were collected from the logs of four workers; of these, 88 were the names of clients who were admitted or re-admitted to the agency during the observation period, and they formed the study group. The remaining 48 clients were already under care when the study began, and they will be considered in Appendix B.

As the Social Service Department did not keep records separately from the Dispensary's own files, it was impossible to be certain of the rate of intake into the agency; but, judging from the workers' logs, nearly 100 clients must have entered or re-entered care during the month of study. This number is around 3 per cent of the estimated number of patients entering or re-entering the Dispensary in the same interval, a figure close to the 2.3 per cent of the Dispensary study group referred for social service.

Entrance to the Service

Only Dispensary patients were eligible for the services of the Social Service Department, although occasionally a client

* Six phone calls from the logs were discarded because they could not be attached to any name. The supervisor's log was excluded because some of her cases overlapped those of the others and because her conditions of work did not allow her to keep her log in sufficient detail for the study. It seems reasonable to assume that the logs used represented the work done in the agency at the time.

came into the service through informal channels or directly from the Welfare Department, and the workers occasionally saw their own old clients if they returned without another referral from a clinic.

Entering the agency was uncomplicated, patients being sent from the clinic to the social service with a note requesting care. Compared to the parent agency, there were few controls at the boundary of this service, although the workers were so busy that the clients often spent a long time in the waiting room before being seen.

The clinic doctors made most referrals for simple financial reasons, but the social workers sometimes found a complex of problems when they interviewed the patient, and these clients tended to be remembered. As one worker said:

> The patient may not be on Welfare, but may say to the doctor, "I can't pay for this medicine"; then the doctor refers them to us . . . but when you talk to them you almost always find that there are multiple problems . . . the children are having trouble in school, or there are marital problems, or they are paying private lawyers and should be using Legal Aid. . . . One woman was fired from a job (in a public utility) that she'd held for a long time right after they found she was married to a Negro. . . .

Although most clinic doctors made general referrals to the Social Service Department, some of them frustrated the workers by issuing the kinds of orders that they were accustomed to giving to nurses. The following description came from an interview with one of the social workers:

> The other day the doctor referred a woman saying that she needed a baby carriage, but I thought she needed a telephone, and she thought she needed a telephone. She had six or seven small children and no phone; her husband had left, and the children had been quite sick, and the neighbor wouldn't let her use her phone, and she was afraid to leave the oldest child, who was seven, with all

the others while she went a block or so to use a pay phone. She was on Welfare and the Welfare worker said she couldn't have a phone unless the doctor recommended it. And he recommended a baby carriage—but that wouldn't work in a blizzard!

Findings

REFERRAL

All 88 clients in the study group had presumably entered the Social Service Department by direct referral from the Dispensary's clinics when a doctor had become aware of some nonmedical problem that was frustrating his therapeutic efforts, and when it occurred to him that the Social Service Department could do something about it (Table 11-1).*

Table 11-1. RELATIONSHIP OF THE SOCIAL SERVICE DEPARTMENT OF THE SYRACUSE DISPENSARY WITH OTHER AGENCIES THROUGH REFERRAL SOURCES, INTERAGENCY CONTACTS, AND REFERRAL TARGETS OF 88 CLIENTS[a]

	Type of relationship with other agencies				
Agency	Referral Source[b]	Target	Arrangements	Information	Eligibility checks
All clients	88	88	88	88	88
Without agency contact	0	61	47	65	84
With agency contact	88	27	41	23	4
Total contacts made	88	33	67	24	4
Medical					
Private physicians and dentists			1	1	
Public health nurses and VNA			2	1	
Hospitals		3	3	4	
Dispensary	88	3			

* Of the 88 clients, 55 had been self-referred to the Dispensary, 10 were parents of children referred by school services, 11 from the Welfare Department, 7 from a hospital social service department, 3 from medical referrals, 1 from the Division of Parole, and 1 from a neighborhood center.

Table 11-1. (Cont.)

Type of relationship with other agencies

Agency	Referral Source[b]	Target	Arrangements	Information	Eligibility checks
Planned Parenthood		2			
Health department			11		
Rehabilitation		1			
Psychiatric clinics		6	2		
Counseling					
Legal Aid			1		
Catholic Charities			1		
Salvation Army				1	
School services			4	2	
Services for the blind			2	1	
Alcoholism services				1	
VA contact office		1		1	
Recreation					
Neighborhood centers		1	1		
YWCA, YMCA		3	1		
Golden Age Clubs		1			
Employment					
Employment offices		3			
Vocational rehabilitation		1			
Workmen's Compensation			1		
Income maintenance					
Service clubs and Red Cross			7	1	
Welfare Department		6	12	9	3
Public housing		1	3		
Social Security					1
State Aid to the Disabled			8		
Surplus food		1	1		
Institutions					
Children's Home			1		
Correction					
Parole and probation			2	1	
Youth Bureau			1		
Other, Nonagencies					
Pharmacies, bank			2	1	

a Period of study for Tables 11-1 through 11-3 was February 15–March 16, 1962.
b All referrals were to the Dispensary, which then referred to the Social Service Department. Of the 88 clients 54 had been self-referred, 10 had come from school services, 11 from the Welfare Department, 7 from a hospital social service department, 4 from medical referrals, 1 from the Division of Parole, 1 from a neighborhood center.

PROBLEMS PRESENTED

In spite of the workers' impressions that their clients had multiple problems, two-thirds of them complained only of not being able to afford the expense associated with illness (Table 11-2). Half of these medically indigent people needed

Table 11-2.   PROBLEMS PRESENTED BY 88 CLIENTS OF THE
SOCIAL SERVICE DEPARTMENT, SYRACUSE DISPENSARY

Problem category	Total	%
All clients	88	100.0
Transition states	*10*	*11.4*
Maladjustment of children[a]	6	6.8
Maladjustment of adolescents[a]	4	4.6
Role failure	*20*	*22.7*
Chronic economic inadequacy (est.)	1	1.1
Inadequate wives and mothers	4	4.5
Marital breakdown	2	2.3
Evidence of crime	4	4.5
Evidence of antisocial behavior	2	2.3
Emotional disturbance (child)	7	8.0
Contingencies (financial)	*58*	*65.9*
Children	27	30.7
Adults	18	20.5
Aged	13	14.8

[a] Including parent-child problems.

some service for children such as the purchase of eyeglasses or arrangements for complicated corrective and rehabilitative procedures. Operations for cleft palates, clubbed feet, and other congenital defects, as well as rehabilitative services of many kinds, were arranged by the department.

Only one-fifth of the clients were found to be suffering from the more serious role failure disorders, and only 10 per cent had transitional problems. The population approaching this agency appeared to have less serious problems than those approaching either Catholic Welfare or the Family Agency, in spite of the workers' impression that many of the clients had multiple problems.

SERVICES OFFERED

Arrangements. Arrangements are among the more controlling of services because they tend to keep the client within the regulative network. As the agency profile shows (Table 11-1), a total of 67 contacts were made with 21 agencies on behalf of 41 clients. The modal arrangement was a complicated plan, usually for a child, between the Welfare Department, the State Health Department's Aid to the Disabled, and the local Health Department. Although medically indigent children were automatically eligible for a wide range of services, the complicated routines of applying for them were beyond the ability of many of their parents.

The agency workers routinely acted in concert with other agencies in the course of giving service, thus enhancing their control over the clients' lives. Apart from making arrangements, they exchanged information about clients with 12 other agencies. As the profile shows, relationships with others in the regulative system were concentrated relatively more on service procedures in comparison with referrals than any other agency studied.

Counseling. Eighteen of the 88 clients in the study group were counseled, 5 of them briefly. The remaining 13 were still in care when the records were searched three months later. These clients were younger than the remainder and were more often complaining of transitional problems: these differences were statistically significant. In spite of its protestations, this agency was finding time to select 20 per cent of its clients for counseling.

Referral Targets. The Social Service Department sent 27 of its 88 clients to a total of 14 agencies, 14 of them by active referral; it could be expected to refer another 8 of the 26 unreferred clients still in care when the records were reviewed. There was practically no overlap between the group of agencies from which these clients had come to the Dispensary in the first place and those to which they were sent, suggesting that the agency was acting as a sorting and allocating center for the medically indigent somewhat as the Family Agency was for an interpersonally disordered group. This agency

seemed somewhat more controlling at the out-boundary than
it was at the in-boundary.

Sixty-eight of the 88 clients in the study group received
one or more of the agency's services and these were related
to the type of problem presented, as Table 11-3 shows. Multiple services and casework counseling were both concentrated
on clients with transitional problems, but arrangements were
most often made for the children and the aged clients within
the contingent group. These differences are statistically significant (Table 11-3). Referral was the only service not connected to problem type, the 27 made being distributed over
all the problem categories.

The Dispensary's Social Service appeared to be giving its
core service, arrangements, to its most vulnerable clients,
children and old people, but its most valued service, counseling, to its most hopeful clients, those with transitional or
developmental problems. In general, however, the preponderance of arrangements over both counseling and referral
suggests that the agency was primarily specializing in muster-
ing resources for its clients, a function that is the core of
medical social work, and one that at least one school believes
to be the major legitimate activity of any social worker
(Wootton, 1959).

A Moderately Controlling, Moderately Specialized Agency

The Social Service Department of the Dispensary could
be considered as playing a formal role in relationship to the
clinic physicians, somewhat reminiscent of the role that public health nurses played for family practitioners when they
dealt with nonmedical problems in the interest of medical
welfare. In a sense, also, the agency had assumed, on behalf
of the clinic physician, an interest in the whole man such as
most of the family doctors professed for their patients. Such
a division of labor between the specific medical task and the
diffuse supportive function can have both strengths and
weaknesses: on the one hand, it is efficient for mobilizing a

Table 11-3. SERVICES OFFERED TO 88 CLIENTS OF THE SOCIAL SERVICE DEPARTMENT, SYRACUSE DISPENSARY, BY PROBLEM TYPE

| Services offered | Total | | Problem category | | | | |
| | No. | % | Transition states | Role failure | Contingencies | | |
					Children	Adults	Aged
All clients	**88**	**100.0**	**10**	**20**	**27**	**18**	**13**
Information only	20	22.7	0	3	6	9	2
One service	*50*	*56.8*	*5*	*12*	*16*	*7*	*10*
Arrangements	31	35.2	2	7	13	2	7
Counseling	6	6.8	3	2	1		
Referral	13	14.8		3	2	5	3
Two services	*15*	*17.0*	*5*	*3*	*5*	*1*	*1*
Arrangements and counseling	4	4.5	2	1			1
Arrangements and referral	6	6.8		1	4	1	
Counseling and referral	5	5.7	3	1	1		
Three services	*3*	*3.4*	*0*	*2*	*0*	*1*	*0*

1. Proportionately more clients with transitional problems received multiple services than did all other clients (P = .027, Fisher's Exact Test).
2. Proportionately more clients whose problems were classed as transitional received counseling than did all of the remainder (P = .00002 by Fisher's Exact Test).
3. Within the contingency group, the aged and the children received more arrangements than the adults ($\chi^2 = 6.5$, d.f. = 1, .02 > p > .01).

variety of services on behalf of the patient; but, on the other, it can split the patient's problems into segments, and, without careful coordination, this segmentation can decrease efficiency, as in the case of the woman who needed a telephone and got a baby carriage.

What seems clear from the study of this agency is that important services were being given to a small fraction of the Dispensary's patient group; whether this fraction was too small in any absolute sense could not be determined from these data.

REFERENCES

Lubove, Roy, 1965. *The Professional Altruist,* Cambridge, Harvard University Press.
Wootton, Barbara, 1959. *Social Science and Social Pathology,* New York, Macmillan.

THE DEPARTMENT OF SOCIAL 12
WELFARE, ADULT SERVICE
AND CHILDREN'S DIVISION

The County Department of Social Welfare was probably the
most misunderstood agency in the regulative system. Because
public misconceptions undoubtedly influenced its function,
some preliminary discussion of the problematic nature of the
agency will serve as an introduction to the findings of the
study.

Welfare Commissioner William Walsh kindly gave his permission
for this study, and John Lascaris, Director of Social Services, and later
Commissioner, made all the necessary arrangements. The staff of this
busy agency cooperated fully with the field workers, Charles Harrington and Ernest Damianopoulos. Erna Christensen, William Baylor,
Carrie Conti, Robert Porter, and Patricia Healy helped to abstract the
records and to analyze the data.

Of all the agencies in the system, the Welfare Department called attention most vividly to the tension between support and control; to the client it was coldly controlling, giving him grudgingly, and under degrading circumstances, only sufficient help to keep him and his family from starving (Coser, 1965). To that part of the public that considers itself "the taxpayer," the Welfare Department, to judge from many letters to the local papers, appeared to be a spendthrift organization staffed with bleeding-heart social workers who squandered the taxpayer's money and, what is worse, undermined the client's independence until he would "rather stay on relief than work." As Glaser (1966) says, "Conservatives do not like welfare agencies because they are expensive and encourage dependency; liberals and radicals dislike them because their requirements restrict freedom and their administration is dull, unimaginative and bureaucratic."*

Historically, the tension about society's obligation to the indigent has appeared in many guises since the state took over from the church the task of providing for the poor. Before the concept of relief in the home was ever entertained, there were arguments about who "deserved" to go to the poor farm; later there were protests about the granting of any "outdoor relief" or financial relief in the home (Pumphrey and Pumphrey, 1961). During the time that relief was given "in kind," and the poor dragged their potatoes and flour home from the relief office as best they could, it was argued that it was wrong to give the poor money instead of food because they would fritter it away. At the time of these studies, relief in the form of a minimum cash income had been accepted, but the granting of relief in their homes to certain categories of people, like mothers of illegitimate children and stranded migrant workers, still continued to be resented. Beneath his apparent niggardliness seemed to lie an essentially laissez-faire ideology; if everyone would pursue his own interests diligently, no one would want (Mencher, 1963). It followed that if he were in want, it must have been through

* For a full account of the activities of county and state welfare departments in New York State at about the period of these studies, see the report of the Moreland Commission (1963).

failure of effort. Accompanying this ideology, however, seemed to run a paradoxical desire to take care of the needy as a voluntary charity. The Welfare Department automatically frustrated this desire, because the taxpayer could neither see nor control the way in which his contributions alleviated the suffering of the poor.

Welfare Stereotypes

Through these ideas, and through the years, had run a single sentiment: it is a disgrace to be so poor that you must depend on others for your sustenance. This sentiment was evident in many statements by private individuals and some public figures at the time of the study.* Although "the poor" in this sentiment seemed like a simple, monolithic category of stigmatized people, they were, in fact, a heterogeneous group around which many factual and conceptual errors had grown up. Public confusion about poverty and dependency appeared to permeate three main areas: the characteristics of the poor, the contribution of the hard-working to the poor, and the nature of dependency.

First, many appeared to believe that the poor were willfully so, even when investigation had shown that only between 2 and 5 per cent of those receiving welfare at any one time were recalcitrant, work-shy, or in any sense purposely poor (Moreland Commission, 1963). The remainder were made up of children, the aged, and those disabled by illness or congenital incapacity. A number were unemployable because they were nearly illiterate,† some seemed to have been incapacitated by years of the narrow, stultifying life of the chronic welfare recipient, and some had learned not to leave the welfare rolls for fear of failing and having to endure the

* During the study, the Welfare Director in Newburgh, New York, attracted national attention by withholding assistance from some categories of eligible clients, apparently to forward himself politically. Although he received a telegram of congratulations from Barry Goldwater, his policy was discontinued as illegal.

† Three-quarters of the heads of the families on the rolls of the Onondaga County Welfare Department at the time of study had not completed grade school.

degradation of applying once more.* The most problematical group and the one most nearly fitting the taxpayer's stereotype was the group receiving the federally subsidized Aid to Dependent Children. Some of these children were illegitimate, and their maintenance in their mothers' homes gave the impression that the Department was actually sponsoring immorality.†

The second error in thinking about welfare concerned the amounts that different classes of people drew from the public purse. Although it was generally believed that those on welfare only took, while the well-to-do only gave, this was not true for several reasons. In the first place, it is important to distinguish between the kinds of people on welfare at one given time and those who appeared and reappeared on the rolls, that is, between the incidence and prevalence populations. Although the majority of the people on welfare rolls on any given day were known to be in some sense disabled, and therefore chronically dependent, many of those entering the rolls were only temporarily in need of aid, usually at "poverty points" in their lives—when their children were small, when sickness occurred, during old age. Most of the lives of most welfare families in Syracuse were spent at work and, therefore, in contributing to the general economic welfare. Indeed, at least half of those families who at some time received public assistance would not have had to do so if the wage-price structure had allowed them to raise families on the small wages of an unskilled or semiskilled worker (Ru-

---

* Garfinkel (1956) has described the conditions necessary for a successful degradation ceremony, and admission to social welfare assistance comes very close to meeting them.

† The controversial ADC program was designed to encourage women, particularly widows, to remain in their homes with their children. As the Social Security program began to provide for families of dead or disabled fathers, the ADC program assisted a correspondingly greater proportion of single women with illegitimate children and children of deserting fathers, some of whom were also illegitimate. There had been developing, at the time of the study, a feeling that these latter women should be encouraged to leave their children in nurseries and enter the labor market. It was believed that if they were working, they would have more incentive to keep from having further illegitimate children.

dolph and Cassetta, 1963). Another large group would probably not have needed public assistance if ordinary fluctuations in the labor market or various kinds of employer-induced economic catastrophes, such as business failures, had not periodically left them out of work (Burns, 1956). Such fluctuations and dislocations in the free labor market were held to be necessary for efficient production and hence, supposedly, raised the gross national product; but the worker whose temporary unemployment contributed to the freedom of the labor market seemed to be held personally responsible for his own failure to stay at work.* Unfortunately, the necessity of relieving poverty in modern industrial society has not been viewed as one of the inevitable costs of a remarkably high productivity, but rather as a charity performed by the hardworking for the shiftless.

While there was little public understanding of the role of temporary unemployment in the economy, there seemed to be even less of its relative cost (Titmuss, 1959). Few people realized that the cost to the taxpayer of a welfare family was probably less than the cost of a well-to-do family who took advantage of all the benefits available to them. Among the most important of these were tax relief for the period of dependency of children during their education and the large hidden subsidies toward that education that came from various branches of the federal government. Although most middle-class people could not have afforded college educations for their children if they had had to bear the full cost themselves, their dependence on the public purse for this purpose did not stigmatize them.

The third conceptual confusion about welfare, and the most serious in its consequences, was the universal tendency to consider financial dependency to be a morally inferior condition that stigmatized the whole man. Dependency is

* In America at the time of these studies many people applying for welfare had counterparts in other industrialized countries who were protected by social insurance. This difference reflected divergent goal structures. In America, economic goals had been paramount; in other countries, notably Russia, Scandinavia, and New Zealand, social or political goals took precedence and various techniques were employed to maintain full employment even if the economy suffered because of it.

usually thought of as the opposite of complete independence, but no one in a complex society can possibly be fully independent, everyone having to depend on others for all kinds of specialized services. The idea of "medical dependency," for example (Lambert *et al.*, 1963), suggests that the process of giving and receiving medical care is co-extensive with and indistinguishable from the issue of who pays for that care, but, in truth, everyone who is not a doctor is dependent upon doctors for medical care. There is no stigma attached to such dependency, which is a natural consequence of a divided labor. To refer to a person as "medically dependent" confuses the need for specialized medical care with the quite separate issue of how health care is to be financed, and highlights the general dislike of financial dependency.

Coser (1965) suggests that, in an achievement-oriented society, anyone who fails to contribute material goods or valued services is automatically stigmatized, but the problem is more complex than that. No one who makes his contributions in such a way that his needs are met all of the time, either by his own efforts or by *indirect* public subsidy, is stigmatized. Having contributed in the past does not help if, when the contribution has ceased, there is no provision for the future. No doubt that is why from time to time old people suffer from malnutrition and neglect because they are too proud to apply for public assistance, and no doubt it is also why they are admired for doing so.

Worker Conflict

All these conceptual confusions had remained surprisingly stable over the years preceding this study, no matter how many or few people were actually on welfare rolls, adding to the frustration of those charged with any part of the task of assisting the poor. Those who worked directly in welfare departments were caught in a classical conflict. As Wilensky and Lebeaux (1958) say, "Any worker who tries to be a good humanitarian and a good agency representative at the same time is in for a torment of conscience." A few workers from time to time identified with the clients and fought the system, but most could not help having a moral aversion to many of the clients and therefore taking the obvious path of identifying themselves with the taxpayer.

In its style, the Onondaga County Welfare Department probably resembled others in the country quite closely, but New York State's regulations were more generous than those of most states, some of which gave relief in their homes only to disabled people. The Onondaga County Welfare Department was financed partly through local taxation and partly through capitation payments from the New York State Department of Social Welfare and the federal Department of Health, Education and Welfare. It was a reasonably complex bureaucracy under the direction of a County Commissioner, employing a number of trained social workers in supervisory positions and a large, shifting group of college graduates without social work training as caseworkers. The department was very sensitive to the local political climate and to public opinion.

Entrance to the Agency

The Adult Division of the Welfare Department was housed in a handsome modern building in the center of Syracuse. Entrance to the building was poorly labeled and people on many kinds of business often had to ask directions. The Intake Division of the Department was located in a reception area that contained two "front" desks, marked "New Cases" and "Active Cases," a number of cubicles, a secretary's desk, and a supervisor's office. The client reported to a worker sitting at one or other of the front desks, told his trouble briefly, and then sat and waited for his turn, at which time his address, rather than his name, was called out. Intake was separate for veterans, although their treatment was identical. It was possible, however, for the applicants to describe their relief payments as "Veteran's Assistance."

In the center of the reception area were five rows of benches and, in addition, other benches were arranged around the walls. About 50 people could sit in the room, and, at the time of these studies, about 30 people—children,

senile old people, young mothers, and dirty, toothless men
waiting for the bus to the County Home—could usually be
found there. Some of the applicants were eating lunches
brought in anticipation of a long wait. Most applicants sat
silently, although occasionally a client might talk to himself
or suddenly start to rant against "the system."

The intake workers' cubicles were not soundproofed, so
that everyone could hear the clients relating their financial
problems as well as other complicating difficulties. During
the intake interview, the worker made a tentative decision as
to whether or not the client was eligible for aid and, if so, for
how much. Before he could give this aid, however, he had to
obtain his supervisor's approval.

The supervisor's office was behind the cubicles and inaccessible to the clients. Besides approving applications, he un-
tangled administrative problems that arose in the course of a
day and dealt with unruliness in the reception room. His
telephone rang constantly.

The secretary's desk was located next to the supervisor's office, and she took incoming telephone calls and rerouted
them when necessary. Most of her activity was concerned
with describing eligibility requirements to applicants who
hoped to apply for assistance by telephone, although she sometimes substituted for one of the intake workers.

If applicants were very ill or were disabled, a worker would
go to their homes to take their applications, but, except for
this rare situation, all clients came through the Intake Division.
If a client was accepted for the County Home, he was sent
there by a bus which left the department every day at the
same hour.

Some clients with special problems were sent immediately
to one or another of the department's own special divisions.
These were concerned with legal issues, employment, medical
matters, and special services to children. An office that distributed surplus foods was also administered by the Welfare
Department. All the special divisions of the Welfare Department accepted referrals from the Adult Division, and the
Children's Division maintained a separate intake of its own,
a practice that sometimes led to failure of coordination within

the department. Clients could be referred around the welfare system of services in much the same way that they were referred around the general regulative system.

Although the Adult Division gave its emergency help quite freely, its eligibility requirements for regular budgeted assistance were complex and exacting. First, the client had to establish his identity and his residence. A client without an address was not eligible for home relief, and could only be given financial assistance in finding a home if he had dependent children. This regulation meant that men, and occasionally women, with no addresses were offered shelter in the County Home. Marriage certificates and the birth certificates of all children were required to establish the identity of the various family members who had legal claims for support from the head of the household.

The second eligibility criterion required that the client be without resources, and that none of his immediate kin be able to assist him; he was likely to be disadvantaged in his search for help if he were a member of a tightly knit family. The client was required to list and sometimes surrender all his assets, including any insurance policies he held; in other words, he had to declare himself destitute. At one time during the study a laborer tried to arrange for assistance for his family during the time he would be in a hospital with a hernia operation. Asked how much money he had left, he replied, "Seventy-five dollars." Following the agency rules, the intake worker replied, "Come back when it is gone."

If there was a medical reason for the application in the first place, the client was usually accepted for assistance and then referred to the medical division where care by one of a panel of family doctors, the Dispensary, or a hospital was arranged. Certain medically fit men who were considered reluctant to work were required to join a work relief program; if they refused they had no recourse but to go to the County Home.

Evidence of past employment, usually an unemployment insurance book, was requested at intake. All employable men were referred to the agency's own Employment Division. Women applicants were usually required to swear warrants of nonsupport against their husbands in order to be eligible for assistance, although this procedure was elective. Some women refused to swear the warrant, perhaps not wishing to add another strain to what was already a tenuous relationship. At about this time the Commissioner of Welfare testified at public hearings that desertion, in his opinion, should be made a federal offense so that the FBI could be called in to find deserting fathers.

After all the necessary documentation had been produced by the client, a verification process followed. This investigation might include calls to landlords to verify rent payments, to banks to check on possible accounts, to previous employers to verify past salaries, and to doctors and clinics to verify statements about illness. It always included visits to the home to observe conditions there. Because of this long process of proving indigency, emergency help, usually a food voucher or money for rent, was often given immediately at intake.*

If the client did not feel that the merits of his case were being properly considered, either at intake or at any time during his contact with the agency, he could, if he knew that it was possible, appeal to the area Office of the State Department of Social Welfare, which would take up his complaint with the local department. During a period of six weeks at the time of the study, 32 complaints were received. In 7 cases the State Welfare Department either interpreted the local department's policy to the client or sent him back to the intake worker; in 21 cases they asked the local department for a report on the case or investigated it on behalf of the client in some other way; and in 4 cases they arranged for a formal hearing of the client's complaint.

Obviously the Welfare Department was both overtly and latently controlling at the in-boundary. No other agency had anything remotely resembling the eligibility requirements of this one, although many others exercised similar latent con-

---

* Two years later the Moreland Commission reported, "The policies and procedures governing the program (in New York State) are among the most complicated, detailed, burdensome, time-consuming and costly in the United States, but they are rigidly adhered to by the casework staff in almost every instance."

trols through public interviews and long waits in crowded, uncomfortable places. Sometimes controls seemed self-defeating; during the study one supervising worker kept a client waiting while she summoned a policeman to arrest him on a nonsupport warrant that he had failed to obey because he had no job, having just emerged from jail where he had been serving a sentence for nonsupport.

Although clients had a potential counter control of the agent in their recourse to the State Department of Social Welfare, only an estimated 1 per cent appeared to be using it. It is impossible to guess how many would have done so if they had known of it, had been unafraid, and had known their legal rights.

Method of Study

A field worker sat at the reception desk of the Adult Division of the Public Assistance Department from August 29 until September 15, 1961, and recorded the transactions between workers and clients. The total time period was not covered and therefore not all applicants were included, but each hour of the day was equally sampled. Two hundred and thirty-two clients, or slightly less than 4 per cent of the total for the year, made application during the period. Of these applicants, 179 had received public assistance in the past. The records of the whole study group were searched immediately upon disposition of each case, and new applications were searched again six months later. Later still, a group of 24 cases was collected from the Children's Division of the Department.

Findings: Adult Division

REFERRAL SOURCE

The agency profile (Table 12-1) shows that 20 different agencies sent clients to the Welfare Department, although the various counseling services accounted for the largest share. Although the agency was locked administratively with the

Table 12-1. RELATIONSHIP OF DEPARTMENT OF SOCIAL WEL-
FARE, ADULT DIVISION, WITH OTHER AGENCIES THROUGH
REFERRAL SOURCES, INTERAGENCY CONTACTS, AND
REFERRAL TARGETS OF 232 CLIENTS[a]

| Agency | Type of relationship with other agencies | | | | |
	Referral Source	Referral Target	Arrangements	Information	Eligibility checks
All clients	**232**	**232**	**232**	**232**	**232**
Without agency contact	179	203	216	223	203
With agency contact	53	29	16	9	29
Total contacts	*53*	*30*	*16*	*9*	*30*
Medical					
Private physician	4	2			
Hospital		3		3	5
Emergency room	2				
Dispensary	4	3	2	1	1
Medical clinics, other	5				
Rehabilitation, physical	1				
Psychiatric clinics	1			1	
Counseling					
Social Service, Dispensary	1				
Hospital social service	7				
Legal Aid or lawyer	8	1			1
Catholic Charities	2				
VA Contact Office	2				
Employment					
Employer	2		2		10
N.Y. State Employment		4	3		
N.Y. State Labor Department					1
Income maintenance					
Welfare out of town	1	4	1		2
Public housing or landlord	2	1	3		2
Social Security office					2
Unemployment insurance		1			1
Red Cross	2				
Union benefits fund					1
Institutions					
Men's shelters	2	7			
Mental hospital	1		1	1	
Correction					
Police and sheriff	1	1	1	1	
Prison, parole, and probation	1	1		1	
Judge and court	4		1	1	3
Other (nonagency)					
Bank, insurance company, Dept. of Motor Vehicles, supermarket		2	2		1

[a] Period of study in Tables 12-1 through 12-5 was August 29–September 15, 1961.

Dispensary and the hospitals, it had a much wider range of referral sources than the Dispensary, perhaps because it offered a less specialized and more urgently needed service.

PROBLEMS PRESENTED

All the clients were in financial distress, and some had other complicating problems. In this agency, because of the intense investigations made, and the extensive records kept, all eligibility-related problems could be expected to be reported, although some personal problems might go unnoticed. Fewer than half the clients reported additional problems serious enough to be placed in the role-failure category, as Table 12-2 shows. A little over a quarter of the total group

Table 12-2. PROBLEMS PRESENTED BY 232 APPLICANTS
TO DEPARTMENT OF SOCIAL WELFARE, ADULT DIVISION

Problem category	No.	%
All clients	**232**	**100.0**
Transition states	*60*	*25.9*
Temporary unemployment only	43	18.5
Marital	10	4.3
Geographic dislocation	7	3.0
Role failure	*112*	*48.3*
Homeless	35	15.1
Economic inadequacy	28	12.1
Inadequate parents	24	10.3
Crime	9	3.9
Marital breakdown	16	6.9
Contingencies	*60*	*25.9*
Adult (insufficient income)	19	8.2
Health	17	7.3
Old	24	10.3

were in transitional distress, usually owing to temporary unemployment, and another quarter were in need for reasons beyond their own control, such as sickness, old age, or an income too small to meet all the requirements of a family.

Among the more seriously affected clients were 35 homeless men, who, out of money, and sometimes with bad hangovers, sought admission to the County Home. Another 28 of the applicants had a long history of joblessness and a chronic inability to keep supporting themselves and their families. As Appendix B will suggest, a considerable proportion of these men had been in mental hospitals. Twenty-four applicants had been unable to supply a reasonably stable home for their children.

SERVICES OFFERED

The core service of the Adult Division of the Department of Social Welfare was material assistance in the form of food, money, residence in the County Home, or clothes and books for school children. Each client was assisted on the basis of a standard budget calculated according to the number of dependent children, the amount of rent allowed, and so on. Clients whose incomes were above the level of a welfare budget were refused aid beyond any emergency help that had been given at intake, even if they were in financial distress at the time.

Sixty per cent of the 232 applicants were offered either some form of direct relief or care in the County Home (Table 12-3), but of the 26 men offered the latter, 10 appeared to refuse it, probably because it was in the country when they preferred to go to one of the Mission Shelters in the city center. Another 33 applicants were offered the services of one of the agency's own specialized divisions.

Forty-four per cent of the applicants wanted supplemental assistance only, and of these more than half were turned down. In contrast, only one-fifth of the 56 per cent who asked for full welfare assistance were refused. In other words, there was a tendency for the core service of the agency to be given to those who needed it most. At the same time, people who were trying to remain partly self-supporting had a good chance of being turned down until they reached a much lower level of functioning (Rudolph and Cassetta, 1963).

The Adult Division made arrangements with outside agencies on behalf of its clients when it was absolutely necessary. As the agency profile shows, the 9 agencies that were involved in arrangements for 16 clients were among the more controlling members of the regulative system. Twenty-nine clients were sent to 12 outside agencies, 6 of them by active re-

Table 12-4. SERVICES OFFERED TO 232 CLIENTS OF THE DEPARTMENT OF SOCIAL WELFARE, ADULT DIVISION

Services offered	Total		Problem category				
	No.	*%*	*Transition states*	*Role failure*	*Old*	*Contingencies Adult*	*Health*
All clients	232	100.0	60	112	24	19	17
No service	57	24.6	15	21	9	9	3
One service	136	58.6	35	69	13	8	11
Relief[a]	107	46.1	31	54	10	6	6
Arrangements	1	.4			1		
Referred elsewhere	14	6.0	3	9	1		1
Special division service	14	6.0	1	6	1	2	4
Two services	35	15.1	8	20	2	2	3
Relief and arrangements	8	3.4	2	3	1	1	1
Relief and referral	10	4.3	1	8	1		
Special division, relief	11	4.7	4	6		1	
Special division, refer	3	1.3		1			
Special division, arrangements	3	1.3	1	2			2
Three services	4	1.7	2	2	0	0	0
Relief, arrangements, referral	2	.9	1	1			
Relief, arrangements, special division	2	.9	1	1			

[a] Includes County Home.

Table 12-3. INTERDEPARTMENTAL RELATIONSHIPS[a]
REGARDING 232 CLIENTS OF DEPARTMENT OF
SOCIAL WELFARE, ADULT DIVISION

| Department | Type of relationship with other department | | |
| | Referral | | Arrange- |
	Source	Target	ments
All clients	**232**	**232**	**232**
Without interagency contact	227	182	222
With interagency contact	5	50	10
Total contacts	*5*	*51*	*10*
Legal division		2	6
Employment Office		6	
Children's Division	3	1	1
Medical Division	1	12	3
County Home		26	
Surplus food office	1	4	

[a] No clients in this study group were offered care in the special counseling service.

ferral, and 1 to jail. As 115, or half of the clients, were still under care and unreferred at the end of the study period, however, another 12 or 15 could be expected to be referred ultimately.

Table 12-4 summarizes the services given to the applicants in the various problem categories. There was a tendency for the agency to give service to more of the applicants classed as role failures than to those with transitional and contingent problems, although this difference did not quite reach statistical significance. Undoubtedly the more severely disordered clients in this agency were desperately in need of help, so much so that many of them developed attachments to their individual workers and appeared to accept their supervisory and controlling activities as the supportive service that they were occasionally meant to be.

Firm, overt control was exercised by the Adult Division over its clients at the in-boundary and throughout the period in which public assistance was given. Periodic visits were made to the clients' homes in order to make sure that all eligibility requirements were still being complied with, and that relief money was being spent in accordance with the budget prepared by the department. As the agency profile shows, information was exchanged with 7 agencies regarding 9 clients, and the eligibility of 29 clients was checked with 12 agencies. No other agency continued to make eligibility checks during the course of care, and no other agency maintained vigilance over collaborating agencies in the way that the Welfare Department monitored the Dispensary's activities through daily eligibility phone calls.* In contrast, almost no continuing control was exercised over clients at the outboundary, complete separation from the service, regardless of the client's need, often being regarded as success.

Although the Welfare Department, taken as a whole, had a marked internal division of labor, it gave a diffuse service to its clients. Through the Adult Division, the whole agency maintained bonds with the rest of the regulative system, no doubt based on the other agents' need for its core function, which was essential to the life of its clients and which no other agency could afford to offer. At the same time, the agency's own goal of reducing its clientele forced it to rely on others for information about its clients, and to use other services wherever possible. In other words, its relationship with other agencies arose from both its unique contribution to a divided labor and its desire not to provide more than just that unique function.

Findings: Children's Division

Although services to children were routinely omitted from study, a group of 24 applications to the Children's Division of the Welfare Department in August and September 1962 were collected for two purposes: first, to look at one of the Welfare Department's special services, and, second, to test a hypothesis regarding the difference between the populations approaching adult and children's services in general. The result of this test is reported in Chapter 20.

* Both agencies would have saved much time, money, and aggravation if block services had been purchased from the Dispensary for Welfare clients.

The Children's Division was charged generally with the protection of children, and it was the only agency studied, except for the police, whose services were available 24 hours a day, New York State law requiring that every complaint about neglect of a child be investigated immediately. The agency used two different strategies of protection: the removal of children from their homes upon a sworn petition of neglect or abuse or upon a request by the parents themselves, and supervision of children in their homes. It also arranged adoptions and supervised children in temporary placements. Although the Children's Division was probably not very much more controlling than the Adult Division, its controls were explicit and legal, whereas the Adult Division exercised much of its control not so much by legal mandate as by administrative ruling. In contrast to the Adult Division, the Children's Division considered that overt support to children was part of its mandate, and some of its intake procedures, such as having children looked after continuously by the same worker, were designed for this end.

The Children's Division maintained a separate intake, and acted almost as a separate agency. Although 6 of the 24 families in the group were receiving assistance from the Adult Division at the time of the study, none had been referred by the Adult Division. As Table 12-5 shows, 5 of the 24 clients entered the service directly, and another 15 were brought in by the police or by the Probation Department; the remaining 4 came from 3 different agencies. Typically, children who were neglected or abused were brought to the attention of the police or other authorities by concerned neighbors or relatives. Either the referring agent or the police themselves then swore a neglect petition against the parents, and the children could be placed directly in temporary, or even permanent, foster or institutional care at the point of intake.

Nineteen of the 24 parents involved in these protection cases were disordered enough to fall into the role failure and deviant behavior category, 11 of them for neglect or abuse of children. In 4 families the parents were ill, and in 1 a hydrocephalic child was dying, and the parents, who could not afford to make private arrangements, asked for terminal care

Table 12-5. RELATIONSHIP OF DEPARTMENT OF SOCIAL
WELFARE, CHILDREN'S DIVISION, WITH OTHER AGEN-
CIES THROUGH REFERRAL SOURCES, INTER-
AGENCY CONTACTS, AND REFERRAL
TARGETS OF 24 CLIENTS

| Agency | Type of relationship with other agencies | | | |
| | Referral | | Arrange- | Infor- |
	Source	Target	ments	mation
All clients	**24**	**24**	**24**	**24**
Without agency contact	5	19	19	18
With agency contact	19	5	5	6
Total contacts	*19*	*5*	*5*	*8*
Medical				
Psychiatric Hospital				1
Child Guidance Clinic				2
Counseling				
Hospital social service	2			1
Family agency				2
School services				1
Institutions				
Mental Hospital	1			
Chronic diseases hospital			1	
Children's group homes		5[a]		
Correction				
Police	8			1
Probation Department	7			
Children's court	1			
Other, nonagency				
Relatives of client			4	

[a] These referrals made in collaboration with the court.

for the child, which the agency arranged in collaboration
with a hospital. In all 24 cases, protection, the core service of
the agency, was provided: in 3, emergency overnight placement in an agency foster home was required; in another 4,
permanent placement in a supervised foster home was made;
in a further 6, placement in a protective institution was arranged in collaboration with other agencies; and in the remaining 11 cases, children were supervised in their homes.
Of these 11 families, however, 10 had children in placement
at the time of the study.

During the course of giving this service, the agency exchanged information with five agencies about eight children,
and made arrangements with four families as well as with the
hospitals and institutions in which the children were placed
(Table 12-5).

Of all the services, this one exercised the most drastic control during care, no doubt reflecting a general belief codified into law, that in some sense children belong not just to
their parents but also to all of society, and, if neglect or abuse
becomes clear, the resources of the regulative system should
be quickly mobilized on their behalf.

A Controlling, Diffuse, Taxpayers' Agency

The Adult Division of the Welfare Department could be
considered the opposite of a recruiting agency, offering as it
did the least service to the fewest people. The department
was an internally specialized agency with its own special divisions, but from the point of view of both the population it
served and the whole regulative system, it was diffuse in
function. Its activities ranged from the administration of a
kind of social insurance for those temporarily out of work to
the care of the chronically ill and the permanent support of
the inadequate. Administratively these clients were all lumped
together as "relief cases" or, as they would have been called
in another day, paupers.

Although the agency had been mandated to "rehabilitate"
its chronic clients, and could get state financial aid for certain
services, there was considerable resistance to "federal inter-
ference" at the state level and to state regulation at the local
level. The department would have liked to exercise local
standards when selecting and excluding clients and still receive reimbursement, but this it could not do. As a result, it
had failed to develop the kinds of services needed for serious
attempts at rehabilitation.

In most of its characteristics, the Onondaga County Welfare Department was typical of most American public assistance systems. Mencher (1963) has pointed out that the form
of administration of financial relief in America at the time

of these studies was essentially outmoded, it being assumed that because welfare populations were generated by the economic system and could not be permanently removed except by economic manipulation, economic and social services should therefore also remain linked to the economic system. This author argued that income maintenance, job finding, and social insurance did not belong under the same administrative roof with prevention, treatment, and rehabilitation services. Most welfare applicants, in other words, should have been treated as economic casualties and dealt with through some extension of unemployment and medical insurances and perhaps through retraining, while the remainder should have been treated as what they essentially were, social and psychological casualties, needing careful diagnosis and long, patient treatment and rehabilitation.

By 1961, "relief cases" had been virtually abolished in such countries as Sweden and New Zealand; but at the time of these American studies, the homogeneous treatment of a heterogeneous population, together with the omnipresent concern for the taxpayer, had led to a service that could not offer genuine support to its clients, even if they were greatly in need of it, and could not modify its form of control over them for fear of wasting money. Of all the agencies studied, this was perhaps the unhappiest, for it was being operated for neither the staff nor the clients but rather to prevent the taxpayer from having starving people on his conscience. As a consequence, no one was really happy about the agency's goals, or satisfied with its means of reaching them.

REFERENCES

Burns, Eveline, 1956. *Social Security and Public Policy,* New York, McGraw-Hill.
Coser, Lewis, 1965. "The Sociology of Poverty," *Social Problems,* Vol. 13, No. 2.
Garfinkel, Harold, 1956. "Conditions of Successful Degradation Ceremonies," *American Journal of Sociology,* Vol. 61, No. 5, March.
Glaser, Nathan, 1966. "The War on Poverty: What Went Wrong?" *New Society,* March.

Lambert, Camille, H. E. Freeman, Robert Morris, and Leon Taubenhaus, 1963. "Public Clinic Care and Eligibility," *American Journal of Public Health,* Vol. 53, No. 8, August.

Mencher, Samuel, 1963. "Perspectives on Recent Welfare Legislation, Fore and Aft," *Social Work,* Vol. 8, No. 3, July.

Moreland Commission, 1963. *Public Welfare in the State of New York,* Albany, New York.

Pumphrey, Ralph, and Muriel Pumphrey, 1961. *The Heritage of American Social Work,* New York, Columbia University Press.

Rudolph, Claire, and Rhondda Cassetta, 1963. "Unemployment and Chronic Inadequacy," paper read before the Annual Meeting of the Society for Applied Anthropology, Albany, New York.

Titmuss, Richard, 1959. *Essays on the Welfare State,* New Haven, Yale University Press.

Wilensky, Harold, and C. N. Lebeaux, 1958. *Industrial Society and Social Welfare,* New York, Russell Sage Foundation.

THE MISSION SHELTER   *13*

All modern communities must find ways of sheltering homeless, wandering men. In the seventeenth century, the Colonial
Poor Laws charged local governments with giving shelter and
work to the homeless, but at that time their numbers were
relatively few. The industrialization and urbanization of the
nineteenth century created additional groups of transient and
seasonal workers who, like the permanent core of wanderers,
needed food and shelter when they had no jobs. In England,
George Orwell (1935, 1950), and in America, Nels Anderson

The Director of the Mission Shelter, Mr. Clarence Jordan, kindly
gave permission for this study. Ian M. Cumming carried out the field
work.

157

(1923, 1940), described vividly the worlds of the homeless and destitute and how they managed to survive on the fringes of society.

Traditionally, the wanderer seeking public assistance has found shelter in a poor farm or county home run by a local government, but he has often been discouraged from remaining long, either by the terms of admission or the conditions of the shelter itself. Since the Middle Ages, but particularly since the last part of the nineteenth century, the churches have concerned themselves with the wandering and alienated man,* partly because of his obvious need and partly because of his lack of spiritual moorings.

In Syracuse in 1961, the homeless man could choose among several services. If he were drunk, he might sober up in jail. If he were a resident of the county, he could go to the Welfare Department's County Home. If he were a transient, he could approach Catholic Charities for a meal ticket and a clothing voucher, or he might get help from the Travelers Aid Society. If he needed a bed, he could approach one of the two shelters run by evangelical religious missions.

The Mission chosen for study was located in downtown Syracuse, and it performed several functions besides providing shelter to about 100 migrant or homeless men each night. Its staff conducted religious services and Sunday school classes, operated a sheltered workshop, ran several recreation and athletic programs for children and youth, operated children's summer camps, and offered counseling, as well as some assistance with food and clothing, to needy families who attended the Mission. There were two branches of the Mission in other parts of the city.

The men's shelter was partly supported by the United Council, but as these funds could not be used for religious activities, the Mission Director hoped eventually to achieve in-

---

* There is no real female counterpart to the homeless man, probably because women's roles are centered on creating and maintaining homes and on establishing social ties with the environment, and therefore women are more adaptable at fitting into other people's families or creating homes of their own.

dependent financing so that he could put into practice his belief that the homeless man could only be rejoined to society through the activation of spiritual ties. Additional funds were raised by donation, by selling furniture that had been given to the Mission and renovated in its workshop, and by charging small sums for lodgings to whoever was able to pay.

Entrance to the Agency

Clients walked into the shelter from the street and signed a register at the front desk, giving their names, birth dates, birthplaces, Social Security numbers, and the names and addresses of next of kin. From the registration desk, the clients went directly to the showers, and, depending on the need, they might be given clean clothes. After cleaning up, all men were free to go to the dormitory, to the lobby of the Mission, or to the chapel for religious services. Any homeless man who was sober could count on a minimum of two or three days' free meals and lodging. If he appeared accessible to the Mission's religious goals and willing to work, he might stay much longer. A few men stayed on, working by day in laboring jobs and paying for their lodgings, and a few worked for their board, room, and spending money in the Mission itself. On an average night, about one-third of the men were said to be travelers, usually truck drivers, who paid a dollar for a bed, and used the Mission as they might have used the YMCA.

Method of Study

An interviewer was allowed to take from the register the names and identifying data of the 63 transient men who had slept in the Mission on the nights of December 28, 29, and 30, 1961. After doing this, he interviewed the foreman of the workshop regarding the 34 men who were working for the Mission either in the workshop or as truck drivers, desk clerks, kitchen help, or maintenance men. These more permanent residents will be described in Appendix B. The Director of the Mission itself was interviewed regarding agency policy.

Results

REFERRAL SOURCE

The Mission made no inquiries and kept no record of how the men reached them, and no eligibility checks were made; in this regard it acted more like a hotel than a social agency. The men were expected to be sober when they came in, although some men who had bad hangovers were taken in if they had been known to the Mission before and if it was felt that they were only suffering a setback in an otherwise successful effort to stop drinking. The doors of the Mission were closed at ten o'clock and no one could enter after that, but, on the whole, the conditions at the in-boundary were only slightly controlling.

Although the men's specific referral sources were unknown, both the Director and the workshop foreman said that most men came on their own or were sent by private citizens, but a steady stream of clients came from agencies concerned with people in acute financial difficulty, such as the Police Department, the Red Cross, the Travelers Aid Society, Catholic Welfare, the Welfare Department, several hospitals, the Dispensary, private physicians, and the other religious missions. The director expressed some tension about accepting men from the other Mission, however, saying that it screened out the "better class of homeless man," and sent on the remainder. Some men were said to come from the County Home, perhaps preferring the Mission because it was in the city instead of the country. A review of the data from the other study agencies reveals a total of seven referrals to the Mission from the agencies for which data were available; they were all from the Police Department and the Adult Division of the Welfare Department.

PROBLEMS PRESENTED

Homeless and wandering men are a heterogeneous group, although to the casual observer they may appear to be simply hoboes and drunks. One group, comprising perhaps half of any mission's population, live in and around the deteriorating centers of the city. These are the skid row group who use missions for temporary shelter. Studies have shown that such men do not wander far from the few familiar streets on which they live (Pittman, 1964). They appear to have a pattern of life that takes them from intermittent work to periods in the County Home, to periodic visits to the Mission shelter, and to jail on charges of drunkenness. Sometimes they live in cheap hotels and work as casual laborers. Many of the skid row men are problem drinkers, although a minority are actually alcoholics (Bogue, 1963); most of them are uneducated and unskilled, and their defining characteristic is inadequacy, both social and occupational. Some are mentally ill or of subnormal intelligence.

Another group of homeless men, probably less than a quarter of any mission's residents at any time, are actually hoboes who have had no address for many years, and are, therefore, ineligible for welfare assistance. Among this group is a handful who have drifted away from middle-class social milieux. The Mission staff was particularly conscious of this downwardly mobile group, both the Director and the shop foreman describing such cases. Most hoboes, however, are uneducated and undersocialized and have never learned an ordinary complement of social roles. Many of them have grown up in broken homes or in children's institutions.

A few of any mission's clients are men in acute distress; migrant workers stranded from families without funds, men in the first stages of alcoholism, and men recently alienated from their families. An unknown number of these become permanently alienated from society, either settling in skid row or drifting from place to place. A final small group are men who are trying to establish themselves in jobs after having been in jail.

Although the problems of the men in the shelter could not be given the standard classification used for the clients of the other agencies, the ages and the residences of next of kin of the 63 transients in the Mission were known. Only 2 of these transient men were under thirty years of age, while 6 were over sixty; the remainder were divided among the decades between thirty and sixty. Seventeen men named next of kin living outside of New York State, and 32 named no next of kin. Of the latter group, 18, or more than half, were born in another state. This group of men from other places would be expected to include hoboes, migrant laborers, and, according to the Mission's Director, truckers stopping for the night, but it was impossible to estimate the proportion of each from the information available. It seems probable, however, that the hoboes would be older than those still functioning in the labor market. Five of the group named next of kin who were living in the Syracuse area.

Six of the 63 transient men at the Mission had been patients in a public mental hospital in New York State; four had been diagnosed as alcoholic, one as schizophrenic, and one as a psychopathic personality. As only one of these men belonged to the out-of-state group, it seems likely that the real rate of mental illness for this transient population would be almost double the 10 per cent discovered. In other words, although the specific problems of each man were not discovered, it seems clear that taken as a group, the men in the Mission Shelter were quite severely disordered.

SERVICES OFFERED

The Mission stated its core function to be spiritual rescue, ". . . reaching those outside the pale of the church for God and for our country," as their annual report put it. The foreman of the workshop explained to the interviewer, "Our first aim here is to reach these men spiritually. This industrial program is just a means to an end, that's all." In line with this firm and overtly stated goal, all efforts were made to use the services of the Mission in such a way as to enhance the possibility of spiritual salvation. A service was held each night and each morning and a Bible study group was conducted each day.

Two major methods were used to control the behavior of the shelter's workers so as to maximize their religious activities. First, while men who did not respond to the spiritual messages were tolerated so long as they were good workers and were in harmony with the over-all temper of the Mission, if they could neither get along with the other men nor accept the spiritual program they were expelled. The threat of expulsion or even the possibility of being refused future admissions acted as a control over the men's behavior. The average length of stay of workers, according to the Director, was about two months.

The second major control used by the staff was the allocation of privileges. The factory foreman explained the procedure when he was asked what would happen if one of his workers went out and got drunk. He replied:

> Well, of course, he can't come back in until he is sober, and then it depends on the individual entirely, his attitude, his ability, whether you feel that you can do anything with him, because you see we have so many men come in these doors that you wish you could help but you don't have accommodations to help, so it depends on the man. If you feel that you can do something with him, even after he comes back, we will bring him back, but he starts in as a transient all over again. He starts in on a room-and-board basis and he works up. After a man is here for so long, he gets seniority rights; he gets on the third floor in the rooms, rather than in the dormitory. So when a man gets drunk and he is out for a night or a day or so, and he comes back, and we do feel that we can take him back on, we put him in the dormitory and room-and-board all over again. If we didn't they would go out and get drunk as many times as they wanted to and come back feeling that they could get away with it. This is somewhat of a punishment to them and they take it as such, too.

Although attendance at evening services was not a prerequisite for shelter, those who went to them rather than remaining in the dormitory or the lobby were served cocoa and doughnuts afterwards. Furthermore, selection of transient men for work in the Mission itself was made at the social gathering following the evening service, so that those who wanted this work were well-advised to attend chapel. Neither the Director nor the factory foreman expected overnight conversions, however, and both were reconciled to the constant backsliding that most of the "regular" men suffered.

The Mission sometimes made arrangements for its clients to receive medical care from a particular physician whom they retained, or from a doctor on the welfare panel; sometimes if a man was physically frail or too old to work, they arranged transfer to the County Hospital or the County Home, but on the whole, they avoided interagency contacts. Their hope was to establish a medical clinic in the Mission so that they would not be dependent upon secular sources for any kind of help with their clients.

The agency's overt control of the clients was paralleled by the latent countercontrol exerted by the most desirable clients through the implied threat of leaving the shelter and going to the rival mission, but their relative powerlessness left the control distinctly asymmetrical.

REFERRALS OUT

It was not possible to tell how many out-referrals were made, although a review of the other study agencies shows three referrals to the Welfare Department and the Dispensary. The Director explained that occasionally a man was sent to the Welfare Department once he had established residence. The over-all number of referrals can be guessed to be low, first, because the Mission staff denied making them; second, because very few agencies served the homeless man; and third, because isolation suited the agency's religious goals. There was no control at the out-boundary.

An Isolated, Diffuse, Controlling Agency

The Mission shelter had cut itself off from the rest of the agency world because its staff believed that its core religious service with the addition of special medical services was all that was needed to save the whole man. No contact with the remainder of the regulative system was thought to be necessary. The goal of spiritual rescue that the Mission set for itself was hard to reach, and the staff was content with a modest success, but from the point of view of the rest of the system their methods looked like goals, and their success consequently seemed greater. The Mission was keeping a large group of disordered, estranged men from starving and freezing to death, a function some other agency would have had to assume had the Mission not been there, and it was providing work in a protected situation to a number of men not ordinarily employable, as well as mobilizing some medical care for a few men who might have died without it. Thus, although the Mission sought almost as peripheral a place in the agency world as its clients had in society, it was not surprising that a substantial number of well-to-do citizens were willing to serve on its Board of Directors, and that there had always been support for its activities during the 75 years of its existence.

REFERENCES

Anderson, Nels, 1923. *The Hobo: The Sociology of the Homeless Man,* Chicago, University of Chicago Press.

Anderson, Nels, 1940. *Men on the Move,* Chicago, University of Chicago Press.

Bogue, Donald, 1963. *Skid Row in American Cities,* Community and Family Study Center, University of Chicago.

Orwell, George, 1935. *A Clergyman's Daughter,* London, Gollancz.

Orwell, George, 1950. *Down and Out in Paris and London,* New York, Harcourt.

Pittman, David J., 1964. "Homeless Men," *Trans-Action,* Vol. 1, No. 2, January.

THE POLICE DEPARTMENT *14*

For the average person, the policeman epitomizes social regulation, and there is evidence that he accepts himself in this light (Sowle, 1962). His job is overtly controlling: keeping the peace and apprehending those who break the law. Nevertheless, in the course of keeping the peace, the policeman often provides overt support, as when he finds a lost child. He sometimes gives support to one person by controlling an-

Police Chief Harold Kelley kindly gave permission for this study; Chief Patrick Murphy, who succeeded Chief Kelley, assisted in interpreting the data; Ian M. Cumming carried out the field work. Much of the material in this chapter has appeared in "Policeman as Philosopher, Guide and Friend," Elaine Cumming, Ian Cumming, and Laura Edell, *Social Problems*, Winter, 1964–65.

other, as when he apprehends a wife-beating husband. This supportive side of police work is, of course, more obvious from the point of view of the client seeking help than from the point of view of the policeman pursuing the law-breaker. Because the studies in this series were all focused on the clients' search for help, the more supportive aspects of the Syracuse Police Department were revealed.

Entrance to the Agency

Any citizen could telephone the police in Syracuse and ask to be connected to any of its departments, but ordinarily they told the officer on the switchboard what they wanted and he connected them to the complaint desk. The complaint officer then reported the call to the appropriate place, which might have been any of the various departments: the general detective division, the homicide or vice squads, the traffic, alcohol, or missing persons bureaus, the youth bureau, or, most commonly, any one of the squad cars on duty. Occasionally the complaint officer referred the caller to some other source of help after hearing the problem. If there was any possibility that the law had been broken or that it might be broken, the complaint would immediately be investigated. Because it is difficult to predict the outcome of a situation that is being described over the telephone, and because failing to investigate a situation that might deteriorate is a serious breach of duty while investigating trivial complaints is not, most complaint officers showed a bias toward investigating doubtful cases. Furthermore, policemen in Syracuse, as in most places (Banton, 1964), are legally responsible for their own actions and are liable to lawsuit in the case of serious error.

Method of Study

A total of 801 incoming telephone calls to the complaint desk were collected over a total of 82 hours. As each complaint was received and disposed of, a description of it was dictated into a tape recorder. Fourteen selected prowl car calls were observed as illustrations of the responses to these complaints. Interviews were conducted with four general detectives concerning their recent cases, and with the detectives in charge of the alcoholism service and the missing persons bureau. Records of all arrests for a 144-hour period were studied.

Findings

THE COMPLAINT DESK

Referral Source. In this study it was impossible to know why the callers decided to approach the police for help. The police themselves take for granted, however, that a certain group of citizens, most of whom are very poor, will call upon them routinely in all kinds of trouble. They also accept the fact that in all socioeconomic groups there are "regulars" who call almost daily with a variety of grievances. Examination of the other core agencies shows that Catholic Charities and the Department of Social Welfare each made a referral to the police during the study period.

Problems Presented. Of the 801 calls to the complaint desk, 88 were excluded from the analysis because they were callbacks on earlier complaints. Of the remaining 713 calls, 33 were requests for information, most of them from the press (Table 14-1). Twenty-eight calls were considered outside the jurisdiction of the police. In one case, for example, a woman called to say that she had had her car repaired and the garage had cheated her. She was advised to call a lawyer. Sometimes, in Syracuse as in other cities (Sudnow, 1965), the complaint officer's own ideas of what was right and appropriate affected his responses. A field note says, "A woman wants protection from her doctor who is trying to commit her to a mental intsitution; the officer replied, 'That's not police business, lady. The police cannot go against any doctor.' "

The remaining 652 calls, recognized as legitimate requests for service, included two major groups: first, routine police business in connection with loss or theft, traffic violations, unlocked doors, fallen power wires, and so on; and, second, re-

Table 14-1.   CLASSIFICATION OF 713 CALLS TO THE COM-
PLAINT DESK OF THE SYRACUSE POLICE DEPARTMENT[a]

Type of complaint	No. of calls	% of total
All calls[b]	*713*	*100.0*
Information only	33	4.6
"Not police business"	28	3.9
Routine police business	255	35.8
Direct support		
Illness, suicide, accident	81	11.4
Incapacitated people	33	4.6
Control of others		
Children's and youths' behavior	104	14.6
Nuisances	33	4.6
Missing persons	11	1.5
Disputes	63	8.8
Violence	43	6.0
Protection	29	4.1

[a] Tables 14-1 through 14-3 are based on calls during 82 selected hours in June and July, 1961.
[b] Calls were considered to be independent, but there was no way of knowing that this was so.

quests for support or assistance with problems of health, safety, or interpersonal relationships.* These calls could not be classified into the categories used in the core agencies because, being emergencies, they were described incompletely and out of context. Table 14-1 lists the contents of 713 separate calls to the complaint desk.

Sixteen per cent of the 713 calls were requests for direct support or control of people who were ill, injured, attempting suicide, or in danger because they were drunk or "psycho"; 40 per cent were requests to the police to do something about the undesirable behavior of others.

One-half of the 283 calls about interpersonal conflict could be considered minor; these included complaints about disturbances made by children, dogs, and noisy adults, or about the behavior of children and youths, usually trespassing, or various kinds of pranks, but occasionally involving some danger. The remaining interpersonal calls were more serious;

* Two coders classifying the calls independently achieved over 90 per cent agreement; differences were reconciled by the author.

they included disputes and fights in both public and private places, and among family members, neighbors, or total strangers. Four per cent of all calls were for protection of children from abuse or neglect,* and of adults from prowlers or angry relatives. A few women who had been shut out of their homes or who had left home after a quarrel called for a "clothing escort" to accompany them into their homes to get their belongings.

Services Offered. The core service of the police complaint department was the protection of the citizenry. This protection was usually provided simply by the blue uniform, an unequivocal symbol of the social order. Although the actual capture and apprehension of law-breakers may stand in the public mind as the crux of police work, most of the policeman's day is spent in more mundane matters such as providing information about what kinds of consequences follow certain kinds of acts, or acting as an outside mediator in situations of conflict.

The dispatch of a policeman to the scene of any complaint is evidence that the complaint officer considers the situation one which could end in a breach of the peace and thus warrants the uniformed presence of an officer of the law.

Table 14-2 shows the services offered to the different groups of callers. In every category except nuisances, more than half of the complaints were investigated by an officer in a squad car. When violence was reported, a car was almost certain to be sent, but when there was only a dispute, the odds were only about even that this would happen. It is possible that some of the calls about violence were later stages of calls about disputes that had received no service. For example, to one complaint, "My boy friend is mad and is going to beat me up," the answer was, "Call us again when he does." This kind of nonchalance was considered to be poor police practice.

Calls about illness, accident, and attempted suicide were almost always investigated or steered to another service, and

---

* If small children were left alone at night without the supervision of an adult or a child who had reached at least the fifth grade, they were considered to be neglected.

Table 14-2. SERVICES OFFERED TO 713 CALLERS BY THE COM-
PLAINT OFFICER OF THE SYRACUSE POLICE DEPARTMENT,
BY TYPE OF COMPLAINT

		Service offered		
Type of complaint	Total calls	Car sent %	Referred %	No service %
Total calls	713	76.8	7.7	15.5
Information only	33	0.0	15.2	84.8
"Not police business"	28	0.0	14.3	85.7
Routine police business	255	69.8	7.1	22.4
Direct support				
Illness, suicide, accident	81	86.4	6.2	7.4
Incapacitated people	33	75.8	0.0	24.2
Control of others				
Children's and youths' behavior	104	85.6	6.7	7.7
Nuisances	33	48.5	15.2	36.3
Missing persons	11	81.8	0.0	18.2
Disputes	63	50.8	17.5	31.7
Violence	43	95.3	0.0	4.7
Protection or escort	29	79.3	0.0	20.7

calls about routine police business, missing persons, and complaints about children were served almost as often. Referral
targets are shown in Table 14-3.

Complaints about nuisances were the most likely to be terminated at the switchboard with advice only. Typically such
calls were made in the evening by women complaining of
noisy neighbors, and the officer usually advised the caller to
sweat it out until a much later hour.

Calls for protection were usually answered, but it was in
this area that the policeman's own preconceptions and standards were most likely to influence his actions. A call from a
Negro slum, for example, appeared to have much less chance
of investigation than one from a middle-class area.* Calls
about neglected children were always investigated. The following example is taken from the notes:

A call came from a very kindly-sounding Italian man

* The officer would be inclined to tell a Negro woman to come to
the D.A.'s office and swear out a warrant, whereas he would send a
car to a white neighborhood.

Table 14-3. REFERRAL TARGETS OF 713 CALLS TO THE
COMPLAINT DESK AND 14 CALLS ANSWERED
BY THE SQUAD CAR

Referral target	Total	Complaint desk	Squad car
All clients	727	713	14
Without referral	665	658	7
With referral	62	55	7
Medical			
County Medical Society	1	1	
Ambulance	4		4
Counseling			
Lawyer	4	4	
Legal Aid	1	1	
Alcoholic services	1	1	
Institutions			
Men's shelter	1	1	
Children's shelter[a]	1		1
Correction			
District Attorney	7	7	
Youth Bureau	6	6	
Chief or Captain	6	6	
Special police bureau	7	7	
Other police department	6	6	
Children's Court	3	2	1
Other, nonagency[b]	14	13	1

[a] Via the Children's Division of the Welfare Department.
[b] Including Telephone Company, SPCA, Better Business Bureau, taxi company, all-night gas station, insurance agency, Public Works Department, and Fire Department.

at about 11 o'clock in the evening. He was reporting that he had found the little boy from next door wandering on the street . . . and he thought the police ought to know about the situation. A car was dispatched and reported that there was nobody home, and in fact, there were three smaller children in the house. . . . The captain dispatched a camera crew, child placement was notified and the children were immediately placed in a temporary home. A stake-out was set for the parents. Meanwhile the pictures had been developed and they showed four undernourished, underclothed little children lying in their own feces on a mattress on the floor. The refrigerator contained two cans of condensed milk and some rotten vegetables; the place was filthy and unheated. As the time went by, anger began to rise and when at about four o'clock in the morning the parents were brought in to the station everybody was in an ugly mood. . . . Had they been the least bit smart, glib, or said almost anything other than "yes" or "no" while they were issued tickets, they would have gotten poked.

In this case, all-out support for the children is accompanied by maximum control of the parents.

THE SQUAD CAR

Certain calls were considered serious enough to warrant a captain following the squad car to the scene, and the field worker accompanied the car to 14 calls in a 23-hour period. Half of these calls would not normally have been investigated by the captain, but as police rules forbade the regular policemen from carrying passengers, the captain agreed to answer a few routine calls.

In handling these cases, the police used three different techniques for solving problems. First, they referred people to other resources; second, they gave concrete information and guidance about what actions were illegal; and third, they acted as mediators in disputes. In 13 of the cases, overt control was evident, but in the fourteenth, the field notes read, "A slightly drunk man is an unwelcome visitor in his ex-wife's home. Police send him home in a cab." The encounter sounds friendly; the importunate visitor may have experienced this police intervention as purely supportive, even though he was, in a sense, under maximum control.

Table 14-3 lists the referral targets of the complaint officer and the squad car policeman. It was known that at least half of the squad car calls were unrepresentative because the captain only went to serious complaints; nevertheless, if he went to as many as one in ten of the calls, it can be assumed that the police were steering about 10 per cent of the people who called the complaint officer to other services, either at the time of the complaint or from the squad car. The range of target agents was somewhat circumscribed, but the police called upon the nonagency world in a greater proportion of their referrals than did any other agency. Examination of data from the other studies shows that Syracuse Psychiatric Hospital, the Dispensary and the Welfare Department, in particular the Children's Division, all received referrals from the police, sometimes through a police surgeon who had been called in to examine the client.

DETECTIVES

Four detectives of the 20 in the department, selected only because they were on duty at the time of the field worker's visit, were asked to describe their 10 most recent cases. It was thought that they might be assigned the more "professional" and hence controlling tasks. For the 2 of them that specialized in theft and forgery this was true, but 15 out of 20 cases described by the 2 general detectives fell into the personal-problem categories, and were similar to the complaint calls except that they were being further investigated because of more serious breaches of the law.

The detective in charge of services to alcoholics reported that he interviewed about 900 alcoholics a year. From these, he took about 150 people on suspended sentence from the court and tried to arrange for counseling service from some other community agency.*

The sergeant in charge of missing persons estimated that he located about 600 people in a year, about half of them children.

ARRESTS

The policeman's most controlling act is the arrest, and in a sense this is a referral to court or jail. During five days at the time of the study, 66 people were arrested, 39 of them for

---

* This outright supportive service was unpopular with the rest of the police, and it has since been closed. Police officers frequently mentioned to the field-worker that it "wasn't police work" and that the detective in charge was "a great cop and wasted on that job."

offenses in the support and control categories. When compared with complaints, arrests fell heavily upon incapacitated people, 26 of the 39 falling into this class. At this rate of arrest, about 5 per cent of the 801 complaint calls would have come under this ultimate control, although the true figure might have been lower because it is unlikely that all arrests were initiated by a complaint call.

A Diffuse, Controlling Citizens' Agency

Although the policeman stood for control, much of his role inevitably involved support. The supportive aspect of police work has also been commented on by Banton, although his excellent study of American and British police forces was conducted from the point of view of the police themselves rather than the applicant for help (Banton, 1964).

There appeared to be several reasons for the apparent disjunction between the policeman's mandate to control and his relatively supportive function. First, the policeman was on duty at times of the day when no other agent was available; second, he dealt with many of the problems of the poor and the ignorant, a group of people that no other agent was anxious to serve (Rudolph and Cumming, 1962); and, third, he had to cope with a wide variety of emergencies, some of which, although potentially needing control, first required support. (All citizens know they can count on emergency help from the police when there is sudden illness at night, and some citizens also take their marital troubles to them.)

The policeman's supportive function did not appear to cause him role conflict probably because it was latent and not recognized either by himself or by the other agents in the integrative system, who characteristically called upon him for his professional controlling function. It was as an agent of control that the policeman participated in a divided labor with social workers, doctors, clergymen, lawyers, and teachers in maintaining social integration. Policemen were often bitter because they were underpaid and overworked and because they saw the law used differently against people like themselves without money and influence, but it is doubtful if they were ever bitter because they did not have an opportunity to be more supportive.

At the time of these studies, some advocates of "professionalization" of police work were saying that policemen should have a better education in law and in concepts of justice, but others believed that as the policemen on the beat spent so much time as amateur social workers they should substitute professional social work skills for the normative actions they now use. If they had done this, however, the policeman would have found himself on both society's side and the client's side, and such a situation would probably have led to role conflict and ultimately to a further specialization within everyday police work that would segregate the elements of overt support and control. As it was, the policeman, for all his complaints, probably accepted the mandate of his role more wholeheartedly and less self-consciously than any other agent in the system.

REFERENCES

Banton, Michael, 1964. *The Policeman in the Community,* New York, Basic Books.

Rudolph, Claire, and John Cumming, 1962. "Where Are Additional Psychiatric Services Most Needed?" *Social Work,* Vol. 7, No. 3, July.

Sowle, Claude R., ed., 1962. *Police Power and Individual Freedom,* Chicago, Aldine.

Sudnow, David, 1965. "Normal Crimes," *Social Problems,* Vol. 12, No. 3, Winter.

11

The Regulative System

There have been some studies of over-all regulative systems: Donnison (1958) and Jefferys (1965) have both described the member agencies of single health and welfare systems, although neither has emphasized the relationships among the members. There have been some studies of the competition among agencies, especially hospitals, for scarce resources (Elling and Roemer, 1961; Thompson and Hawkes, 1962), but most of these have focused upon adaptive and instrumental rather than integrative and regulative activities. Levine and White (1961) identified one integrating mechanism, "domain consensus," by which they meant the implicit agreement among agencies about what each should be doing, and Litwak and Hylton (1962) have suggested that certain agencies appear to be assigned special coordinating functions within the total system. Haurek and Clark (1967) have suggested that the transfer of appropriate clients is essential for the integration of any specialized system of agencies.

In this Part the pattern of exchange of clients and patients among the study agencies and between them and the rest of the system is described, and three "levels" of agency activity are tentatively identified. Estimates of the rate of flow of clients around the system are then made; the variety of contacts made by the various agencies for a number of purposes is explored; and, finally, the implications of all these activities for the integration of the system are considered. First, however, a new classification of the study agencies will be presented.

REFERENCES

Donnison, D. V., 1958. *Welfare Services in a Canadian Community,* Toronto, University of Toronto Press.

Elling, Ray, and Milton I. Roemer, 1961. "Determinants of Community Support," *Hospital Administration,* Vol. 6, No. 3, Summer.

Haurek, Edward W., and John P. Clark, 1967. "Variants of Integration of Social Control Agencies," *Social Problems,* Vol. 15, No. 1, Summer.

Jefferys, Margot, 1965. *An Anatomy of Social Welfare Services,* London, Michael Josef.

Levine, Sol, and Paul E. White, 1961. "Exchange as a Conceptual Framework for the Study of Interorganizational Relationships," *Administrative Science Quarterly,* Vol. 5, No. 4, March.

Litwak, E., and Lydia Hylton, 1962. "Interorganizational Analysis: A Hypothesis on Co-ordinating Agencies," *Administrative Science Quarterly,* Vol. 6, No. 4, March.

Thompson, James D., and Robert W. Hawkes, 1962. "Disaster, Community Organization and Administration Process," *Man and Society in Disaster,* eds., G. W. Baker and D. W. Chapman, New York, Basic Books.

THE AGENCIES RECLASSIFIED *15*

Throughout Part I, the study agencies were arranged under the common-sense operating categories used both by lay people and the professionals in the agencies themselves: medical, counseling, recreational, employment, income maintenance, institutions, and correctional. In this chapter, a new grouping of agency services will be developed using five variables: the relative control exerted by each agency over its clients, the specificity of each agency's function, its relative level of professionalization, the size and pace of the agency operation, and the accessiblity of the agency to the client.

Control

A quasi-score was computed for 15 separate services of the 12 study agents and agencies based on impressions gathered from their over-all practices. The control level was estimated from a composite of three subscores of from 0 to 2 derived from the level of control that the agency appeared to exert at: (1) the in-boundary, (2) the out-boundary, and (3) during care. From the resulting score was subtracted the estimated countercontrol of the client over the agency. Table 15-1 shows that the entire counseling group, clergymen, Cath-

Table 15-1.   QUASI-SCORES REFLECTING RELATIVE AGENCY-CLIENT CONTROL[a] IN FIFTEEN AGENCY SERVICES

| Agency | Control point | | | Total control | Client counter control | Control score |
	In	Dur-ing	Out			
Family doctors	–	1	1	2	2	0
Planned Parenthood	–	1	–	1	1	0
Private psychiatrists	1	1	–	2	2	0
Clergymen	–	2	–	2	1	1
Catholic Welfare	–	2	–	2	1	1
Family Agency	2	–	1	3	2	1
Dispensary	2	–	–	2	1	1
Psychiatric clinics	2	1	–	3	1	2
Catholic Charities	2	–	–	2	–	2
Mission Shelter	–	2	–	2	–	2
Social Service, Dispensary	1	1	1	3	–	3
Welfare, adult	2	2	–	4	1	3
Police	1	2	1	4	1	3
Home Care Service	2	2	2	6	–	6
Welfare, children	2	2	2	6	–	6

[a] Based on the discussion of controlling mechanisms in Chapter 1.

olic Welfare, the Family Agency, and private psychiatrists, had low control scores as did family doctors, the Planned Parenthood Center, and the Dispensary. Medium levels of control were indicated for psychiatric clinics, Catholic Charities, and the Mission Shelter. The Social Service Department of the Dispensary, the Adult Division of the Welfare Department,

and the Police Department were at the more controlling end
of the spectrum, but the highest scores were accrued by the
two agencies dealing with the most helpless clients, the Children's Division of the Welfare Department and the Home
Care Service.

Professionalization

Professionalization, according to Goode's comprehensive review of the subject (1960), has two "sociologically causal"
characteristics, a prolonged training in a body of abstract
knowledge and a collectivity orientation, that is, a concern
for the client that transcends the agent's own self-interest. In
the regulative system, an over-all collectivity orientation is
taken for granted, but, while no agent is self-oriented in the
sense of putting personal gain before all other considerations,
some are oriented to the well-being of the client and others to
the general welfare of society. This distinction is, however, the
same as the one made throughout between support and control and it will not be considered in estimating professionalization.

Although theoretical training is necessary for the existence
of a profession, in everyday practice it can sometimes be
spread very thin. At the time of these studies, social work, for
example, required two years of professional training after the
baccalaureate degree,* but in any given agency, as long as
there was one such trained worker acting as supervisor, most
of the work could be done by in-service trained staff members.
Welfare departments, for example, hired college graduates
without postgraduate training for casework positions.

In the nursing profession, in-service training was used during wartime in order to relieve staff shortages, but ultimately
many hospitals staffed their wards with these "subprofes-
sionals" under the supervision of registered nurses. Eventually
nurses' aides and licensed practical nurses gave the care that
had hitherto been given by registered nurses, and were recog-

---

* By the time of writing, the introduction of ladder-like careers of
various levels of training for all service professions was under active
consideration in some community colleges and universities.

nized as an institutionalized part of the nursing hierarchy.

In general, the level of professionalization of any group has tended to ebb as the services of the specialty have become scarce, although the training requirements of the leaders have increased as their supervisory and administrative responsibilities have grown.

Professionalization does not have a simple relationship with length of training, however. While services such as medicine obviously require years of technical training, other services, such as performing marriages and burying the dead, obviously do not. Nevertheless, there is such a strong belief that these rituals should be performed by a duly qualified person that the expectation is codified into law. The clergy, for example, are among those in whom the authority to perform marriages is legally vested, although marriage itself is essentially a contract and does not need the blessing of the church in order to be binding. Nevertheless, the legal authority to perform marriages adds to the professionalization of the clergy because it gives recognition and legitimacy to the convergence of legal and religious interests on the formation of new families.

For the agencies in the study series, a quasi-score, intended to reflect the level of professionalization of the staff taken as a whole, was estimated from several characteristics: (1) whether or not a college degree was either customary or mandatory for practice; (2) whether in-service training to perform the agency function was *ever* given; and (3) whether or not the profession had an exclusive mandate for performing its core function.

Membership in a professional organization that controls standards and practices was not included in the score because such a membership is characteristic of all guilds and some businesses as well as the professions.

Among the study agencies, only the Mission Shelter was completely unprofessionalized according to the three criteria used (Table 15-2), but both social casework services, the public health nursing service, the police, and the Welfare Department had only one of the three characteristics.

Table 15-2. QUASI-SCORE REFLECTING PROFESSIONALIZATION
OF SERVICES OF FIFTEEN AGENCIES

Agency	Degree required or customary	In-service training never given	Exclusive mandate	Professionalization score
Mission Shelter	–	–	–	0
Police	–	–	1	1
Catholic Welfare	1	–	–	1
Family Agency	1	–	–	1
Social Service, Dispensary	1	–	–	1
Home Care Service	1	–	–	1
Catholic Charities	1	–	–	1
Welfare, adult	–	–	1	1
Clergymen	1	–	1	2
Welfare, children	1	–	1	2
Psychiatric clinics	1	.5[a]	.5[a]	2
Private psychiatrists	1	1[a]	1[a]	3
Family doctors	1	1	1	3
Planned Parenthood	1	1	1	3
Dispensary	1	1	1	3

[a] The clinics were commonly assumed to practice a medical specialty, but in fact they were also offering a counseling service. For this reason, their score is a compromise between the two functions. Private psychiatrists appeared to be conducting a much more "medical" type of practice. (See Chapters 3 and 7.)

Although casework is generally considered to be a profession and caseworkers have long been preoccupied with professionalization, they are, nevertheless, closer to being a guild inasmuch as the core of their practice is not derived from an abstract body of knowledge but from a codified system of activities taught by masters to apprentices. Viewed in this light, the clergymen of the study series were obviously more highly professionalized than the social workers, although their professional status derived from their sacred rather than their counseling roles.

The medical specialties had the highest professionalization scores. The position of psychiatric clinics was problematical; in 1961 outpatient clinics specialized in psychotherapy, which was done by social workers and psychologists as well as psychiatrists. In these clinics, psychiatrists came closest to being pure counselors, and their tendency to be marginal to the medical world was at its most visible (Smith, 1958).

Specificity of Function

In a system of divided labor and interdependency of function, the members would be expected to develop clearly defined roles and clearly specifiable functions. Furthermore, specialized skills would be encouraged, and diffusion of roles discouraged, because it would lead to an over-all loss of skill and to competition for clients.

For the purposes of these studies, specialization was taken to be a composite of two practices: (1) the limiting of service to one core function, over and beyond the referrals that all agencies are expected to make if the system is to work at all, and (2) the aiming of services toward the client's specialized problem or particular behavior rather than toward modification of the whole man or his condition. Table 15-3 orders the 15 agency services from the least to the most specific according to these criteria. The highest score for specificity of func-

Table 15-3. QUASI-SCORES REFLECTING RELATIVE SPECIFICITY OF FUNCTION OF FIFTEEN AGENCY SERVICES

Agency	Single service only	Core service *not* to the whole man	Specificity score
Catholic Welfare	–	–	0
Family Agency	–	–	0
Clergymen	–	–	0
Psychiatric clinics	–	–	0
Welfare, children	–	–	0
Family doctors	–	–	0
Mission Shelter	–	1[a]	1
Welfare, adult	–	1	1
Social Service, Dispensary	–	1	1
Home Care Service	–	1	1
Dispensary	–	1	1
Private psychiatrists	1	.5	1.5
Catholic Charities	1	1	2
Police	1	1	2
Planned Parenthood	1	1	2

[a] Core service taken to be shelter, not religious conversion.

tion was accrued by the police, Catholic Charities, and the Planned Parenthood Center; the casework agencies, psychiatric clinics, family doctors, and clergymen had the lowest, and the remaining agencies were in between.

Table 15-4 groups the 15 agencies according to the three characteristics: specificity of function, level of professionalization, and the estimated net control over the clients. Except

Table 15-4. SPECIFICITY OF FUNCTION, LEVEL OF PROFESSION-ALIZATION, AND CONTROL OVER CLIENTS OF FIFTEEN AGENCY SERVICES

	Lower Professionalization	Control score[a]	Higher Professionalization	Control score[a]
Diffuse Service	Catholic Welfare Family Agency	1 1	Clergymen Family doctors Psychiatric clinics Welfare, children	1 0 2 6
Specific Service	Social Service, Dispensary Catholic Charities Mission Shelter Welfare, adult Police Home Care Service	3 2 2 3 3 6	Private psychiatrists Planned Parenthood Dispensary	0 0 1

[a] Score representing net control of agency over client; see Table 15-1.

for services to children, all the high-control agencies were alike in offering specific services and requiring relatively low levels of professionalization. This group of agencies was drawn from several of the common-sense operating categories, while the specific-function, highly professionalized agencies all offered medical services, and exerted little control over the patients.

Among the agencies offering relatively diffuse services, all but the Children's Division of the Welfare Department, a special case, had low-control scores. Children's services differ from those for adults for several reasons: first, all services to children are socializing as well as regulative in function; second, minor children belong, in a sense, to everyone, and issues of "motivation for care" are irrelevant; third, there are legal prescriptions about the care and protection of minor children.

From this classification, the medical specialists clearly emerged as a group, but the remaining cells were not so obviously homogeneous.

Size and Pace of Agency Operation

The size of the agency and the pace at which it handles clients can be expected to affect agency-client relationships. Table 15-5 shows both the rate of intake into the 15 services

Table 15-5. ESTIMATED SIZE AND ACTIVITY OF FIFTEEN AGENCY SERVICES

	Size and activity		
Agency type	*Intake per month (incidence)*	*Data source*	*Estimated active cases (prevalence)*
Diffuse low control			
Clergymen (one)	2–15	e	10–100
Family doctors (one)	300–400	e	1200
Catholic Welfare	35	s	150–200
Family Agency	54	r	150–200
Psychiatric clinics (two)	30	s	50–100
Specific low control			
Private psychiatrists (one)	33[a]	e	50–400[a]
Planned Parenthood	59	r	3000–4000
Dispensary	810	s	13,000–15,000[c]
Specific high control			
Mission Shelter	600	s	100
Catholic Charities	51	s	0
Police	5000–6000	s	0
Social Service, Dispensary	88	r	100–200
Welfare, adult	509	s	5000–6000
Home Care Service	10	s	50–100
Welfare, children	36[b]	r	2500–3000[c]

e = estimated from all available information, both in these studies and in the literature.
s = calculated from the time taken to collect the study group or from the agency statistics.
r = taken from the agency's records.
[a] Adapted from Bahn, *et al.* (1965).
[b] Families.
[c] Individuals.

during the study period and the approximate numbers of active clients at that time. It is obvious that the services varied enormously; at one extreme was the Police Department, which might be called an expelling agency because it admitted large numbers of clients but retained none; and at the other, the Children's Division of the Welfare Department, which admitted only a trickle of clients, but retained the majority of them. All the expelling agencies were among the specific-function, controlling group.

Adding the concept of retaining and expelling to the first three characteristics, the agencies can be grouped under four categories:

1. The diffuse, low-control, client-oriented, counseling types of agencies that included the two major caretaking agents, doctors and clergymen, as well as all of the counseling services—that is, the Family Agency, Catholic Welfare, and the psychiatric clinics.

2. The specialized medical agencies characterized by low control and high professionalization: private psychiatrists, the Planned Parenthood Center, and the Dispensary. All the members of this group, like the counseling group, dealt with clients and patients in a one-to-one supportive manner when performing their core function.

3. The specific-function, high-control, expelling agencies: the Mission Shelter, the Police Department, and Catholic Charities. In these agencies clients were offered a specialized service under conditions of high, but temporary, control.

4. The high-control, "keeping" agencies, the Welfare Department, both Adult and Children's services, the Dispensary's Social Service, and the Home Care Service, whose core functions—arrangements, income maintenance, and protection—involved them not only in controlling the client, but also in coordinating their own functions with those of other agents and with the public. It was characteristic of these agencies that they were the most controlling of the individual client, but at the same time, the most system-integrative, in the sense that they were the link between those agents that worked in dyadic relationships with clients and the remainder of the regulative system. Paradoxically, support to the individual requires isolation, which puts a strain on the system, while

coordination and integration of the system, when carried out through service activities, implies enmeshing the client in a network of control.

Accessibility of the Agency

When the agencies were examined in the light of their accessibility to the client, that is, the proportion of new clients entering the agency without a referral, the counseling group were found to include agencies that the client could approach directly, that is, doctors and clergymen, and those, such as casework agencies and psychiatric clinics, that he usually approached via an intermediary (Table 15-6). The only agents

Table 15-6. PROPORTION OF NEW APPLICATIONS TO FIFTEEN AGENCY SERVICES REFERRED BY SELF, INFORMAL NETWORK, AND OTHER AGENCIES

Service	Data source	New clients per month	Self	Other informal	Agency
Counseling type					
Clergyman (one)	e	0–10	70.0	15.0	15.0
Family doctor (one)	e	0–10	40.0	45.0	15.0
Catholic Welfare	s	25	34.7	12.2	53.1
Family Agency	r	49	20.8	12.2	67.0
Psychiatric clinic (one)	r	6	5.0	14.0	81.0
Medical specialties					
Private psychiatrist (one)	e	6[a]	10.0	20.0	70.0
Planned Parenthood	r	59	4.9	48.5	46.6
Dispensary	s	432	14.2	3.7	82.1
Controlling-Expelling					
Mission Shelter	e	25–50	80.0	10.0	10.0
Catholic Charities	r	23	91.3	0.0	8.7
Police	e	unknown	80.0	15.0	5.0
Controlling-Keeping					
Social Service, Dispensary	s	72	0.0	0.0	100.0
Welfare, adult	s	116	37.0	22.0	40.8
Home Care Service	s	10	0.0	0.0	100.0
Welfare, children	s	29	0.0	0.0	100.0

(The column header above the percent columns reads: %[b] referred by)

e = estimated from available information.
s = calculated from study group data, agency statistics, etc.
r = from agency records.
[a] Adapted from Bahn *et al.*, 1965.
[b] Calculated, where possible, from the new applications in the study group; the remainder are estimates.

besides doctors and clergymen that were freely accessible to clients were the three controlling-expelling agencies, the Mission Shelter, Catholic Charities, and the police.

Using this concept of accessibility as a final characteristic, the 15 agency services were regrouped as follows:

1. Gatekeeper Agencies
   a. Caretakers
      Doctors
      Clergymen
   b. Emergency centers
      Catholic Charities
      Mission Shelter
      Police
2. Counseling Agencies
   Family Agency
   Catholic Welfare
   Psychiatric Clinics
3. Medical Specialties
   Planned Parenthood
   Dispensary
   Private psychiatrists
4. Protective Controlling Agencies
   Welfare Department
      a. Adult Service
      b. Children's Division
   Home Care Service
   Social Service Dispensary

Each of these four major groups of agencies had distinct combinations of characteristics: all the gatekeeper agencies, for example, could be called front-line services. In a sense they were reminiscent of what Robert Frost once said about home, "When you have to go there, they have to take you in." Put another way, the client could choose the gatekeeper agent, while the remainder of the agencies were more likely to choose the client.

Between the two types of gatekeepers, however, there were obvious differences: caretakers were supportive and diffuse in function and expected to maintain contact with the client; emergency centers were controlling and specific, kept few, if any, records, and did not keep their clients in care. On the whole, the emergency services were serving the poorer clients, the caretakers the more affluent.

The counselor group differed from the caretakers in being relatively inaccessible; but, like the two caretakers, they offered a supportive service to the whole man. Medical specialties differed from all other agencies in their combination of high professionalization and highly specific function. They were not usually accessible directly to a client; even a service as isolated from the agency world as Planned Parenthood received half of its new patients through agency referrals. Medical practice did not always offer this kind of specific service, however; at one time all doctors were locked into the lay referral system, not the professional network. With the development of medical knowledge and the increase in specialization, however, medicine became the model of a modern division of labor, each specialist offering a service no one else could give and each dependent upon the others for their specific contribution.

Finally, the protective, controlling group of agencies were those that took over from the gatekeepers problems that were of long duration or problems that threatened either the welfare of the individual or the strength of the social fabric.

Final Classification

The classification presented so far includes only the study agencies. The process of classifying those agencies from which clients came in to the study agencies and to which they were referred revealed that two distinct subcategories of service were missing: first, agents giving supportive counsel to clients regarding some particular problem but not concerned with the whole man, and hence forming a subcategory of specific counseling agents; and second, protective controlling agencies whose major obligation was to protect society by controlling the client rather than, as in the case of the agencies studied, to protect the client himself.

The expanded typology and the agencies included then became:

1. Gatekeepers:
    a. Caretakers: doctors and clergymen.
    b. Emergency services: including the three study agencies and others like them, as well as the Travelers Aid Society, emergency functions of the Red Cross, ambulance services, the emergency rooms of hospitals, the Surplus Food office (not always used for emergencies, but available), various service clubs and voluntary organizations that supplied emergency funds for various purposes.
2. Medical specialists: including all public and private specialized medical clinics and services, such as the chest X-ray service, the hearing clinic, and the gamut of hospital clinics.
3. Counselors:
    a. Diffuse counseling agencies: including the study agencies and others in the same category, school counseling services, recreation facilities with broad interests in personal development such as the YMCA, neighborhood houses, and even Golden Age Clubs, psychological services, including aftercare clinics and child guidance clinics, Friendly Visitors Association (because of the diffuseness of their goals), and social services for various handicapped groups such as the blind.
    b. Specific counseling agencies: including lawyers, public health nursing services focused on health training, vocational rehabilitation, employment services of every kind, alcoholism services (because of the avowed *specific* goal of improvement in the drinking pattern through whatever means), and the Veterans Administration Contact Offices.
4. Protective controlling agencies:
    a. Client-oriented: The income-maintenance services, including the Welfare Department; hospital services, including psychiatric hospitals but not state hospitals; group placements for children, maternity homes, the Public Housing Authority, homes for the aged, the District Attorney's Office (as used by plaintiffs to

prefer charges of neglect, abuse, etc.), all medical social services, and all of the social insurances that require eligibility to enter and continue in care, such
as Workmen's Compensation, Social Security, and
Unemployment Insurance; all kinds of sheltered
workshops. Voluntary services like Meals on Wheels
and the Loan Closet were included under this category, although they fall somewhere between a social
service and a business, depending upon the fees
charged.

b. Society-oriented: All detention services, parole and
probation services, judges and courts, the Youth Bureau of the Police Department, and all state mental
hospitals.

REFERENCES

Bahn, Anita, M. Conwell, and P. Hurley, 1965. "Survey of Private
Psychiatric Practice," *Archives of General Psychiatry,* Vol. 12,
No. 3, March.

Goode, William J., 1960. "Encroachment, Charlatanism, and the
Emerging Profession: Psychology, Sociology, and Medicine,"
American Sociological Review, Vol. 25, No. 6, December.

Smith, Harvey L., 1958. "Contingencies of Professional Differentiation," *American Journal of Sociology,* Vol. LXIII, No. 4,
January.

THE EXCHANGE OF CLIENTS AND PATIENTS   *16*

Limitations of the Data

There are a number of problems with inferring client exchanges from data such as these. In the first place, it was not possible in all agencies to discover exactly where clients had come from. It was no coincidence that in the caretaker agencies, with their privileged, two-person relationship, it was impractical to intercept clients or to examine records. Although some questions were asked about referral practices, the answers could not be interpreted in quantitative terms. Similarly, the emergency services were difficult to study; it was not feasible, for example, within the framework of these

193

studies to discover who suggested to people that they should call upon the police for help. In one emergency service, Catholic Charities, some observations were possible, however, because the agency was merged administratively with Catholic Welfare.

In agencies where records of referral sources were kept, accuracy was still problematical. Some agencies placed more value than others upon knowing their recruitment sources, and some had more time to spend on meticulous record keeping. Furthermore, any agency was more likely to record a client's referral source at his first appearance than at subsequent ones, and consequently new referrals of old clients could easily be lost. Old clients were, however, more likely to enter an agency without a formal referral; throughout this chapter in-referrals are diluted by the informal entry of former clients in order to reflect the everyday comings and goings of clients in the system.

Referrals out of agencies were even harder to discover than referrals in for various reasons: records do not always require this information; referral may come at any point in the duration of care and may be buried in any part of the record; and, when the client is informally steered, no record may be kept at all.

Agencies differ in the amount of *risk* of referral to which they expose their clients: agencies that keep clients a long time have more opportunity to refer than those that do not; agencies such as Planned Parenthood that see their clients only every six months are less likely to refer them than are agencies that see them every week and become familiar with collateral problems. In these studies, some of the clients were still in care at the time the records were reviewed, and hence were still at risk of being referred. For this reason, out-referral figures were adjusted to reflect both the number of unreferred clients whose cases were still open at the time of record review and the proportion of referrals that the agency made at intake, during service, or at termination.* As Table

* The rate of referral for all clients who got past the intake phase and whose cases were closed was calculated. This rate was then applied to open cases. No closed cases had been referred from either service

16-1 shows, agencies differed both as to the time of referral and the type of referral made. There are many sources of error in making adjustments of this kind, especially in assuming equal chances of referral at any time after intake and equal likelihood of hitting various target agencies, but the figures they yield probably reflect what actually happened better than the uncorrected ones.

Interpreting out-referrals is hindered by the possibility that when an agency refers a client, the client may not act on that referral. When he is only steered to another source, the chances of his reaching it probably depend as much on his own sense of urgency and the type of agency to which he is directed as upon the referring agency's intention. During the two-month span in which Catholic Charities was studied, for example, 38 of the 102 applicants for financial relief were advised to apply to the Welfare Department. Of the 232 welfare applicants studied over a period of two weeks, however, only two had been referred from Catholic Charities, whereas nine or ten might have been expected from that source. This particular discrepancy probably arose because some clients had tried unsuccessfully in the past to get welfare assistance and felt it was hopeless to try again.

In general, there is an important principle involved in the discrepancy between in- and out-referrals: whereas in-referrals are events, or consummated choices, out-referrals are unconsummated choices or potential events. For this reason, although corrected out-referrals are considered as events in this Part, considerable caution is needed in interpreting their meaning. Later, out-referrals, along with arrangements and information exchanges, will be viewed as agency choices, and the system will be looked at from a sociometric point of view.

A final problem, common to analyses of both in- and out-referrals, is the handling of multiple referrals. A choice can be made among the referring agents involved to ensure in-

---

of the Department of Social Welfare, but some open cases had been referred during care; therefore the adjustment was based on time in care. In the Home Care Service an additional adjustment was made for the expected deaths of the one-third of the patients with terminal illnesses.

Table 16-1. PROPORTION OF APPLICANTS REFERRED AND STEERED AT INTAKE, DURING CARE, AND AT TERMINATION BY TEN AGENCY SERVICES

Agency service	Total Applicants	Total Referred and Steered No.	Total Referred and Steered %	% referred			% steered		
				At intake	During care	At termination	At intake	During care	At termination
Emergency									
Catholic Charities	102	57	55.9	4.9	—	—	51.0	—	—
Medical specialists									
Planned Parenthood	103	3	2.9	—	1.0	1.9	—	—	—
Dispensary	214	32	15.0	0.9	1.4	2.8	0.9	3.7	5.1
Diffuse counseling									
Family Agency	54	17	31.5	20.4	1.9	5.6	3.7	—	—
Catholic Welfare	69	29	42.0	4.3	—	—	31.9	5.8	—
Psychiatric clinic	551[a]	53	9.6	9.1[b]	—	—	0.5	—	—
Protective control									
Welfare, adult	232	29	12.5	0.4	1.7	—	6.9	3.4	—
Welfare, children	24	5	20.8	—	20.8	—	—	—	—
Home Care Service	66	11	16.7	1.5	—	15.2	—	—	—
Social Service, Dispensary	88	27	30.7	8.0	6.8	2.3	4.5	3.4	5.7

[a] Intake cohorts from both clinics, method of referral.
[b] Estimated on the basis of referral targets, most of which require a formal referral.

dependence, but the links among the agencies will be underestimated accordingly. In this Part, a person who is referred to two agents is considered throughout to be two people, because he represents two events in the system, and the system is the focus of interest.

In all the tables in this Part the study agencies and the referral sources and targets were grouped in the revised classification of agency types. Clergymen and doctors were entered into all tables even though no figures were directly available about their practices. Instead of percentages, check marks were entered wherever one or more of these caretaker agents said that he exchanged clients with another agency, and X's were entered wherever the other studies in the series showed caretakers as sources or targets of referral. For example, some family doctors said that they referred clients to the Family Agency for adoption services, so this referral pattern was marked with a check; some clients in the Family Agency study group were referred by doctors, so an X was also entered for this referral type. The same procedure was used for the Mission Shelter, private psychiatrists, and for in-referrals to the Police Department.

The Pattern of Exchange

In Tables 16-2 and 16-3, it is immediately clear that the caretaker group, according to both its own statements and all available evidence, were sending clients to more kinds of agencies than they themsleves received clients from. Among the emergency services, this asymmetrical pattern was evident in the Police Department, and was very striking in Catholic Charities, but did not characterize the Mission Shelter, which, although an emergency service, was, by its own intention, not an allocating center.

The exchange pattern for the medical specialist agencies was the opposite of that of the gatekeeper group; all three of the agencies received the majority of their patients by referral and from a wide variety of other agencies. Only the Dispensary referred more than a trickle of patients elsewhere,

Table 16-2. PER CENT OF APPLICANTS RECEIVED BY THE FIFTEEN AGENCY SERVICES FROM VARIOUS SOURCES

Agency service	Total applicants	% received from						Protective control		% Multiple Referrals[f]
		All agents	Caretaker[e]	Emergency	Medical Specialist	Diffuse counsel	Specific counsel	Client	Society	
Caretakers										
Family doctors	—	—	—	—	c	—	[d]	c	—	—
Clergymen	—	—	[d]	[d]	—	[e,d]	—	[d]	[d]	—
Emergency										
Mission Shelter	63	[e,d]	—	[e,d]	—	—	—	[e,d]	—	—
Catholic Charities	102	7.8	4.9	c	—	—	—	2.9	—	—
Police	(713)	—	—	—	—	—	—	c	—	—
Medical specialists										
Private psychiatrists	—	[e,d]	[d]	—	[e,d]	[e,d]	[d]	[d]	[d]	—
Planned Parenthood	103	51.5	15.5	—	10.7	—	1.9	23.3	—	—
Dispensary	214	67.3	10.3	13.1	10.3	7.9	3.7	21.5	0.5	3.7
Diffuse counseling										
Family agency	54	63.0	35.2	—	—	5.6	7.4	14.8	—	9.3
Catholic Welfare	69	50.7	34.8	1.4	—	2.9	4.3	5.8	1.4	1.4
Psychiatric clinic	207[a]	71.5	21.3	—	18.8	8.2	1.9	20.8	0.5	—
Protective control										
Welfare, adult	232	22.8	1.7	3.9	4.3	0.4	5.2	4.7	2.6	—
Welfare, children	24	79.2	—	33.3	—	—	—	12.5	33.3	—
Home Care Service	66	106.1[b]	18.2	—	12.1	—	69.7	6.1	—	6.1
Social Service, Dispensary	88	100.0	—	—	100.0	—	—	0.0	0.0	—

[a] Intake cohort from second clinic combined with dropout group from first clinic.
[b] This row adds to more than 100 per cent because of multiple referrals. The per cent of clients referred to the agency by more than one agent is shown in the last column.
[c] Indicates that referrals of this kind were found in the study agencies.
[d] Indicates that the agent stated that he received referrals from this source.
[e] It is not always possible to distinguish family doctors (caretakers) from medical specialists, although the number of clients referred by privately practicing specialists to agency services is probably small.
[f] This reflects the discrepancies between people referred and number of referrals as shown in profile tables, Chapters 4 through 14.

Table 16-3. PER CENT OF CLIENTS SENT BY THE FIFTEEN AGENCY SERVICES TO VARIOUS TARGETS, ADJUSTED FOR CASES STILL AT RISK OF REFERRAL

Agency service	Total clients	% sent to						Protective control		% Multiple referrals[c]	Adjustment factor
		All agents	Care-taker	Emergency	Medical Specialist	Diffuse counsel	Specific counsel	Client	Society		
Caretakers											
Family doctors	—	—	d	c	c, d	c, d	d	c, d	d	—	—
Clergymen	—	—	d	d	c, d	c, d	d	c, d	d	—	—
Emergency											
Mission Shelter	63	—	—	d	c, d	—	—	c, d	d	—	—
Catholic Charities	102	58.8	2.0	8.8	2.9	—	13.7	30.4	1.0	2.9	None
Police	(713)[a]	(13.4)	(0.1)	(2.5)	—	—	(0.7)	(3.0)	(7.1)	—	—
Medical specialists											
Private psychiatrists	—	—	—	—	—	c	—	—	—	—	—
Planned Parenthood	103	4.5	1.5	—	1.5	1.5	—	—	—	—	1.5
Dispensary	214	24.3	—	0.6	0.6	—	0.6	22.5	—	3.7	1.3
Diffuse counseling											
Family Agency	54	40.7	—	—	—	18.5	5.6	16.7	—	9.3	None
Catholic Welfare	69	43.5	2.9	—	—	2.9	11.6	23.2	2.9	1.4	None
Psychiatric clinic	207[b]	9.7	0.7	—	1.9	1.4	0.5	4.3	0.7	—	—
Protective control											
Welfare, adult	232	30.2	2.2	8.6	3.0	—	5.2	9.9	1.3	0.4	2.5
Welfare, children	24	52.0	—	—	—	—	—	52.0	—	—	2.5
Home Care Service	66	24.2	—	—	—	—	22.7	1.5	—	—	1.5
Social Service, Dispensary	88	43.9	—	1.1	6.1	15.9	8.0	14.8	—	6.8	1.3

[a] Police data in parenthesis because they could not be included on Table 16-4.
[b] Intake cohort from second clinic combined with dropout group from first clinic.
[c] Indicates that referrals of this kind were found in the study agencies. Not included in total to preserve comparability with Table 16-2.
[d] Indicates that the agent stated that he received referrals from this source.
[e] This reflects the discrepancies between people referred and numbers of referrals as shown in profile tables, Chapters 4 through 14.

and most of the 24 per cent of its clients that it did refer were sent to the Welfare Department.

Counseling agencies, like medical specialists, received most of their clients by referral, the majority from caretakers. Unlike medical specialties, the two casework agencies referred more than 40 per cent of their clients elsewhere. The psychiatric clinic, however, received many more clients by referral than it sent to other agencies, and it resembled the medical specialists in the asymmetry of referral practice.

As the majority of referrals from counseling agencies were made at the time of intake, these agencies were obviously performing an allocating function for some clients. On the other hand, the quite high rate of passage of clients among the counseling services themselves probably meant, because of the relatively unspecialized nature of counseling itself, that some sorting and screening for desirable clients was occurring.

The protective controlling agencies, except the Welfare Department, received almost all their clients by referral, and between one-quarter and one-half of their client groups were referred elsewhere. Clients came to these agencies from a wide variety of other sources and the target agencies were also scattered—except for the Children's Division of the Welfare Department, which referred only to foster homes and children's institutions.

The only two agencies for which there were data that recorded a higher proportion of out-referrals than in-referrals were the Adult Division of the Welfare Department and Catholic Charities, both agencies that supplied money to people in financial trouble. Their patterns of client exchange probably reflected the battle of eligibility rules that was being waged among agents whose budgets were smaller than the demands made upon them. Much of the exchange reflected the circulation of clients around the Welfare Department, Catholic Charities, the Surplus Food Office, the Red Cross, and so on, as they searched for an agency whose criteria they met, and which was prepared to serve them.

There was a tendency, noticeable in Tables 16-2 and 16-3, for agencies to exchange clients with other agencies at approximately the same level of control. Besides this selection tendency, there was a marked diminution of the proportion of clients referred into and out of agencies as they became more controlling in character. Part of this effect may have been a result of the sampling of agencies; perhaps the whole gamut of correction agents was undersampled by including only the police, and perhaps the supportive medical agencies were oversampled. There were, however, many more medical than correction agents, partly because ill health is of universal concern and affects almost everyone, whereas deviant behavior is of universal concern but affects only a minority. The suggestion in these tables that a much greater proportion of clients were circulated, sorted, and exchanged among the more supportive agents than among the more controlling corresponds with what is known: those disorders that require support are less threatening and therefore more open to negotiation about treatment, both on the part of the agent, who has no legal obligation to act in any particular case, and on the part of the client, who is seeking support rather than being sought out for control. On the other hand, the scarcity of the most controlling agents in the referral pattern may mean that they were cut off from the more supportive end of the spectrum of agents, gathering all necessary services in one place instead of entering into a division of labor with others unlike themselves. The implications of this pattern will be discussed in Chapter 17.

Levels of Referral

Looking at the agency services in terms of the revised typology obscures certain obvious features of the regulative system—that doctors send patients to hospitals for instance, and that nurses act under doctors' instructions—but it does highlight the relative position of the various types of services in the system. In Figure 1, the exchange of clients and patients is charted using only those exchanges that were 10 per cent or more of the agency's own total intake. The solid lines represent the in-referrals, or patterns of events, and the dashed lines, the out-referrals, or choices made by agencies on behalf of clients.

The figure suggests the possibility of a three-level system in which agencies did not exchange many clients at their own level but rather sent them to other levels. Gatekeepers of all kinds formed the primary level, and they sent clients both to the second level, which included the specific and diffuse counselors and the medical specialists, and to the protective controlling agencies at the third level. Agencies at the second and third levels exchanged clients between levels, but the only exchange within the second level was the referral of patients by medical specialists to the psychiatric clinics, which were, themselves, marginal to the medical world. When the agency choices were added to the events, some additional potential exchanges appeared; emergency services advised clients to go both to emergency services and to other services similar to their own. Inasmuch as the dashed choice lines do not coincide entirely with the solid "event" lines in this figure, the channeling of clients between the levels must be interpreted as a compromise between the agency's choice for the client and his own wishes in the matter.

The pattern of movement shown in Figure 1 suggests at first glance a movement of clients from support to control; this pattern was visible in many of the agency profiles, and had been noted before in the paths of patients to mental hospitals in an early study in this series (Cumming, 1962). There is a possibility, however, that such an orderly progression is an illusion. It is clear from Figure 1 that only the first agency level contributed to the one-way movement from support to control, while agencies at level three returned clients to level two and probably to level one. It is almost certain that many clients were finding their own way back to the first level where, by definition, they could return without a formal referral. Cumming's earlier observation that patients who ended in mental hospitals had taken a fairly orderly path from supportive to controlling agents perhaps cannot be generalized. On the one hand, the mentally ill patients in that study were not so much seeking help as being ejected from society because they could not be contained within the network of everyday expectations and obligations that ordinarily controlled their behavior. On the other hand, it is possible

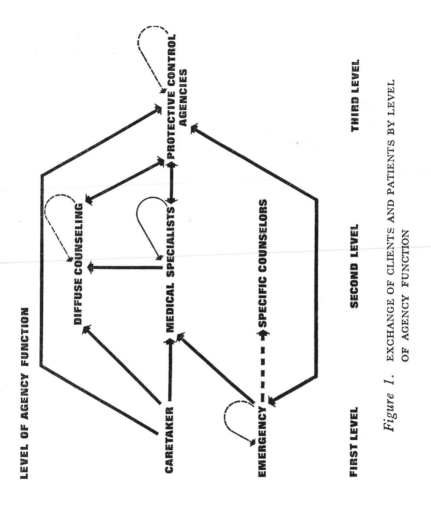

LEVEL OF AGENCY FUNCTION

PROTECTIVE CONTROL AGENCIES

DIFFUSE COUNSELING

MEDICAL SPECIALISTS

SPECIFIC COUNSELORS

CARETAKER

EMERGENCY

FIRST LEVEL   SECOND LEVEL   THIRD LEVEL

Figure 1. EXCHANGE OF CLIENTS AND PATIENTS BY LEVEL
OF AGENCY FUNCTION

that referrals to gatekeepers from agencies at other levels were always made because of new problems and therefore represented a new path toward care, but this could not be determined from these data.

In Chapter 17, the over-all rate of flow of clients and patients throughout the system will be analyzed, using monthly rates of exchange, and the magnitude of the flow between the levels will be examined.

REFERENCE

Cumming, Elaine, 1962. "Phase Movement in the Support and Control of the Psychiatric Patient," *Journal of Health and Human Behavior,* Vol. 3, No. 4, Winter.

THE SCALE OF THE
EXCHANGE OF CLIENTS

An examination of the *rate* of exchange of clients among agencies gives a different picture from that developed by comparing the proportions of clients referred by the various agencies. Examining the number of clients exchanged per unit of time allows statements to be made about what exchanges are likely to be taking place at any given moment. By looking at the system in this way, the effect of agency size on the overall pattern of exchange can be estimated, and the various exchanges can be seen in their actual scale.

The tables in this chapter do not include referrals into the Police Department or referrals into or out of the offices of doctors, clergymen, or private psychiatrists, because the rates were unavailable. Monthly rates of referral in and out of the remaining study agencies were estimated from the best information available about the numbers of clients approaching each agency in the month of study (see Table 15-5). Referral rates were calculated in proportion to those found in the study groups, and the out-referrals were adjusted for anticipated future referrals in the manner used in Chapter 16. Although errors and inaccuracies in the estimates make it impossible to draw inferences about any but the larger patterns of client flow, these larger patterns not only set the general tone of the system but also acted as an important adhesive force among agencies. Each pair of agencies connected by a major flow of clients would have had to maintain some knowledge of each other's rules, norms, working preferences, and administrative habits and accommodate to them through some consensual process. Large volumes of interaction might have been a way to ensure the smooth working of a division of labor based on a "domain" consensus, rather than on a central administrative framework. Among some casework and counseling agencies, where only a small flow of clients was received, other integrative mechanisms were no doubt needed, among them perhaps the professional activity of social workers, which would tend to solidify norms and develop consensus.

The Major Pattern

Table 17-1 summarizes the rate of flow of clients into the study agencies, and it reveals a major pattern: as far as intake alone was concerned, two agencies, the Dispensary and the Adult Division of the Welfare Department, accounted between them for three-quarters of the client flow; the Dispensary receiving an estimated 545 patients by referral each month, and the Adult Division of the Department of Welfare receiving 115 clients. Although these figures are estimates, the difference between these two agencies and all the others was great enough to give credence to their relatively great weight in the system.

The rate of flow of clients refers, of course, to the incidence

Table 17-1. ESTIMATED NUMBER[a] OF REFERRALS PER MONTH RECEIVED
BY TEN AGENCY SERVICES FROM VARIOUS SOURCES

| | Monthly Total | | Received from | | | | | | | |
| | | | Gatekeepers | | Medical specialist | Counseling | | Protective control | | |
Agency service	Appli-cants	In-re-ferrals	Care-takers	Emer-gency		Diffuse	Specific	Client	Society
All services	1682	896[b]	143	133	207	74	69	240	30
Emergency									
Catholic Charities	51	4[b]	3					2	
Medical specialists	869	575	92	102	89	65	31	192	4
Planned Parenthood	59	30	9		6		1	14	
Dispensary	810	545	83	102	83	65	30	178	4
Diffuse counseling	119	73	37	1	6	6	6	16	1
Family Agency	54	34	19			3	4	8	
Catholic Welfare	35	18	12	1		1	1	2	
Psychiatric clinic	30	21	6		6	2	1	6	1
Protective control	643	243	11	30	112	3	32	30	25
Welfare, adult	509	115	9	18	22	3	26	24	13
Welfare, children	36	29		12				5	12
Home Care Service	10	11	2		2		6	1	
Social Service, Dispensary	88	88			88			0	

[a] Based on Table 15-5 and the tables in Chapters 4–13.
[b] This row does not add because of rounding.

populations received by these agencies; some agencies admitting only a small number of clients or patients nevertheless had large numbers in care. Planned Parenthood, for example, an agency that tended to keep its patients once they had been admitted, had a total patient population of around 3000 at the time when it was admitting only about 60 patients each month. A discussion of the differences between the incidence and prevalence populations follows in Appendix B.

Tables 17-2 through 17-5 show in detail the source of the clients entering the study agencies. The caretaking group of agencies made its biggest contribution to the medical specialties (Table 17-2) and most of this was taken up by the estimated 83 referrals per month from individual medical doctors to the Dispensary. In a parallel, but much smaller, flow of clients, clergymen made their major contribution to counseling agencies; each of these client movements probably reflected a division of labor in operation. Some familiar patterns disappeared when rates were calculated; although family doctors, for example, contributed heavily to the family agency in terms of the latter's own intake, these referrals were apparently a minor part of the over-all out-flow from medical doctors.

Even greater than the flow of patients from doctors to the Dispensary was the movement of patients from emergency room care to the Dispensary for follow-up medical care. On a somewhat smaller scale was the activity of police who brought about 12 neglected and abused children to the attention of the Children's Division of the Welfare Department each month, the two mission shelters, which steered about eight patients to the Dispensary, and the family doctors who advised nine patients per month to apply to the Welfare Department. When the volume of traffic alone is considered, the major movement of clients through the gatekeeper agents was obviously by people searching for medical care. This finding is a confirmation of the family doctors' own report that their major referral activity was to sources of specialized medical care (Chapter 3).

Table 17-2. ESTIMATED NUMBER OF REFERRALS PER MONTH RECEIVED BY TEN AGENCY SERVICES FROM GATEKEEPER AGENCIES

| | Monthly total | | | Received from | | | | | | |
| | | | Total from Gate-keepers[a] | Caretakers | | Emergency | | | | |
Agency service	Appli-cants	In-re-ferrals		Family Doctors	Clergy-men	Catholic Charities	Mission Shelters (2)	Red Cross	Emer-gency rooms	Police
All services	1682	896	276	113	26	3	12	9	91	18
Emergency										
Catholic Charities	51	4	3		3					
Medical specialists	869	575	194	89	3	0	8	4	87	4
Planned Parenthood	59	30	9	6	3			4		
Dispensary	810	545	185	83			8	4	87	4
Diffuse counseling	119	73	38	18	20	0	0	1	0	0
Family Agency	54	21	19	11	8					
Catholic Welfare	35	34	13	2	11			1		
Psychiatric clinic	30	18	6	5	1					
Protective control	643	243	41	11	0	3	4	4	4	14
Welfare, adult	509	115	27	9		3	4	4	4	2
Welfare, children	36	29	12							12
Home Care Service	10	11	2	2						
Social Service, Dispensary	88	88	0							

[a] The row totals are taken from Table 17-1; when the row does not add to the total, the error is due to rounding.

Table 17-3. ESTIMATED NUMBER OF REFERRALS PER MONTH RECEIVED BY TEN AGENCY SERVICES FROM MEDICAL SPECIALISTS

Agency service	Monthly Total		Received from					
	Applicants	In-referrals	Total From Medical Specialists[a]	Planned Parenthood	Private Psychiatrist	Dispensary	Rehabilitation clinic	Other special clinic (7)
All services	1682	896	207	3	3	100	2	98
Emergency								
Catholic Charities	51	4	0					
Medical specialists	869	575	89	3	0	1	0	85
Planned Parenthood	59	30	6	3		1		2
Dispensary	810	545	83					83
Diffuse counseling	119	73	6	0	3	1	0	1
Family Agency	54	34	0					
Catholic Welfare	35	18	0					
Psychiatric clinic	30	21	6		3	1		1
Protective control	643	243	112	0	0	98	2	12
Welfare, adult	509	115	22			9	2	11
Welfare, children	36	29	0					
Home Care Service	10	11	2			1		1
Social Service, Dispensary	88	88	88			88		

[a] The row totals are taken from Table 17-1; when the row does not add to the total, the error is due to rounding.

Minor Patterns

Medical specialists contributed much less to the over-all client flow than did gatekeepers (Table 17-3). About half of all the referrals into the study agencies by medical specialists was the estimated 83 patients sent from other specialized public clinics to the Dispensary. Another 88 patients were estimated to go from the Dispensary to its own Social Service Department each month. Except for scattered referrals to the Welfare Department, all this movement was internal to the medical world or between it and its articulating agency, the medical social work department. Here again, a reasonable division of labor appears to have been at work, although the question of whether all the movement seen was necessary, or whether some represented needless changes of service for the client, cannot be answered from these data.

It is usual to consider the public health nurse's service as an extension of the physician's function and, although the focus of this study was upon the educative, or specific-counseling, aspects of her job, she was clearly playing a medical-adjunctive role (Table 17-4). Nurses appeared in the major pattern, sending patients to medical care and to their own Home Care Service. Their linkages to the nonmedical world, which were important, and which will be discussed in Chapter 18, were not focused on any one target, and hence were not a feature of the broad outlines of the pattern.

The majority of the 270 clients referred from the protective-controlling agencies to the study group came from agencies concerned with the protection of the individual, and most of these moved from the Welfare Department to the Dispensary. The pattern of flow from the agencies charged with the protection of society was quite different; most of the clients coming from this group went to other protective-controlling agents (Table 17-5). In other words, the correction agencies appeared here, as in Part I, to be circulating clients among themselves rather than dividing their work with other types of agencies. These findings draw attention to what is already known about the culture of correction systems: their

Table 17-4. ESTIMATED NUMBER OF REFERRALS PER MONTH RECEIVED BY TEN AGENCY SERVICES FROM COUNSELING SERVICES

| | Monthly total | | Received from | | | | | | | | | |
| | | | Diffuse counseling | | | | | Specific counseling | | | | |
Agency service	Applicants	In-referrals	Total from counselors[a]	Catholic Welfare	Family agency	School Services	Psych. clinics (2)	Employment	VA contact office	Voc. Rehabilitation	Lawyers and Legal Aid	Public Health Nursing (2)
All services	1682	896	143	1	1	65	9	18	5	2	22	26
Emergency Catholic Charities	51	4	0									
Medical specialists	869	575	96	0	0	61	4	11	0	0	0	20
Planned Parenthood	59	30	1									1
Dispensary	810	545	95			61	4	11				19

Diffuse counseling											
119	*73*	*12*	*0*	*1*	*4*	*3*	*3*	*1*	*0*	*4*	*0*
Family Agency											
54	34	7			1	2	1			3	
Catholic Welfare											
35	18	2			1	1	1	1		1	
Psychiatric clinic											
30	21	3	1	1	2	1	1	1			
Protective control											
643	*243*	*35*	*1*	*0*	*0*	*2*	*4*	*4*	*0*	*18*	*6*
Welfare, adult											
509	115	29	1			2	4	4		18	6
Welfare, children											
36	29	0									
Home Care service											
10	11	6									
Social Service Dispensary											
88	88	0									6

[a] The row totals are taken from Table 17-1; when the row does not add to the total, the error is due to rounding.

Table 17-5. ESTIMATED NUMBER OF REFERRALS PER MONTH RECEIVED BY TEN AGENCY SERVICES FROM PROTECTIVE-CONTROLLING SERVICES

Agency service	Monthly total		Total from protective control agents[a]	Received from									
	Appli-cants	In-re-ferrals		Client-oriented							Society-oriented		
				Hos-pitals	Soc. Service, Dis-pensary	Wel-fare	Half-way house	Psych. hospital	Public hous-ing	Social Secur-ity	Mental Hospital	Proba-tion and parole	Courts
All services	1682	896	270	112	14	101	4	4	7	1	4	19	12
Emergency Catholic Charities	51	4	2			2							
Medical Specialists	869	575	196	85	12	90	4	0	1	0	0	4	0
Planned Parenthood	59	30	14	9	1	3			1				
Dispensary	810	545	182	76	11	87	4					4	

Diffuse counsel-ing	*119*	*73*	*17*	*8*	*0*	*6*	*0*	*2*	*2*	*1*	*0*	*2*	*1*
Family Agency	54	34	8	3		4				1		1	
Catholic Welfare	35	18	3	1		1		1				1	
Psychiatric clinic	30	21	6	4		1		1	1	1		1	1
Protective control	*643*	*243*	*55*	*19*	*2*	*3*	*0*	*2*	*4*	*0*	*4*	*13*	*11*
Welfare, adult	509	115	37	15	2	2			4		2	2	9
Welfare, children	36	29	17	3							2	11	2
Home Care Service	10	11	1	1		1							
Social Service, Dispensary	88	88	0										

[a] The row totals are taken from Table 17-1; when the row does not add to the total, the error is due to rounding.

exclusiveness leads to alienation of the clients and to some extent of the workers themselves from the mainstream of social life, so that the purpose of the agency, to restore the client to normative control, tends to be subverted by this practice.

Articulating Agencies

In Table 17-4, which shows the movement of clients from counseling agencies to the target agents, two important features stand out: the flow of 61 patients per month from the school services to the medical system, and the contribution by the specific counseling services, particularly lawyers, of 22 clients per month to the protective controlling agencies.

The school counseling service can be looked upon as an articulating structure forming a bridge between socializing and regulative institutions. As schools in America in 1961 were in frequent interaction with families, they provided a pathway into the regulative system that bypassed gatekeeper agencies. In one sense, the school was itself a gatekeeper agent for the health and welfare systems, taking responsibility for the welfare of the whole child. At a time when there was a large immigrant population, no doubt the school played an even more crucial caretaking role, but even in 1961, among a study population most of which had been in the country two or three generations, it still acted as dispatcher for a number of children who might not have received health care without it.

Lawyers, like school counselors, are in a sense articulating agents for the regulative system, as well as being themselves regulators of both institutional and individual affairs. Although the source of their clients was not discovered in these studies, it seemed likely that some were recruited from the nonagency world and fed to the counseling and protective-controlling agencies.

The various employment services, both private and public, as well as the personnel offices of industry, were performing a more clear-cut articulating function, connecting the occu-

pational world to the regulative system. Although all employment agencies were grouped together, the tables show that
the personnel offices sent clients into the system and the employment agencies received them from it; their articulating
roles were thus separate and distinct.

In each of the articulating structures there was a combination of regulative and nonregulative functions: the school
was essentially a socializing institution, but it maintained
nurses, social workers, and special teachers, who provided
both direct service and a bridge to the regulative system.
Lawyers dealt with instrumental matters, usually business, but
within their own profession they had specialists who dealt in
interpersonal matters as well as made referrals to other services. Employment agencies served employers and in so doing
served clients, and the same is true of the personnel offices of
business and industry. Clergymen played essentially the same
type of articulating role when they referred clients from their
own ministrations to those of the system at large.

Choices versus Events

Table 17-6 summarizes the out-referrals, or choices, made
by the agencies on behalf of their clients. The police emerge
here, along with family physicians and schools, as a major
gatekeeping agency. Although much of their daily activity
was supportive, their referrals tended to direct clients to the
controlling end of the system, which may be one reason for
the public image of the controlling "cop." Two-thirds of the
policemen's referrals were to jail, and most of the remaining
one-third were to various legal agencies, revealing the policeman as a major connection between the correctional and
other segments of the system. Detailed tables of out-referrals
are not presented here because in Chapter 18 they will be
considered, along with arrangements, eligibility checks, and
information exchanges, as choices made by the agencies
among themselves.

Theoretically, if one agency sends a certain number of clients to another agency each month, and if they all go, that

Table 17-6. ESTIMATED NUMBER OF REFERRALS PER MONTH SENT TO VARIOUS TARGET AGENCIES BY TEN AGENCY SERVICES, CORRECTED FOR PROPORTION OF CLIENTS STILL AT RISK OF REFERRAL[a]

	Monthly Total		Gatekeepers		Medical Specialists	Counseling		Protective control	
Agency service	Applicants	Referrals[a]	Care-takers	Emergency		Diffuse	Specific	Client	Society
All services	1682	499	14	55	33	27	55	307	8
Emergency									
Catholic Charities	51	31	1	5	1			16	1
Police	(5500)[b]	(366)	(4)	(69)			(23)	(59)	(212)
Medical specialists	869	199	1	5	6	1	5	181	0
Planned Parenthood	59	3	1		1	1			
Dispensary	810	196		5	5		5	181	
Diffuse counseling	119	42	1	0	2	12	7	18	2
Family Agency	54	22				10	3	9	
Catholic Welfare	35	16	1		1	1	4	8	1
Psychiatric clinic	30	4			1	1		1	1
Protective control	643	226	11	45	24	14	36	92	5
Welfare, adult	509	163	11	44	16		27	60	5
Welfare, children	36	19						19	
Home Care Service	10	2					2		
Social Service, Dispensary	88	42		1	8	14	7	13	

Sent to

[a] Corrected throughout with the adjustment factor used in Table 16-3.
[b] Estimated monthly calls to the Police Department. This row not included in total so as to allow comparison with Table 17-1.

number should appear as in-referrals in the other agency. That is to say, if Agency *A* sends 30 clients per month to agency *B,* but only two clients enter Agency *B* by referral from agency *A,* there has been a discrepancy between the agency's choice of action for the client and the client's own choice of behavior. A discrepancy between such choices and events was found when in-referrals were compared with out-referrals (Table 17-7). Among those agencies between which only a few clients were exchanged, there was no reason to expect a very good fit because of chance alone, to say nothing of the crudeness of the adjustment factors used. Among those between which there was considerable exchange, there was a tendency, shown in Table 17-7, for both the in- and out-referrals to be fairly high, but there were still enormous discrepancies. Some of these discrepancies were known to reflect administrative conventions that made the records misleading: for example, a welfare worker might tell his client to go to the Dispensary, and his appearance there might have been recorded as a referral at the time that his welfare status was checked, but the welfare worker might never have entered this event into the client's record, partly because he was too busy and partly because he tended to look upon the Dispensary as an extension of his own service. A discrepancy between the Dispensary and its Social Service Department may have been of the same order. In theory, in order to enter the Social Service Department, a note from a Dispensary clinic was necessary, but old clients who had their "own workers" might bring new problems into the Social Service Department without benefit of a referral from clinics and thus some episodes of service would not get into the record.

Some discrepancies, such as the difference between the numbers of clients steered or referred from the Catholic agencies to the Welfare Department, and from the Family Agency to the psychiatric clinics, probably reflected the clients' reluctance to follow the agencies' advice. In other words, the movement of clients was a resultant of at least two forces, agency pressure and client motivation.

Table 17-7. DISCREPANCIES BETWEEN ESTIMATED NUMBERS OF CLIENTS PER MONTH RECEIVED FROM AND SENT TO THE STUDY AGENCIES[a] CORRECTED FOR CASES STILL OPEN

Referred to	Total	Referrals from (in parentheses)								
		Catholic Charities	Mission Shelter	Dispensary	Family Agency	Catholic Welfare	Psychiatric clinic	Welfare Adult	Social Service, Dispensary	Police Dept.
Total	247 (163)	3 (17)	4 (N.D.)	99 (79)	1 (7)	1 (6)	7 (2)	99 (18)	14 (23)	18 (15)
Catholic Charities	2 (0)							2 (0)		
Mission Shelter	N.D. (42)							N.D. (38)		N.D. (4)
Planned Parenthood	5 (3)			1 (0)				3 (0)	1 (3)	
Dispensary	110 (21)	0 (1)	4 (N.D.)				4 (1)	87 (16)	11 (4)	4 (0)
Family Agency	5 (1)						1 (1)	4 (0)		

Agency							
Catholic Welfare	1 (0)					1 (0)	
Psychiatric clinic	4 (14)	1 (0)	1 (5)		1 (0)	0 (8)	
Welfare, adult	18 (85)	3 (15)	8 (54)	0 (2)	1 (6)	2 (0)	2 (8)
Welfare, children	12 (11)						12 (11)
Home Care Service	2 (0)	1 (0)	1 (0)		1 (0)		
Social Service, Dispensary	88 (25)		88 (25)				
Police Department	N.D. (3)	N.D. (1)			N.D. (2)		

a The children's division of the Welfare Department, Planned Parenthood, and Home Care Service did not report referrals to the other study agencies, although they received referrals from other agencies.

N.D. = No data.

Figures in parentheses () are corrected out-referrals.

Overview

Figure 2 suggests the major outline of the movement of clients around the system; only in-referrals of more than ten each month are included. The centrality, in terms of both the rate of flow of clients and the numbers of agency contacts, of the Welfare Department and the Dispensary is immediately apparent in this figure. The major suppliers to these huge services were family doctors, hospitals and their clinics and emergency rooms, the police, and the schools. The police and doctors appeared to have been major allocating agencies, while the flow of clients from clergymen, the diffuse counseling agencies and public health nursing services was relatively minor in quantity, even though their connections were widespread.

Whether other large movements of clients were undetected because of the nature of the agencies sampled is not known. Partly because of the general knowledge of the system and partly because any very large client flow would be expected to find its way into this system of services in some way, it is probable that most major currents are represented here. There is no doubt, however, that the size of the movement of clients among unsampled agencies cannot be estimated; for example, the number of people moving back and forth between lawyers and family doctors cannot be guessed from this study. The same is true of employment services and school services; it is possible that some groups of unsampled services were involved heavily with one another, but it is improbable that any movement of clients, except perhaps around the correctional services, was completely overlooked.

Figure 2 highlights the differences among the articulating agents. While the schools and the employment services linked the nonagency to the agency world, the police and lawyers linked the more controlling to the more supportive elements of the system, thus playing an internal integrative role.

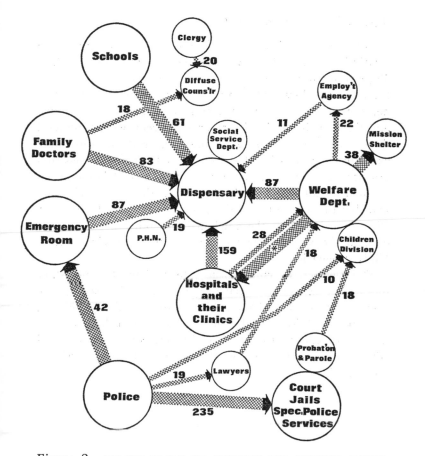

Figure 2. MAJOR FLOW OF CLIENTS PER MONTH AMONG
AGENCY SERVICES

* Connections between hospitals and their clinics are shown as
major pathways although they do not appear in the tables. This is
because the intervening agency, the medical division of the welfare
department, is not in the agency sample.

Agency Levels Reconsidered

The agency levels suggested in Figure 1 can be seen more clearly in Figure 2. Of the 968 exchanges represented, 472, or 49 per cent, were clients going from gatekeepers to agencies at the other two levels. Of the remainder, 286 exchanges, or 30 per cent of the total, were clients going between levels two and three. Thirty-eight clients, or 4 per cent, went from level three back to the gatekeepers, and 172, or 18 per cent, were exchanged by agencies at the same level. These findings suggest that there was indeed a gross division of labor that accounted for all but about 12 per cent of the client exchanges, and that there were two major patterns of flow in the system: clients moving from the gatekeepers to other agencies, and, once in the system, moving between two basically different kinds of agencies.

This chapter, by emphasizing rate of flow, does not show the variety of contacts made by such agencies as Catholic Welfare and the Social Service Department of the Dispensary, both of which contacted many agencies regarding a small number of clients. In the next chapter, which is concerned with choices among agencies, this aspect of the system will be considered.

AGENCY CHOICES 18

The choice of one agency by another for any kind of interaction almost automatically reflects a system of understanding among the various agencies regarding one another's core
services, eligibility rules, and other boundary conditions. Different kinds of interactions among agencies require different
kinds of understandings: if, for example, one agency calls
upon another to provide a collateral service for one of its
own clients, a considerable consensual base is required. Information exchanges require fewer shared assumptions, perhaps
only the belief that the records of certain kinds of clients can
appropriately be known to a wide audience. Eligibility checks
rest on an understanding that the client's private life is to be

in part relinquished before he can receive what he is asking. Not all agencies can be approached for information bearing on eligibility, particularly agents such as doctors and lawyers whose relationships with clients are essentially supportive.

When an agency is chosen as a referral target and an active referral is made, this transaction can represent a refined consensus about which agencies should serve what clients. If, on the other hand, the client is steered, the choice might indicate nothing except an urge on the part of the referring agency to be rid of the client.

Although choices among agencies resemble choices made by individuals of one another for various purposes, it is probably not safe to regard the resemblance as more than a rough parallel. In individual choices of partners for various activities, issues of responsiveness, reciprocity, and interpersonal rewards are paramount. In the agency world, with its complex flow from place to place of clients and patients, the meaning assigned to any balance of choosing over being chosen is problematical. Isolation for an agency such as Planned Parenthood does not carry the same implications as isolation of a child in a classroom. In other words, agency staff members presumably got their personal rewards from interpersonal relationships and their professional satisfaction from reaching their goals, rather than from some calculus of giving and getting clients. The agency itself survived or was submerged for reasons apart from the quid pro quo of client exchange, unless that exchange reduced its client flow too much, an unlikely event when there were shortages of all kinds of professionals. Within limitations, however, a sociometric approach to agency choices can point up the integration of agencies in a system of divided labor.

Throughout this chapter, the rates, particularly of arrangements, should be considered minimal because there was not sufficient information about when choices were made to adjust for cases remaining open. In some agencies, such as the Dispensary's Social Service, and the Home Care Service, more arrangements certainly were made before the cases were closed. Referrals out to other agencies, which have been considered in Chapters 16 and 17 as evidence of client flow, will be considered here as agencies' choices of one another as targets for their clients.

Arrangements

Information about arrangements, that is, choices by agencies for collateral services, was available for nine of the agency services, and it was found that 251 arrangements were made in connection with the 952 applications for these services. The monthly rate at which arrangements were made with gatekeeper agencies was low (Table 18-1); even private physicians were approached only by the Home Care Service, which was, after all, dependent upon family physicians for guidance. The highest rate of arrangements were found to have taken place with client-focused protective agencies, usually the Welfare Department or hospitals, and with medical specialists, usually the various hospital and Health Department Clinics.

The Dispensary, although making arrangements for only a small proportion of its patients, actually contributed 16 per cent to the monthly total, exceeded only by the Welfare Department and its own Social Service. Although the Home Care Service made an average of two arrangements for each client, its patient intake was so low that it did not contribute as much as the Dispensary to the over-all activity. Although arrangements with client-focused protective services and medical specialists dominated the picture, a substantial minority of the arrangements were made with specific counseling agencies, and these were distributed over many kinds of services such as those offered by lawyers, public health nurses, vocational rehabilitation and employment offices, and so on. In general, arrangements were made with all kinds of agencies except the caretakers, and this versatility reflects a division of labor between the study group and the remainder of the system.

Information Exchanges

Agencies exchanged information about 150 of the 952 applicants without at the same time making arrangements or re-

Table 18-1. ESTIMATED NUMBER OF ARRANGEMENTS MADE EACH MONTH WITH VARIOUS TYPES OF AGENCIES BY NINE SERVICES

| Agency service | Monthly total | | Monthly arrangements with | | | | | | | |
| | Appli-cants | Arrange-ments[a] | Gatekeepers | | Medical Special-ists | Counsel | | Protective control | | Non-agency |
			Care-takers	Emer-gency		Specific	Diffuse	Client	Society	
All services	1652	167	4	18	24	25	14	63	14	7
Emergency										
Catholic Charities	51	2		1	0			1		
Medical specialists	869	27	0	4		8	0	11	4	0
Planned Parenthood	59									
Dispensary	810	27		4	1	8		11	4	
Diffuse counseling	89	13	0	1		2	3	6	2	
Family Agency	54	6				1	2	2	1	
Catholic Welfare	35	7		1	1	1	1	4	1	
Protective control	643	125	4	12	23	15	11	45	8	7
Welfare, adult	509	35		2	4	11		9	4	4
Welfare, children	36	2						2		
Home Care Service	10	21	3	1	8	1	1	6	1	1
Social Service, Dispensary	88	67	1	9	11	3	10	28	3	2

[a] Total is not the sum of the row or column because of rounding errors in the cells.

ferrals. Such a pooling of knowledge about the client's life is one way of controlling his behavior; since such controls were taken into account when the agencies were classified, it is not surprising that the majority of the information checks were made by and with controlling agencies. At the same time, information exchanges offer the agencies an opportunity to consolidate and reaffirm their norms about agency actions. Table 18-2 shows that 40 per cent of all the estimated monthly exchanges of information were calls from the Dispensary to hospitals, the Welfare Department, and the Social Security Office. The only other major flow of information was among the four controlling agencies of the same type. There was a general tendency for agencies to exchange information with others in their own category, probably because norms about confidentiality and clients' rights are similar in agencies dealing with similar problems in similar ways. This process does not, however, suggest a division of labor in the way that the distribution of arrangements does, but rather a solidarity based on similarity of function and mutual aid between people with similar problems and outlooks. The tendencies in these tables are, of course, only suggestive; no statistical tests are applied to them because the figures are estimates and because the results were not predicted; but it is reasonable to expect that in a divided labor, arrangements have the effect of coordinating the system while information exchanges have the effect of reinforcing norms and strengthening areas of consensus.

Eligibility Checking

Whereas information exchanges, like arrangements, are usually made in the clients' interests, eligibility checking is meant to protect the agency from illegal use. Such checking is, of course, irrelevant for some agencies, however, because criteria for entry are nonspecific. Among the nine services, six made some eligibility checks, but only the Welfare Department and the Dispensary made them at anything like a significant rate (Table 18-3). In any month, most of the eligibility checking was carried out by these two agencies. Although the Welfare Department almost certainly made more exhaus-

Table 18-2. ESTIMATED NUMBER OF INFORMATION EXCHANGES MADE EACH MONTH WITH VARIOUS TYPES OF AGENCIES BY NINE SERVICES

	Monthly total		Gatekeepers		Medical	Counsel		Protective control		Non-agency
Agency service	Applicants	Informa-tion[a]	Care-takers	Emer-gency	Special-ists	Specific	Diffuse	Client	Society	
All services	1652	152	5	7	16	5	20	92	9	2
Emergency										
Catholic Charities	51	3	1			1	1	1	1	
Medical specialists	869	73	0	0	11	0	0	62	0	0
Planned Parenthood	59	1						1		
Dispensary	810	72		1	11			61[b]	1	1
Diffuse counseling	89	14	1	1	1	1	6	4	0	1
Family Agency	54	10			1		6	3		
Catholic Welfare	35	4	1	1		1		1		1
Protective control	643	62	3	6	4	3	13	25	8	1
Welfare, adult	509	20	2	2	2		2	7	7	
Welfare, children	36	12		2			8	3		
Home Care Service	10	6	2		2			2		
Social Service, Dispensary	88	24	1	2		3	3	13	1	1

[a] Total is not the sum of the row or column because of rounding errors in the cells.
[b] Fifty-four of these contacts were with hospitals, the remainder with the Welfare Department and the Social Security office.

Table 18-3. ESTIMATED NUMBER OF ELIGIBILITY CHECKS MADE EACH MONTH WITH VARIOUS TYPES OF AGENCIES BY NINE SERVICES

| | Total | | Monthly eligibility checks with | | | | | | | |
| | | | Gatekeepers | | Medical special-ists | Counsel | | Protective control | | Non-agency |
Agency service	Appli-cants	Eligi-bility[a]	Care-takers	Emer-gency		Specific	Diffuse	Client	Society	
All services	1652	589	1	0	3	27	1	548	8	3
Emergency										
Catholic Charities	51	8				1	1	6	1	
Medical specialists	869	509	0	0	0	0	0	509	0	0
Planned Parenthood	59	1						1		
Dispensary	810	508						508		
Diffuse counseling	89	1	0	0	0	0	0	1	0	1
Family Agency	54	0								1
Catholic Welfare	35	1						1		1
Protective control	643	71	1	0	3	26	0	32	7	2
Welfare, adult	509	66			2	26		28	7	2
Welfare, children	36	0								
Home Care Service	10	1	1		1					
Social Service, Dispensary	88	4						4		

[a] Total is not the sum of the row or column because of rounding errors in the cells.

tive eligibility checks and had more demanding criteria for admission than the Dispensary, the Dispensary far surpassed it in numbers of individual checks because patients were required to have their credentials reviewed for every episode of illness.

The Dispensary made all its checks with the Welfare Department, however, and therefore they could not have had anything like the effect on the over-all system that the Welfare Department's wide-ranging eligibility procedures must have had.

Purchase of block service from the Dispensary by the Welfare Department would certainly have reduced the total rate of eligibility checking manyfold, and thus would have changed the pattern. At the time of writing, it was not known what effect upon this stream of jurisdictional exchanges Medicare and Medicaid would have.* It seems obvious, however, that eligibility checking was, with the single exception of the Dispensary, a less common activity than either information exchanges or arrangements.

Combined Choices

Table 18-4 summarizes the number of choices estimated to have been made in every month by the nine study agencies for the making of arrangements, the exchanging of information, the checking of eligibility, and the referral or steering of clients. Both referrals and eligibility checks were made for about one-third of each month's incoming client group, and arrangements were made or information exchanged about 10 per cent. Arrangements were made by all agency types, but the protective controlling and counseling groups made a somewhat greater number than the others. Catholic Charities specialized in referrals, making them for an estimated 70 per cent of their clients, but all agencies made some. Information was exchanged by the counselors regarding 16 per cent of

---

* By the time of going to press it seemed certain that checking was reduced by these new programs because eligibility, once established, was more or less permanent and did not have to be re-established for each episode of illness.

Table 18-4. PER CENT OF ESTIMATED MONTHLY CHOICES MADE BY NINE AGENCY SERVICES FOR REFERRAL, ARRANGEMENTS, INFORMATION EXCHANGE, OR ELIGIBILITY CHECKS

Agency service	Estimated applicants per month	% of clients for whom choices were made regarding			
		Arrangements	Referral	Information	Eligibility
All services	1652	10.1	30.2	9.2	35.7
Emergency					
Catholic Charities	51	3.9	60.8	5.9	15.7
Medical specialists	869	3.1	22.8	8.4	58.6
Planned Parenthood	59	—	2.9	1.7	1.7
Dispensary	810	3.3	24.2	8.9	62.7
Diffuse counseling	89	14.6	42.7	15.7	1.1
Family Agency	54	11.1	40.7	18.5	—
Catholic Welfare	35	20.0	45.7	11.4	2.9
Protective control	643	19.4	35.1	9.6	11.0
Welfare, adult	509	6.9	32.0	3.9	13.0
Welfare, children	36	5.6	52.8	33.3	—
Home Care Service	10	100.0	20.0	60.0	10.0
Social Service, Dispensary	88	76.1	47.7	27.3	4.5

their clients, which was the highest rate among the agencies. Eligibility checking was the special province of the Dispensary, and arrangements were most often made by the counselors, the Home Care Service and the Dispensary's Social Service, all agencies employing social workers.

The tables so far have set forth the proportions and quantities of different kinds of choices; in Table 18-5 the variety of interagency choices is shown. The nine services varied in the scope of their choices, with the controlling group, except for the Children's Division, choosing from among a wider variety of agencies, the counselors and the one emergency service being intermediary and the medical specialists having the smallest variety of contacts with the fewest categories of agencies. Figure 3 summarizes these data pictorially with each line indicating contact with one agency, and with the character of the concentric circle touched by that line reflecting the nature of the target agency. In this figure, the familiar patterns show up in a somewhat different light: the Children's Division and the medical specialist agencies appeared to be essentially receivers, chosen by a number of the study agencies but themselves choosing a small variety and small number of others. The diffuse counseling agencies, particularly Catholic Welfare, chose a wider variety of other agencies, while the Home Care Service, the Social Service Department of the Dispensary and Catholic Charities acted as dispatcher agencies making many kinds of contacts with a wide variety of other services. The Welfare Department, like the Dispensary, was an over-chosen agency with ties both to the rest of the system and to the nonagency world.

Three of the four controlling agencies—the Home Care Service, the Dispensary's Social Service, and the Adult Division of the Welfare Department—appeared to provide most of the articulation with the nonagency world, and could therefore be considered as performing an integrative function between the regulative system and the rest of society.

Recapitulation, Re-evaluation, and Prediction

The over-all picture that has emerged from the reanalyses presented in this Part is at once a description of the past and

Table 18-5. TOTAL NUMBER OF DIFFERENT AGENCIES[a] CHOSEN BY NINE SERVICES FOR ARRANGEMENTS, REFERRALS, INFORMATION AND ELIGIBILITY, TAKEN TOGETHER

Agency service	Total	Gatekeepers		Medical Special-ists	Agency chosen Counsel		Protective control		Non-agency
		Care-takers	Emer-gency		Specific	Diffuse	Client	Society	
Catholic Charities	22	2	4	3	3	2	5	3	
Planned Parenthood	5	1		1		1	2		
Dispensary	13		2	3	1		6	1	
Family Agency	16			1	3	5	6	1	
Catholic Welfare	22	2	2	2	5	1	7	2	1
Welfare, adult	26	1	3	1	4	1	6	5	5
Welfare, children	7		1			3	3		
Home Care Service	33	2	3	2	5	4	9	1	7
Social Service, Dispensary	35	1	4	4	6	8	7	3	2

[a] Agents such as doctors are grouped, as are employers, schools, lawyers, and patient clinics, hospitals, and nursing homes.

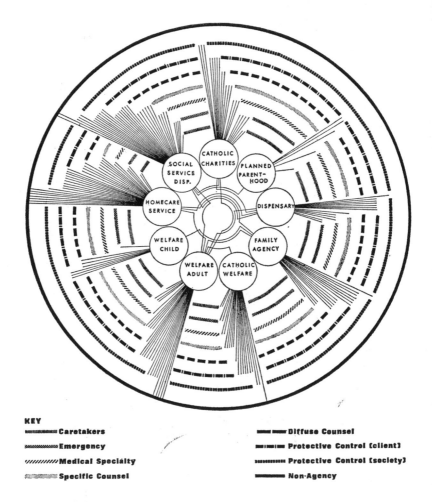

KEY

|||||||||||||| Caretakers
▨▨▨▨▨▨ Emergency
/////// Medical Specialty
▨▨▨▨▨ Specific Counsel

▬▬ ▬ Diffuse Counsel
▬■▬■▬ Protective Control (client)
|||||||||||| Protective Control (society)
▬▬▬▬ Non-Agency

Figure 3. NUMBERS OF TYPES OF AGENCIES CHOSEN BY
NINE SERVICES FOR REFERRAL, ARRANGEMENT,
INFORMATION, AND ELIGIBILITY CHECKS

a prediction of the future; its details are hypotheses, although not formally labeled as such. A summary of the major findings, together with further speculation about their meaning, is presented below.

MAJOR FINDINGS: HYPOTHESES FOR FUTURE TESTING

1. It was possible to classify the agencies according to the specificity of their function, the professionalization of their staffs, the control exerted over clients, and the duration of client-agency encounters. These characteristics were used selectively, rather than systematically, but the resulting classification, although logically vulnerable, proved useful in analyzing the flow of clients through the system.

2. Three agency "levels" were tentatively identified: first, those caretaking and emergency services to whom clients came directly without formal referral and through whom they flowed into the remainder of the system; second, all medical specialties practiced outside hospitals and all varieties of counseling services; and third, all those agencies that exercised protective control of the client either for his own safety or for that of society.

Within these three levels, a minority of the transfer of clients took place; between them, a major flow was found. This pattern suggested that a gross division of labor existed in the system, with broadly different orders of problems being solved within each class of agency, possibly by supportive techniques at Level II, controlling at Level III, and both at Level I. It also raised the possibility of an intra-level competition and a diffusion of function among agencies. Concretely, problems that took a client to a medical clinic might result in his being referred to a hospital but were unlikely to send him to a lawyer or a family agency; problems that took him to a religious charity might propel him eventually to a family agency or to the Welfare Department but it was unlikely, although not impossible, that he would end up, through a formal referral, back in the care of a family physician or a clergyman. In Part III, where a "trouble score" is assigned to each client, the relationship of this score to his career in the regulative system will be examined.

3. The regulative system did not appear to do its work in a vacuum; it was attached to the rest of society through articulating agencies and through ties to the instrumental world generated inside the system. Articulating agencies were those whose core function was something other than the support or control of individuals, but who directed certain people into the system in the course of their own jobs. These agencies included schools, employers, employment agencies, lawyers, and clergymen.

Contacts were initiated by the more controlling agencies with a wide variety of public and private business concerns. In concrete terms, the school might send a near-sighted child to a clinic, but the clinic social worker arranged for the payment of his glasses with the optician.

4. The majority of the clients in the system at any given time were seeking either medical care or financial assistance or were being controlled in some way by the police. The character of the entire regulative system must have been affected by the sheer magnitude of these three activities.

5. There was a gradient of activity throughout the system. The more supportive the services, the heavier the traffic among the agencies. How much of this circulation around supportive agencies resulted from screening and sorting of clients and how much from a division of labor was unclear, but it might reasonably be proposed that the more alike the agencies between which clients moved, the more likely was the movement to represent rejection of the client. Conversely, the more controlling the service and the more threatening to the social order the client, the fewer the options available to either client or agent, and, therefore, the less the traffic. In concrete terms, a man with a low back pain could have visited his family physician, an orthopedic clinic, a psychiatrist, a marriage counselor, and an employment agency in his search for relief, but a burglar had no choice, once he was caught, but to go with the policeman to detention. Once detained, those who offended the social order appeared to get sealed off at the controlling end of the system. Specialized medical, counseling, and protective services were presumably added to these agencies so that their clients would no longer

have to circulate. The implications of such a practice for the culture of the correctional system are weighty. Any subsystem in any sector of society develops its own values; the more specialized it is, the more it must engage in an active division of labor with other specialized services if it is not to develop a parochial subculture. The question of when a parochial subculture is to be desired and when avoided was raised by these findings, but could not be answered.

6. It seemed reasonable to propose that in a consensual system, all things being equal, values would tend to become formed and fixed in those parts of the system where there were regular exchanges of large numbers of clients and frequent interactions regarding them. If the changes were reciprocal, a melding of the norms from each agency would be expected to take place, as it seemed to have occurred between the Welfare Department and the Dispensary. If the flow of clients was in one direction, any exchange of norms would be one-sided: when policemen take patients to the emergency rooms of hospitals, for example, they learn more about hospitals than the hospital staffs learn about the Police Department. It follows that the boundary conditions around agencies —that is, intake procedures, eligibility requirements, and policies regarding confidentiality—all play a vital part in structuring the relationships among agencies and hence developing the values of the regulative system. For example, when a public service is offered as a charity, as was the case in the Welfare Department at the time, a halo of ideas about clients is developed; these ideas are then reflected in intake regulations and eligibility criteria, and these in turn tend to reinforce the image of the client as dependent and inadequate. Under a system of social insurance where the service is given as a right, respect for the client might be expected to be reflected in more attractive ways of delivering the service and in interagency collaborations focused more on the service and less on the client's right to it.

In agencies where applicants were few and interactions of all kinds with the rest of the system relatively infrequent, contacts such as the professional meeting and the interagency committee were perhaps used for the development of domain consensus. If this were the case, it would be expected that the staffs of the big, busy agencies would be the least often involved, all things being equal, in exchanges that were not directly concerned with actual clients, and the smaller agencies would be more often involved in staff-centered exchanges.

7. There did not seem to be a good fit between client action and agency intentions; most client flow might tentatively be considered a resultant of these two vectors rather than the product of either one or the other alone.

III

The Population and
Its Problems

The purpose of Part III is to carry forward the exploration of the division of labor between the agencies at the three levels identified in Part II from the point of view of the characteristics of the populations approaching them. Because there was only one agency at the first level for which sufficient data were collected, most of the analyses will be limited to comparisons of the two streams of clients approaching and leaving Levels II and III, and considerations of the services they were offered by these two groups of agencies.

Because the agencies at Level III were more controlling and their services less optional than those at Level II, it was predicted that the individuals in the population approaching them would be more vulnerable, more troubled, and therefore more in need of service than those in the population approaching Level II. In Chapter 19 the age, sex, marital status, and type of household of the groups of families and individuals approaching the study agencies will be compared, both with one another and with the United States census reports of the Syracuse urbanized area for 1960.

In Chapter 20, the populations will be compared in terms of the kinds of problems presented at the agencies and in terms of the clients' past experience with three controlling services: welfare assistance, placement services for children, and mental institutions. The prediction that a greater proportion of clients approaching the protective controlling agencies at Level III will have experienced these kinds of trouble will be tested.

In Chapter 21, a trouble score will be developed from the characteristics described in Chapter 20, and a prediction that the population approaching Level III agencies will have had higher scores will be tested. The fate of the clients—that is, the proportion of them receiving service at the agencies to which they applied—will then be analyzed and this analysis will be related to the client flow described in Part II.

In Chapter 22, changes in the Syracuse regulative system that took place after these studies were completed will be described briefly, and the major conclusions of the studies recapitulated.

AGE, SEX, AND MARITAL STATUS OF CLIENTS AND PATIENTS

19

Probably no one passes his whole life quite without need of formal regulation, but those who can afford it are likely to seek private sources of support or control. Family doctors are approached for medical care, lawyers or clergymen for counsel and advice, special schools for problem children, and either banks or kinsmen for loans of money in emergencies. Those who cannot reach these private sources must turn to more public places.

The regulative agents who serve the well-to-do are always hesitant to make information available to outsiders, because of both self-interest and their feelings of solidarity with their clients. Those who deliver the publicly supported forms of care, being torn between loyalty to the clients and an attachment to the society that engages them in their regulative tasks, are more willing to divulge information. Because of this persistent difference in the availability of information from different kinds of services, the populations to be described in this and subsequent chapters will overrepresent the poorer segment of those who make contact with the regulative system.*

Individuals and families are known to require more formal regulation at some times in their lives than at others; young children need medical attention, adolescents run out of money, and old people become disabled (Anderson, 1958). The tables in this chapter explore the differences in age, sex, and marital status of the population applying to ten of the study agencies.

There was enough information about the clients approaching both of the Catholic agencies, the Planned Parenthood Center, the Syracuse Dispensary and its Social Service Department, the Family Agency, both the Adult and Children's Divisions of the Welfare Department, and the Home Care Service, to allow comparisons of the study populations from these nine agencies. In addition, there was a limited amount of information about the 63 transient men in the Mission Shelter.

Throughout Part III the unit of analysis is the client rather than the application. Although no client has been counted twice in one agency, problems of independence are raised by related families appearing in several agencies, and they will be discussed in Chapter 21.

Age, Sex, and Marital Status

The combined study populations of 1010 applicants included 500 families as well as 250 men and 260 women who

---

* Some researchers have taken pains to include the well-to-do in specific studies (Jaco, 1957; Gardner and Hopkins, 1963), but in general the amount of information dwindles as the affluence of the patient or client increases.

were not married at the time of application (Table 19-1). The figures in all the tables are minimal because some of the applicants were seeking care for their families as well as for themselves. Throughout this section, the unit of analysis will be the family* and the nonmarried applicants will be looked upon as one-person families.

As Table 19-1 shows, just under 5 per cent of the whole group of applicants were less than twenty years of age,† 25 per cent were in their twenties, 23 per cent in their thirties, 18 per cent in their forties, 12 per cent in their fifties, and 18 per cent were sixty or over. Within each marital status, the ages of the applicants differed. Nonmarried men were over-represented in the three oldest age groups and had an average age of close to fifty years, nonmarried women were clustered in the twenties and the sixties and had an average age of just under forty-one, and male spouses were over-represented in the two decades from twenty to forty and had an average age of a little more than thirty-seven years.††

This distribution of age and marital status gives a suggestion of the kinds of problems arising at different times in the life span: men become more disadvantaged by the nonmarried state as they get older (Cumming and Henry, 1961; Townsend, 1957); married couples need help to clothe, educate, and sometimes control their children; and unattached women are most susceptible to social, economic, and health problems when they are very young and when they are old.

When the part of the combined study population that was over twenty years old was compared with the corresponding population of the Syracuse urbanized area (U.S. Census of Population, 1960) the study population was found to be younger than expected with an over-representation of both men and women below the age of forty (Table 19-2). About

---

* Except for the Home Care Service, because a separate record for each spouse was kept in the agency when both were in care.

† The husband's age was assigned throughout to married couples even when the wife applied for assistance.

†† A test of the difference in proportion of nonmarried men over 60 years of age approaching the Welfare Department and the Mission Shelter yielded $x^2 = 10.8$; d.f. $= 1$; P $<$ .001. Between the Mission Shelter and the Dispensary, $x^2 = 5.75$; d.f. $= 1$; P $<$ .02.

Table 19-1. AGE, SEX, AND MARITAL STATUS OF 1010 APPLICANTS APPROACHING TEN STUDY AGENCIES

Age[a]	Total		No.			%		
			Nonmarried		Married	Nonmarried		Married
	No.	%	men	women	couples	men	women	couples
All Applicants	1010	100.0	250	260	500	100.0	100.0	100.0
< 20	44	4.4	6	22	16	2.4	8.5	3.2
20–29	257	25.4	15	79	163	6.0	30.4	32.6
30–39	234	23.2	42	38	154	16.8	14.6	30.8
40–49	177	17.5	60	40	77	24.0	15.4	15.4
50–59	120	11.9	64	18	38	25.6	6.9	7.6
60 and over	178	17.6	63	63	52	25.2	24.2	10.4
Average age	41.1		48.9	40.7	37.4			

[a] Age of husband assigned to married couples.

Table 19-2. COMPARISONS OF THE AGE AND SEX OF 2295
APPLICANTS AGED TWENTY YEARS AND OVER, ESTIMATED
TO HAVE APPROACHED NINE STUDY AGENCIES IN
ONE MONTH, WITH THE POPULATION OF THE
SYRACUSE URBANIZED AREA, 1960[a]

| | No. | | % | |
Age and Sex	*Study group*	*Syracuse*	*Study group*	*Syracuse*
Total population	2295[b]	*211,559*	*100.0*	*100.0*
20–29	737	42,399	32.1	20.0
30–39	668	47,397	29.1	22.4
40–49	398	41,343	17.3	19.5
50–59	179	33,341	7.8	15.8
60 and over	313	47,079	13.6	22.3
Total men	*1053*	*100,483*	*100.0*	*100.0*
20–29	292	20,582	27.7	20.5
30–39	314	22,991	29.8	22.9
40–49	188	20,022	17.9	19.9
50–59	107	16,020	10.2	15.9
60 and over	152	20,868	14.4	20.8
Total women	*1242*	*111,076*	*100.0*	*100.0*
20–29	445	21,817	35.8	19.6
30–39	354	24,406	28.5	22.0
40–49	210	21,321	16.9	19.2
50–59	72	17,321	5.8	15.6
60 and over	161	26,211	13.0	23.6

[a] Mission Shelter excluded because the rate of application was not accurately enough known.
[b] For this table, married couples have been allocated to the male and female categories, and as the wife's age is taken to be the same as her husband's, the table *overestimates* the ages of the study group women.

70 per cent of both the study group and the adult population of the Syracuse urbanized area were married, but in view of the youth of the study population, this represents a deficit of married couples in the study population. The relative surplus of nonmarried people suggests an extra vulnerability of the study population.

Individual Agency Comparisons

As Table 19-3 shows, the different types of agencies were being approached by different populations. The one emergency service, Catholic Charities, like the Mission Shelter,

Age,[a] Sex, and Marital Status	Total	Mission Shelter	Catholic Charities	Planned Parenthood	Dispensary	Family Agency	Catholic Welfare	Welfare Adult	Welfare Children	Home Care Service	Social Service, Dispensary
All Applicants	**1010**	**63**	**97**	**103**	**214**	**54**	**69**	**232**	**24**	**66**	**88**
Nonmarried men	*250*	*63*	*64*	—	*34*	*4*[b]	*14*[b]	*55*	*2*	*4*	*10*[b]
Under 40	63	15	18	—	8	0	9	9	2	0	2
40–59	124	42	13	—	14	3	3	26	0	0	3
60 and over	63	6	33	—	12	1	2	20	0	4	5
Nonmarried women	*260*	*0*	*7*	*4*	*72*	*14*[b]	*14*[b]	*83*	*10*	*16*	*40*[b]
Under 40	139	—	6	4	42	10	6	48	8	0	15
40–59	58	—	1	0	11	3	3	25	2	0	13
60 and over	63	—	0	0	19	1	5	10	0	16	12
Married couples	*500*	*0*	*26*	*99*	*108*	*36*[b]	*41*[b]	*94*	*12*	*46*	*38*[b]
Under 40	333	—	16	96	77	18	23	68	9	2	24
40–59	115	—	10	3	22	17	16	23	3	8	13
60 and over	52	—	0	0	9	1	2	3	0	36	1

[a] Husband's age assigned to married couples.
[b] The Social Service Department of the Dispensary received a greater proportion of nonmarried female applicants than either of the two counseling agencies, both of which received a greater proportion of married couples than would have been expected by chance alone ($\chi^2 = 12.14$; d.f. = 2, P < .01).

was receiving a disproportionate number of nonmarried men, the majority of whom were living alone (Table 19-4). Indeed, among the nonmarried applicants to the ten agencies 90 per cent of the men, compared to only 26 per cent of the women, lived alone. In four of the agencies—Catholic Char-

Table 19-4. LIVING ARRANGEMENTS OF 250 NONMARRIED MEN AND 260 NONMARRIED WOMEN APPROACHING TEN STUDY AGENCIES

Agency Approached	Nonmarried Men	Nonmarried Women	Living Alone Men	Living Alone Women	% Alone Men	% Alone Women
All Nonmarried Applicants	250	260	224	68	89.6	26.2
Caretaker agencies						
Catholic Charities	64	7	62	3	96.9	42.9
Mission Shelter	63	—	63	—	100.0	—
Medical specialties						
Planned Parenthood	—	4	—	—	—	0.0
Dispensary	34	72	26	16	76.5	22.2
Diffuse counseling						
Family Agency	4	14	2	3	50.0	21.4
Catholic Welfare	14	14	10	6	71.4	42.9
Protective control						
Welfare, adult	55	83	49	23	89.1	27.7
Welfare, children	2	10	1	1	50.0	10.0
Home Care Service	4	16	2	8	50.0	50.0
Social Service, dispensary	10	40	9	8	90.0	20.0

A greater proportion of nonmarried men than women lived alone among the groups approaching:
1. Catholic Charities P = .0049; Fisher's Exact Test.
2. Dispensary $\chi^2 = 26.2$; d.f. = 1, P < .001.
3. Welfare, adult $\chi^2 = 47.5$; d.f. = 1, P < .001.
4. Social Service, Dispensary $\chi^2 = 14.5$; d.f. = 1, P < .001.

ities, the Adult Division of the Welfare Department, the Dispensary, and its Social Service Department—the differences in the living arrangements of the nonmarried men and women applicants reached statistical significance. This difference arose not only because this population contained a number of unmarried or deserted women with small children, but also because women can be fitted into households as extra members more readily than men.

The Planned Parenthood Center, not surprisingly, received only women, the majority of them married. The study groups from the Family Agency and Catholic Welfare did not differ from one another in age or marital status, but when they were combined and compared with the group approaching the Social Service Department of the Dispensary, the difference in function of the two kinds of agencies was suggested by the surplus of nonmarried women applying for medical social work and the preponderance of married couples approaching the two counseling services.

The Adult Division of the Welfare Department and the Dispensary had appeared, during the observation period, to be receiving very similar populations, but the group approaching the Dispensary was older and included more nonmarried women than the group approaching the Welfare Department. Both of these differences were statistically significant.

The Children's Division of the Welfare Department received only one-half of its applications for protective services from married couples, most of the remainder coming from nonmarried women.

Agency Level Comparisons

Statistical comparisons of the populations approaching agencies at the three levels identified in Part II could not be made without weighting the individual study groups by the rate of intake into the agencies. This was done by treating the groups as if they were strata in a sample (McCarthy, 1951). The Catholic Charities study group was omitted because it was the only Level I agency being compared, and the remaining population was considered as two groups approaching two kinds of agencies.

Comparison of the populations approaching Levels II and III showed that proportionately more nonmarried people than would have been expected by chance were applying to the protective controlling agencies of Level III and proportionately more married couples were approaching the medical specialties and counseling services of Level II. When the agencies themselves, rather than the populations, were com-

Table 19-5. COMPARISON OF THE PROPORTION OF NONMARRIED APPLICANTS
APPROACHING EIGHT STUDY AGENCIES AT LEVELS II AND III

Agency Level	Study Groups			Annual Estimates		
	Total Number	Nonmarried No.	%	Total[a] Number	Nonmarried No.[b]	%
Level II	*440*	*156*	*35.5*	*11,496*	*5225.3*	*45.5[c]*
Planned Parenthood	103	4	3.9	708	27.6	3.9
Dispensary	214	106	49.5	9,720	4811.4	49.5
Family Agency	54	18	33.3	648	215.8	33.3
Catholic Welfare	69	28	40.6	420	170.5	40.6
Level III	*410*	*220*	*53.7*	*7,716*	*4486.5*	*58.1[c]*
Welfare, adult	232	138	59.5	6,108	3634.3	59.5
Welfare, children	24	12	50.0	432	216.0	50.0
Home Care Service	66	20	30.3	120	36.4	30.3
Social Service, Dispensary	88	50	56.8	1,056	599.8	56.8

[a] Estimated as in Chapter 15.
[b] Expected number derived by multiplying total annual number of applicants by the per cent of nonmarried applicants in the corresponding agency.
[c] A larger proportion of the applicants approaching the agencies at Level III than at Level II were unmarried at the time of application (Critical Ratio = 3.15; P = .002).
When each agency in Level II is compared with each agency in Level III, 13 of the 16 comparisons show the Level II agencies to receive a smaller proportion of nonmarried applicants (P = .05. Sign Test, two-tailed).

pared using a Sign Test (McKinnon, 1964), there was a statistically significant difference between the two levels (Table 19-5). This means that the proportion of nonmarried people approaching agencies at Level II was smaller than the proportion approaching Level III and that the difference was not a result of the populations in the large agencies swamping those in the small ones.

Although the one emergency service at Level I cannot be said to represent other gatekeeper agencies, let alone the caretaking agents, the eight agencies at Levels II and III were chosen for their representativeness of services, and the finding that they were attracting different populations supports the tentative conclusion of Part II that there was an overriding division of labor between them. This possibility will be pursued in the next two chapters where further characteristics of the various study groups will be briefly considered.

REFERENCES

Anderson, Odin, 1958. *The Health of a Nation,* Chicago, University of Chicago Press.

Cumming, Elaine, and William E. Henry, 1961. *Growing Old,* New York, Basic Books.

Gardner, Elmer A., and Roger A. Hopkins, 1963. "Development of a Flexible Control System in the Maintenance of a Patient Case Register," Proceedings of the Retrieval Section of the Conference on Data Acquisition and Processing in Biology and Medicine.

Jaco, E. Gartly, 1957. "Social Factors in Mental Disorders in Texas," *Social Problems,* Vol. IV, No. 4, April.

McCarthy, Philip J., 1951. *Sampling, Elementary Principles,* Bulletin No. 15, New York State School of Industrial and Labor Relations, Cornell University.

McKinnon, William J., 1964. "Table for both the Sign Test and Distribution-Free Confidence Intervals of the Medians for Sample Sizes to 1,000." *Journal of the American Statistical Association,* Vol. 59, No. 307.

Townsend, Peter, 1957. *The Family Life of Old People: An Inquiry in East London,* New York, The Free Press.

United States Census of Population, 1960. *General Population Characteristics, New York,* U.S. Department of Commerce, Bureau of the Census.

THREE KINDS OF TROUBLE *20*

This chapter considers applicants to the nine study agencies in terms of three kinds of trouble: whether they had ever received public assistance; whether they, or members of their immediate families, had undergone hospitalization for mental illness or mental retardation; and whether they had experienced episodes of having their children placed outside their homes. It also compares the agencies in terms of the proportion of clients drawn from each of the problem categories used in Part I. The three troubles chosen for analysis all represent grave disruptions of either family structure or personal integrity, and all indicate that formal controls had been exercised over the client and his family, probably with

253

a minimum degree of compensating support. These are not, of course, the only indices of trouble; such important disruptions as imprisonment, expulsion from school, and illegitimacy are also indications of social and personal breakdown that occurred in the lives of many of the clients in the study. The choice of the three particular problems used here was made because the necessary information was available, but there is no reason to believe that the use of other indices would have led to qualitatively different conclusions.

Welfare Assistance

In Chapter 12, the impact upon the individual of the process of applying for public assistance was discussed briefly; in this chapter, a history of having received public assistance will be taken to be an index of trouble. In two of the nine agencies—Planned Parenthood and the Home Care Service—where a welfare history was noted at intake, the agencies' own records were used; in the remaining seven agencies, the records of the Onondaga County Welfare Department were searched. When records contained accounts of welfare histories in other counties, these were included. Only histories of *past* applications of clients approaching the Welfare Department itself were used in order to maintain comparability. The number of clients reported as having a welfare history in Tables 20-1 and 20-2 is minimal because, besides the problem of underreporting in the two agencies whose own records were used, some clients may have received assistance in other counties, and this may not have been put in their records; nevertheless, 62 per cent of the population approaching the nine agencies were found to have received welfare assistance in the past or were receiving it at the time they applied at one of the other study agencies.

When the study groups approaching each agency were compared (Table 20-1), those approaching Catholic Charities had a surprisingly small proportion of clients with a welfare history; perhaps because the mobility of many of the men making application obscured the true proportion.

The two counseling agencies were apparently serving dif-

Table 20-1.   PROPORTION OF APPLICANTS WITH A HISTORY
OF WELFARE ASSISTANCE AMONG 947 APPLICANTS
TO NINE AGENCIES

Agency Type	Total	With Welfare History	
		No.	%
All Applicants	**947**	**589**	**62.2**
Gatekeeper			
Catholic Charities	97	54	55.7
Medical specialties	*317*	*181*	*54.1*
Planned Parenthood	103	23[a]	22.3
Dispensary	214	158[a]	73.8
Diffuse counsel	*123*	*47*	*38.2*
Family Agency	54	11[b]	20.4
Catholic Welfare	69	36[b, c]	52.2
Protective control	*410*	*307*	*74.9*
Welfare, adult	232	179	77.2
Welfare, children	24	17	70.8
Home Care Service	66	37	56.1
Social Service, Dispensary	88	74[c]	84.1

[a] Not tested because Planned Parenthood figure minimal.

[b] A greater proportion of Catholic Welfare than of Family Agency applicants had a public assistance history ($\chi^2 = 11.7$; d.f. $= 1$, $P < .001$).

[c] A greater proportion of the Social Service Dispensary than Catholic Welfare applicants had a public assistance history ($\chi^2 = 17.3$; d.f. $= 1$, $P < .001$).

ferent populations, as more than half of the applicants approaching Catholic Welfare had a history of public assistance compared with only one-fifth of those applying to the Family Agency. (The Social Service Department of the Dispensary, a social work agency of still a different character, received application from a greater proportion of welfare clients than either of the counseling agencies, 84 per cent of their applicants falling into that category.) All these differences were statistically significant.

Within the medical specialties, a differentiation of client groups similar to that among the counseling agencies appeared; just over 20 per cent of the Planned Parenthood patients had a welfare history compared with almost 75 per cent of those from the Dispensary, although the former figure is undoubtedly too low; even if it were doubled, however, the difference would still be striking. In contrast, the numbers of applicants with a welfare history among the four protective controlling agencies ranged only from 56 to 84 per cent. Not even the Home Care Service clients, whose own records were used, or those approaching the Welfare Department itself, differed significantly from the others.

To test the prediction that a higher proportion of troubled clients would be found approaching Level III than Levels I and II, the study populations were weighted to reflect the application rate at each agency (Table 20-2). Fifty-six per cent of the applicant group to the one gatekeeper agency, Catholic Charities, had a welfare history compared to 67 per cent and 78 per cent of the other two groups. Catholic Charities was omitted from the comparison, however, because it could not be assumed to represent other gatekeeper agencies. When the remaining two levels were compared, the population approaching Level III was found to have a significantly greater proportion with welfare histories than that approaching Level II. Although the agencies at Level II were more variable among themselves with regard to the proportion of applicants who had had public assistance than those at Level III, a Sign Test showed that the Level II agencies themselves, as well as the populations approaching them, were significantly different. This finding confirms the impression given by the high proportion of nonmarried applicants approaching Level III that these agencies were consistently receiving more vulnerable clients, more in need of protective control.

In summary, the Level III agencies had the highest proportion of clients with a welfare history, the Level II agencies an intermediate proportion, and the one Level I agency the lowest, although the latter may not have been typical of others in the gatekeeper group.

Mental Illness and Mental Retardation

Any mental illness or mental retardation that requires treatment in a state hospital or training school is a disruptive force to the group in which it occurs. When the affected person has a key role to play, mental illness can result in a major disordering of the social structure, such as when women cannot manage their homes or when men cannot keep jobs. If

Table 20-2. COMPARISON OF PROPORTIONS OF 850 APPLICANTS WITH WELFARE HISTORIES APPROACHING AGENCIES IN LEVELS II AND III

Agency Level	Study groups			Annual estimates		
	Total number	With welfare history No.	%	Total[a] number	With welfare history No.[b]	%
Level II	*440*	*228*	*51.8*	*11,496*	*7,683*	*66.8[c]*
Planned Parenthood	103	23	22.3	708	158	22.3
Dispensary	214	158	73.8	9,720	7,173	73.8
Family Agency	54	11	20.4	648	132	20.4
Catholic Welfare	69	36	52.2	420	219	52.1
Level III	*410*	*307*	*74.9*	*7,716*	*5,977*	*77.5[c]*
Welfare, adult	232	179	77.2	6,108	4,715	77.2
Welfare, children	24	17	70.8	432	306	70.8
Home Care Service	66	37	56.1	120	67	55.8
Social Service, Dispensary	88	74	84.1	1,056	888	84.1

[a] Estimate taken from Table 19-5.
[b] Expected number derived by multiplying the total estimated annual number of applicants in each agency by the percent found in the corresponding agency to have had welfare histories.
[c] A larger proportion of applicants to Level III than to Level II had welfare histories when the numbers in each study group were weighted according to the annual rate of application to that agency (Critical Ratio = 3.16, P < .001). Thirteen out of sixteen possible comparisons of the agencies at the two levels showed those at Level III to have a higher proportion of applicants with welfare histories (P = .025, Sign Test, one-tailed).

the affected person does not have a key role, mental illness can still be a major burden or stress, even though it does not actually disrupt the social structure.

Paradoxically, the chronic forms of mental illness are often more destructive than the acute forms because full recovery is unusual. Chronic illnesses include much schizophrenia, most alcoholism, mental deficiency of the more severe kinds, personality and character disorders, and various organic illnesses. These illnesses can cause grave social disruption because the regulative system fails to produce its full intended effect, and residual characteristics that hamper role performance may be permanent.

Some diseases are more disruptive at some times of the life cycle than at others; an organic brain disease or a severe character disorder is a calamity when it affects the father of a young household, but only a burden and a stress when it affects an old man whose roles have already become peripheral.

The names of the 1010* clients and their 3059 significant kin—that is, primary kin, or other kin if they were living in the household or if they were involved in the client's presenting problems—were searched in the central files of the New York State Department of Mental Hygiene, and 17.5 per cent, or 177 families, were found to have had a total of 195 different affected members.† This number underestimates the prevalence of mental illness in this group for two reasons: first, some mental illness may not have been treated in hospitals, or may have been treated in hospitals in another state; and second, not all significant kindred were named in the case records. It is not certain just how high this minimum figure of 17.5 per cent of affected families was because studies of lifetime accumulated rates of hospitalization for people in different age groups were lacking, even though a substantial literature on the over-all incidence and prevalence of symptoms of mental illness was slowly being accumulated (Dohren-

---

* This is the only comparison in this chapter in which the applicants to the Mission Shelter are used.

† When affected people appeared as significant kin in more than one case, they were assigned only to the case upon which they were judged to have the greatest impact.

wend and Dohrenwend, 1965) ; nevertheless, the proportion of affected families was considered prima facie high for New York State at that time.*

The amount of social disruption represented by these illnesses is suggested by the finding that 149, or 76.4 per cent, of the 195 affected family members or their ex-spouses were the applicants themselves, while the 46, or 23.6 per cent, who were children, siblings, parents or other relatives represented at the very least stress and burden on the applicant families.

Although the diagnostic distribution seen in Table 20-3 cannot easily be interpreted without a detailed analysis of other characteristics of the affected people, it is clear that most of these family members were suffering from serious and often chronic disorders. Twenty-four per cent of the patients were diagnosed as schizophrenic and 17 per cent as mentally retarded; about 14 per cent each were diagnosed as depressed, behavior-disordered, or alcoholic; 9 per cent were diagnosed as suffering from organic disorders, and only 7 per cent as psychoneurotic.

When the proportion of families with hospitalizations for mental disorders applying to each of the ten study agencies was examined, a rather even distribution of this index of trouble was found, with the marked exception of the Children's Division of the Welfare Department. In that agency 12 of the 24 applicant families had suffered hospitalization of 15 members, 6 of them children (Table 20-3). This proportion of affected families is significantly higher than the proportion of the group approaching the Social Service Department of the Dispensary, which had the next highest rate, 25 per cent having had hospitalizations.

The rate of mental illness among families applying to the Children's Division was of particular interest because in a preliminary description of these populations (McCaffrey, 1963) it had been noted that the proportion of mentally ill men (16.7 per cent) in the study populations was considerably

* Personal communication, Abbott Weinstein, Director, Division of Statistics and Data Processing, New York State Department of Mental Hygiene.

Table 20-3. PSYCHIATRIC DIAGNOSES OF 195 MEMBERS OF APPLICANTS' FAMILIES APPROACHING TEN AGENCIES

		Agency Approached									
Diagnosis	Total	Mission Shelter	Catholic Charities	Planned Parenthood	Dispensary	Family Agency	Catholic Welfare	Welfare Adult	Welfare Children	Home Care Service	Social Service, Dispensary
All Applicants	1010	63	97	103	214	54	69	232	24	66	88
With affected members											
Number	177	6	21	10	31	9	17	42	12	7	22
Per cent	17.5	9.5	21.6	9.7	14.5	16.7	24.6	18.1	50.0[a]	10.6	25.0[a]
Total affected members	195	6	24	10	34	9	19	48	15	7	23
Diagnosis											
Schizophrenia	46	1	4	2	8	3	8	14	3		3
Depression	27		1	4	6	4	2	6	1		3
Psychoneurosis	13			1	3		3	1	3	2	
Behavior disorder	28	1	6		4	1	1	9	3		3
Alcoholism	29	4	7	1	3		1	6	1	2	4
Mental deficiency	33		3		6	1	4	8	3		8
Organic disorders	16		3	1	4			4	1	3	
Undiagnosed	3			1							2

[a] Proportionately more of the families approaching the Children's Division of the Welfare Department than of those approaching the Social Service Department of the Dispensary had a mentally ill family member ($\chi^2 = 4.45$, d.f. = 1, .05 > P > .02).

greater than that of women (8.9 per cent). It had also been noted that because children's services had been omitted from the sample of agencies, none of the group was *directly* concerned with supporting families in which the mother was failing in her core role of caring for her children, although several offered support, or control, to families in which the wage earner had failed in his core role of providing sufficient income, or in which the marriage itself was foundering. It was predicted, therefore, that a study of the Children's Division of the Welfare Department, an agency whose core service was the protection of children, would reveal a surplus of families in which women had failed in their central roles and that this could sometimes be because of mental illness. Of the nine affected adults in the agency, five, or 55.6 per cent, were women, compared with 31.3 per cent among the remaining agencies. Although the agency, as predicted, was attracting a population with a surplus of affected women, the proportion was not significantly different from that of the other agencies. The absolute surplus of affected members compared to the other agencies was, however, statistically significant, and this finding illustrates a profoundly held American value: drastic circumstances must prevail before an agent of society is given a legal mandate to violate family privacy by removing children from their parents' custody, even for their own protection. It will be recalled that in the classification of the agencies presented in Chapter 15, the Children's Division accrued the highest Control Score.

When the ten agencies were compared in terms of the diagnoses of the affected patients (Table 20-3), no very striking pattern emerged, but when the populations approaching the agencies at Levels II and III were weighted and compared, the predicted pattern of a higher proportion of affected families applying to Level III became clear (Table 20-4). The client group approaching Catholic Charities, however, contained a higher proportion of clients with this characteristic than did the groups approaching the other two levels. A comparison of the proportion of affected families approaching each individual agency in Level II with each agency in Level III also showed a statistically significant difference.

Table 20-4. COMPARISON OF PROPORTION OF APPLICANTS WITH HISTORIES OF HOSPITALIZATION FOR MENTAL ILLNESS APPROACHING AGENCIES IN LEVELS II AND III

Agency Level	Study groups			Annual estimates		
	Total number	*With mental illness* No.	*With mental illness* %	*Total*[a] *number*	*With mental illness* No.[b]	*With mental illness* %
Level II	*440*	*67*	*15.2*	*11,496*	*1,689*	*14.7*[c]
Planned Parenthood	103	10	9.7	708	69	9.7
Dispensary	214	31	14.5	9,720	1,409	14.5
Family Agency	54	9	16.7	648	108	16.7
Catholic Welfare	69	17	24.6	420	103	24.6
Level III	*410*	*83*	*20.2*	*7,716*	*1,598*	*20.7*[c]
Welfare, adult	232	42	18.1	6,108	1,105	18.1
Welfare, children	24	12	50.0	432	216	50.0
Home Care Service	66	7	10.6	120	13	10.6
Social Service, Dispensary	88	22	25.0	1,056	264	25.0

[a] Estimated as in Table 19.5;
[b] Calculated as in Table 20-2.
[c] A larger proportion of applicants to Level III than Level II agencies had histories of mental hospitalization when the numbers in each study group were weighted by the rates of application to that agency (Critical Ratio = 3.04, P = .003).
Twelve of the sixteen possible comparisons of the agencies at the two levels showed those at Level III to have a higher proportion of applicants with histories of mental hospitalization (P = .05, Sign Test, one-tailed).

In summary, 17.5 per cent of the 1010 applicants to ten agencies had suffered, among other troubles, hospitalizations of family members for mental disorders. Among the populations approaching Level III agencies, the proportion of applicants with this characteristic was significantly higher than among those approaching Level II agencies. The individual agencies also differed between the two levels, as had been predicted.

Child Placement

Children can be separated from their families for a variety of reasons, and sometimes a separation is the only solution to a major family problem; nevertheless, the placement of children always reflects family disruption because it means that the family as a socializing agent has broken down, at least temporarily. As the socialization of children is the major task of modern families, the removal of children from the home, even if it does solve a problem, must be considered an index of serious trouble.

Information about the placement of children was less reliable in these studies than information about welfare assistance or hospitalization for mental illness because it was derived only from the agencies' own files without a cross-check with placement agencies. Furthermore, in order to record a placement in a client's file, the agency had both to know that placement had occurred and to consider it a significant datum. For these reasons, the figures in Tables 20-5, 20-6, and 20-7 are underestimates of the numbers of placement episodes that these clients had experienced. Even with this under-reporting, however, 100, or slightly more than 10 per cent, of the families approaching nine of the study agencies had placed children outside the home at least once and had had this information recorded in their files. Of these families, 28 had experienced more than one episode of this kind of family dispersion (Table 20-5).

One-quarter of all the placements of children from these families had been in foster homes, another quarter were with relatives of the family, the latter probably representing

Table 20-5.   TYPE OF PLACEMENTS EXPERIENCED BY THE
CHILDREN OF 100 OF THE 947 APPLICANTS APPROACH-
ING NINE AGENCIES

Placement Type	Total	No. with placement Once	Multiple	% with placement Once	Multiple
Total	**100**	**72**	**28**	**72.0**	**28.0**
Individual Placement	*48*	*44*	*4*	*91.7*	*8.3*
Foster home	25	23	2	92.0	8.0
With relatives	23	21	2	91.3	8.7
Group Placement	*52*	*28*	*24*	*53.8*	*46.2*
State schools[a]	15	10	5	66.7	33.3
Mental hospitals	7	1	6	14.3	85.7
Correctional institutions	14	5	9	35.7	64.3
Other institutions	11	7	4	63.6	36.4
Placement type unknown	*5*	*5*	*0*	*100.0*	—

[a] For the retarded; this category includes private placement of the retarded.

adaptive efforts on the part of the families. The remaining
placements were divided among various kinds of group placements.

Among the 100 affected families, 50 were applicants to the
Welfare Department, and 19 to the Children's Division*
(Table 20-6). As the Adult Division of the Welfare Department had an interest in the whereabouts of children for financial and jurisdictional reasons and as the Children's Division
had an interest because of its protective function, it was likely
that a reasonably complete reporting had taken place in these
two agencies. Catholic Charities, an agency that did not require detailed family histories before offering help, had recorded placements for 7 per cent of its applicants, and
Catholic Welfare, with a policy of minimum invasion of the
clients' privacy, had recorded placements for 15 per cent of
its applicant group, a figure higher than that for the Adult
Division of the Welfare Department. Because of these discrepancies, and because only the Children's Division, itself a

---

* There is some loss of independence in these analyses because of
the Children's Division's placement function, although an attempt was
made to separate current from past placements.

Table 20-6. PER CENT OF 947 APPLICANTS APPROACHING NINE SOCIAL AGENCIES WHO HAVE HAD CHILDREN PLACED OUTSIDE THE FAMILY

Agency	All Applicants	No. with placement			% with placement		
		Once	Multiple	Total	Once	Multiple	Total
All Applicants	947	72	28	100	7.6	3.0	10.6
Emergency							
Catholic Charities	97	6	1	7	6.2	1.0	7.2
Medical specialties							
Planned Parent-							
hood	103	6	0	6	5.8	—	5.8
Dispensary	214	9	0	9	4.2	—	4.2
Counseling							
Family Agency	54	4	3	7	7.4	5.6	13.0
Catholic Welfare	69	7	3	10	10.1	4.3	14.5
Protective control							
Welfare, adult	232	21	10	31	9.1	4.3	13.4
Welfare, children	24	9	10	19	37.5	41.7	79.2
Home Care Service	66	0	0	0	—	—	—
Social Service,							
Dispensary	88	10	1	11	11.4	1.1	12.5

placement agency, differed radically from the remainder, caution in interpreting the findings seems necessary. Nevertheless, when the populations were weighted for intake rate and compared, the group approaching Level III agencies was found, as predicted, to contain a very much greater proportion of applicants who had placed their children (Table 20-7). When the agencies themselves were used as the units of analysis, however, no significant difference emerged between those at Level II and those at Level III. This discordance may reflect a cross-cutting division of labor among agencies in which the drastic recourse of placing children was the special province of certain agencies in both levels; it also may only reflect the greater tendencies of some agencies to record this kind of information. Finally, the very fact that an agency had access to this kind of information suggested a weakness of the boundaries of the client family and a high level of control on the part of the agency. In other words, the placement of children could be viewed as an index of trouble, not only because of the disruption of the home but also because of the public notice that had been taken of the dispersion of the family when the item was entered into the agency record.

In summary, there was some evidence that the placement of children outside the home was a trouble visited upon families who had moved into the more controlling sector of the regulative system, but this evidence was somewhat weaker than it was for the other signs of family disorder; it may have reflected not so much general family breakdown among the population approaching Level III agencies as a special kind of trouble in which some agencies at both levels were specialized.

Problem Type

The degree of trouble that the client had been experiencing just prior to his application to the study agencies was reflected in the type of problem he presented. These problems were classified in Part I as transition states, or problems inherent in the life cycles of individuals and families, contingencies, or problems generated by the environment or by the nature of the human organism, and role failures, or serious problems in meeting the demands of central life roles. Tables 20-8 and 20-9 summarize the proportions of clients presenting these problems who applied to the different agencies.

Table 20-8 shows that the medical specialists were rather similar to one another in having about three-quarters of their clients complaining of contingent problems, about one-fifth of role failures, and the remainder of transitional problems. Both medical agencies differed from the two counseling agencies, which in turn were somewhat similar to one another in having a majority of clients complaining of role failure. Although every effort was made to keep the three trouble indices from influencing the problem category, it was obviously not always possible to disentangle failure in a central life role from the effects of such things as a welfare history, the placement of a child, or hospitalization for a mental disorder. In a sense, then, the label of role failure summarized the other trouble indices, and it is therefore not surprising that the populations approaching the Level III agencies were found, when they were weighted for the rate of intake, to have received significantly more clients with this label. Catholic Charities, however, had a much higher proportion of such clients than the groups approaching the other two agency levels, suggesting that the label itself may have been unwittingly influenced by an emergency character of the presenting problems.

When the agencies were considered as units, the difference between those in Level II and those in III failed to reach significance. The variance in the proportion of clients classified as role failure among the agencies at the two levels suggests that for this characteristic, as for child placement, there was an over-all division of labor between the two major levels, which resulted in a higher proportion of applicants approaching Level III complaining of these serious problems, while within each level there was a secondary division of labor such that certain agencies like the Welfare Department and the Family Agency specialized in problems of this general type but of different subcategories: economic inadequacy

Table 20-7. COMPARISON OF PROPORTIONS OF APPLICANTS WITH EPISODES OF PLACEMENT OF CHILDREN OUTSIDE THE HOME APPROACHING EIGHT AGENCIES IN LEVELS II AND III

Agency level and type	Study groups			Annual estimates		
	Total number	With placement episodes No.	With placement episodes %	Total[a] number	With placement episodes No.[b]	With placement episodes %[b]
Level II	*440*	*32*	*7.3*	*11,496*	*594*	*5.2*[b]
Planned Parenthood	103	6	5.8	708	41	5.8
Dispensary	214	9	4.2	9,720	408	4.2
Family Agency	54	7	13.0	648	84	13.0
Catholic Welfare	69	10	14.5	420	61	14.5
Level III	*410*	*61*	*14.9*	*7,716*	*1,293*	*16.8*[b]
Welfare, adult	232	31	13.4	6,108	819	13.4
Welfare, children	24	19	79.2	432	342	79.2
Home Care Service	66	0	—	120	0	—
Social Service, Dispensary	88	11	12.5	1,056	132	12.5

[a] Estimated as in Table 19-5.
[b] Expected number derived as in Table 20-2.
[c] A larger proportion of applicants to Level III than to Level II agencies were found to have had children placed outside the home when each study group were weighted according to the annual rate of application to that agency (Critical Ratio = 5.3, P < .001).

Table 20-8. PER CENT OF 947 APPLICANTS TO NINE AGENCIES WITH THREE KINDS OF PROBLEMS

| | Total | Number | | | Per cent | | |
		Transition states	Contingencies	Role failure	Transition states	Contingencies	Role failure
All applicants	**947**	**142**	**459**	**346**	**15.0**	**48.5**	**36.5**
Emergency							
Catholic charities	97	32	10	55	33.0	10.3	56.7
Medical specialty							
Planned Parenthood	103	9	75	19	8.7	72.8	18.4
Dispensary	214	6	164	44	2.8	76.6	20.6
Counseling							
Family Agency	54	14	3	37	25.9	5.6	68.5
Catholic Welfare	69	11	20	38	15.9	29.0	55.1
Protective control							
Welfare, adult	232	60	60	112	25.9	25.9	48.3
Welfare, children	24	0	5	19	—	20.8	79.2
Home Care Service	66	0	64	2	—	97.0	3.0
Social Service,							
Dispensary	88	10	58	20	11.4	65.9	22.7

Table 20-9. COMPARISON OF PROPORTION OF APPLICANTS WITH PROBLEMS CATEGORIZED AS ROLE FAILURE APPROACHING EIGHT AGENCIES IN LEVELS II AND III

Agency level and type	Study groups			Annual estimates		
	Total number	Classified role failure No.	Classified role failure %	Total[a] number	Classified role failure No.[b]	Classified role failure %
Level II	*440*	*139*	*31.6*	*11,496*	*2,815*	*24.5[c]*
Planned Parenthood	103	20	19.4	708	138	19.5
Dispensary	214	44	20.6	9,720	2,002	20.6
Family Agency	54	37	68.5	648	444	68.5
Catholic Welfare	69	38	55.1	420	231	55.0
Level III	*410*	*153*	*37.3*	*7,716*	*3,536*	*45.8[c]*
Welfare, adult	232	112	48.3	6,108	2,950	48.3
Welfare, children	24	19	79.2	432	342	79.2
Home Care Service	66	2	3.0	120	4	3.3
Social Service, Dispensary	88	20	22.7	1,056	240	22.7

[a] Estimated as in Table 19-5.
[b] Estimated as in Table 20-2.
[c] A larger proportion of applicants to Level III than to Level II agencies were presenting problems serious enough to be classed as role failures when the numbers in each study group were weighted according to the rate of applications to that agency. (Critical Ratio = 5.76, P < .001).

tending to appear at the former and marital breakdown at the latter. A review of Tables 10-3 and 12-2 suggests that this was indeed the case.

In summary, this chapter has presented evidence that there was an over-all division of labor between the protective controlling agencies at Level III and the medical and counseling agencies at Level II that resulted in their applicant groups differing. The population approaching Level III agencies included a higher proportion of members with each of a number of different kinds of troubles. The group approaching the one gatekeeper agency also appeared to include more members with serious disorders than the group applying to Level II agencies, but this finding cannot be generalized even to other emergency services, and it is extremely unlikely that the caretakers, family doctors, and clergymen were seeing populations with anything like this amount of trouble. Within this over-all division of labor, there was evidence that a secondary specialization was occurring: while welfare assistance and mental hospitalization were troubles that were clearly more common among the clients of Level III agencies, there was some evidence that troubles like the placement of children and the presentation to the agency of problems of serious role failure, although occurring more frequently among the groups approaching Level III, were also characteristic of applicants to some of the agencies in Level II.

In the next chapter, a "trouble score" will be developed from the three indices of trouble reported above, and the question of what kinds of treatment clients with different degrees of trouble were receiving at the two agency levels will be examined in order to throw further light on the division of labor between the agencies at the two levels.

REFERENCES

Dohrenwend, Bruce P., and Barbara S. Dohrenwend, 1965. "The Problem of Validity in Field Studies of Psychiatric Disorder," *Journal of Abnormal Psychology*, Vol. 70, No. 1, February.

McCaffrey, Isabel, Elaine Cumming, and Claire Rudolph, 1963. "Mental Disorders in Socially Defined Populations," *American Journal of Public Health*, Vol. 53, No. 7, July.

THE OUTCOME

21

This chapter summarizes the information in Chapter 20 by using a score that combines the three indices of trouble and examines the kinds of services given to clients in the light of their trouble scores.

Summary of Troubles

A trouble score of from 0 to 3 was assigned to each client by giving one point for each of the characteristics examined in Chapter 20: having a welfare history, having had a hospitalization of himself or a family member for a mental disorder, and having had children placed outside the home. The

72

classification of the client's presenting problem as a failure in a central life role was not included in the score because it had been assigned on the basis of a subjective judgment and did not often reflect a single concrete event. Table 22-1 shows the relationship between the trouble score and the three problem types. Although a higher proportion of the clients with the label role failure had trouble scores of 2 and 3 than would have been expected by chance, the relationship was not as close as might have been expected if the two methods of summarizing the clients' problems had been tapping the same areas of trouble. This discrepancy probably arises because the trouble score, by definition, reflected the *content* of the clients' predicaments and the problem type reflected a judgment about the seriousness of the problems and possibly their acuteness or chronicity.

When the trouble scores of the study groups approaching the different agencies were calculated (Table 21-2), there was considerable variation among the agencies. The two medical specialties differed strikingly, with the Dispensary seeing a much larger proportion of troubled clients than Planned Parenthood, although the difference may be exaggerated by under-reporting of welfare histories among Planned Parenthood patients. Between the two counseling agencies, there was a parallel difference with Catholic Welfare seeing a larger proportion of troubled clients than the Family Agency. Both of these differences were statistically significant. The protective controlling agencies were equally variable, ranging from the Children's Division with 71 per cent of its clients having a trouble score of 2 or 3 to the Home Care Service where only 8 per cent had such a high score. Even allowing for possible under-reporting of welfare histories in the latter agency, this is a very large difference.

Among the clients approaching Catholic Charities, the one gatekeeper agency, 16.5 per cent had a high trouble score; this figure was higher than the weighted proportion of 13.4 per cent of high scores for all of the agencies at Level II, but lower than the 27.5 per cent for those at Level III (Table 21-3). As had been predicted, a larger proportion of the group approaching Level III had high trouble scores than

Table 21-1. RELATIONSHIP BETWEEN PROBLEM TYPES AND TROUBLE
SCORES OF 947 CLIENTS APPLYING TO NINE AGENCIES

Problem Type	Total	No.					Trouble score %			
		0	*1*	*2*	*3*		*0*	*1*	*2*	*3*
All applicants	*947*	307	458	144	38		32.4	48.4	15.2	4.0
Transition states	*142*	61	63	14	4		43.0	44.4	9.9	2.8
Contingencies	*458*	158	230	60	10		34.5	50.2	13.1	2.2
Role failure	*347*	88	165	70	24		25.4	47.6	20.2	6.9

Proportionately more clients with problems serious enough to be classed as role failures than clients in the other two categories had scores of 2 or
3. ($\chi^2 = 21.1$, d.f. = 1, P $<$ .001.)

Table 21-2. TROUBLE SCORES OF 947 APPLICANTS TO NINE AGENCIES

Agency Type	Total	No.				%			
		0	1	2	3	0	1	2	3
Total	947	307	458	144	38	32.4	48.4	15.2	4.0
Gatekeeper									
Catholic Charities	97	36	45	11	5	37.1	46.4	11.3	5.2
Medical specialist									
Planned Parenthood	103[a]	71	25	7	0	68.9	24.3	6.8	0
Dispensary	214[a]	50	135	25	4	23.4	63.1	11.7	1.9
Diffuse counsel									
Family Agency	54[b]	35	13	4	2	64.8	24.1	7.4	3.7
Catholic Welfare	69[b]	27	25	13	4	39.1	36.2	18.8	5.8
Protective control									
Welfare, adult	232	46	131	43	12	19.8	56.5	18.5	5.2
Welfare, children	24	1	6	9	8	4.2	25.0	37.5	33.3
Home Care Service	66	27	34	5	0	40.9	51.5	7.6	0.0
Social Service,									
Dispensary	88	14	44	27	3	15.9	50.0	30.7	3.4

[a] A greater proportion of Planned Parenthood than Dispensary clients had a trouble score of 0. ($\chi^2 = 60.6$, d.f. = 2, P < .001.)

[b] A greater proportion of Family Agency than Catholic Welfare clients had trouble scores of 0. ($\chi^2 = 6.99$, d.f. = 1, .02 > P > .01.)

Table 21-3. COMPARISON OF PROPORTION OF APPLICANTS APPROACHING EIGHT AGENCIES AT LEVELS II AND III WHO HAD HIGH (2 OR 3) TROUBLE SCORES

Agency Level	Study group			Annual estimates		
	Total number	Trouble scores 2 and 3 No.	Trouble scores 2 and 3 %	Total[a] number	Trouble scores 2 and 3 No.[b]	Trouble scores 2 and 3 %
Level II	**440**	**59**	*13.4*	**11,496**	*1545.2*	*13.4*[c]
Planned Parenthood	*103*	7	6.8	708	48.1	6.8
Dispensary	*214*	29	13.6	9,720	1321.9	13.6
Family Agency	*54*	6	11.1	648	71.9	11.1
Catholic Welfare	*69*	17	24.6	420	103.3	24.6
Level III	**410**	**107**	*26.1*	**7,716**	*2122.7*	*27.5*[c]
Welfare, adult	*232*	55	23.7	6,108	1447.6	23.7
Welfare, children	*24*	17	70.8	432	305.9	70.8
Home Care Service	*66*	5	7.6	120	9.1	7.6
Social Service, Dispensary	*88*	30	34.1	1,056	360.1	34.1

[a] Estimated as in Table 19-5.
[b] Estimated as in Table 20-2.
[c] A larger proportion of applicants to Level III than to Level II agencies had Trouble Scores of 2 or 3 when the number in each study group were weighted according to the rate of application to that agency. (Critical Ratio = 5.2, P <.001.)

Twelve of the sixteen possible comparisons of the agencies at the two levels showed those at Level III to have a higher proportion of applicants with trouble scores of 2 and 3. (Sign Test, one-tailed, P = .05.)

of the group approaching Level II, and the difference was statistically significant. When each of the four agencies in Level II was compared with each of the four in Level III, those in Level II were found to have a lower proportion of clients with high trouble scores, and this difference also was statistically significant.

In summary, the agencies differed among themselves in the proportion of their applicants who had two or more indices of trouble, and therefore, in a sense, specializing in the population from which they drew; at the same time, there was an over-all specialization between the two levels in which the protective controlling agencies at Level III receive a larger proportion of clients with multiple troubles than those at Level II.

The Problem of Independence

Before the interagency comparisons of populations reported in this Part were made, multiple applications by the same person were removed from the study groups, but certain other kinds of duplications remained. First, the same clients sometimes appeared in more than one agency; second, different members of the same family sometimes appeared in the same agency; and third, members of the same family sometimes appeared in different agencies. In all, 55 families making 114 of the 1010 applications to the ten agencies, or 11.3 per cent of the study group, were in one of these three categories.

These duplications and redundancies were not removed because the system itself was the focus of study, and families making multiple applications gave it an essential part of its character. Furthermore, in any comparison between two individual agencies, these overlapping cases would be expected to lessen the differences so that the results reported would be on the conservative side. On the other hand, if multiple applications had tended to be *within* agency levels, the differences *between* levels would have been exaggerated, but as two-thirds of the 114 related applications were made to agencies at different levels, this did not appear to be a problem.

Specifically, 16 of the 114 clients applied only to Level II agencies, 24 only to Level III agencies, 2 only to Level I, and the remaining 72 to agencies at different levels. In view of this distribution of the multiple applications, it does not seem likely that any loss of independence they represented was affecting the differences reported.

Services Given

In the chapters of Part I, analyses of the services given to patients showed considerable variability, with counseling agencies being, by and large, the most selective in giving their core service, protective controlling agencies less so, and the medical agencies least of all. Table 21-4 summarizes these findings and shows the medical specialties to be much alike in serving almost everyone, the counselors similar to one another in serving between one-half and two-thirds of their clients, and three of the protective controlling agencies giving service to almost all applicants, while the fourth, the Welfare Department, served only 58 per cent of its applicants.

When the populations approaching Levels II and III were weighted to reflect intake, the Level II agencies were found to be giving their core services to proportionately more of the group approaching them than were those at Level III (Table 21-5). Although this difference between the two populations was highly significant, the agencies in the two groups did not differ from one another when the 16 comparisons of individual agencies were made. In other words, because of the different rates of flow through the various agencies, although a larger proportion of the stream approaching Level III agencies was refused service, a comparison of the practices of individual agencies did not show a statistically significant difference. This discrepancy highlights the difference in the populations approaching the two levels and at the same time draws attention to the wide range of admissions criteria within each level; thus, the very busy Adult Division of the Welfare Department, which served only 58 per cent of its clients, overwhelmed the three small controlling agencies, which served all of their small flow of clients. By the same token,

Table 21-4. PROPORTION OF 947 APPLICANTS SERVED BY NINE SELECTED AGENCIES

Agency Type	All applicants	No.				Service given %			
		Served and referred	Served	Referred	Not served	Served and referred	Served	Referred	Not served
Total	947	115	627	89	116	12.1	66.2	9.4	12.2
Gatekeeper									
Catholic Charities	97	22	28	35	12	22.7	28.9	36.1	12.4
Medical Specialist									
Planned Parenthood	103	2	101	0	0	2.0	98.0	0	0
Dispensary	214	25	181	6	2	11.7	84.6	2.8	0.9
Diffuse counsel									
Family Agency	54	6	27	11	10	11.1	50.0	20.4	18.5
Catholic Welfare	69	9	29	20	11	13.0	42.0	28.9	15.9
Protective control									
Welfare, adult	232	12	123	17	80	5.2	53.0	7.3	34.5
Welfare, children	24	0	24	0	0	0	100.0	0	0
Home Care Service	66	11	54	0	1	16.7	81.8	0	1.5
Social Service, Dispensary	88	28	60	0	0	31.8	68.2	0	0

Table 21-5. COMPARISON OF PROPORTION OF APPLICANTS APPROACHING EIGHT AGENCIES AT LEVELS II AND III WHO RECEIVED THE CORE SERVICE OF THOSE AGENCIES

Agency Level	Study groups			Annual estimates		
	Total number	Received core service No.	%	Total[a] number	Received core service No.[b]	%
Level II	*440*	*380*	*86.4*	*11,496*	*10695.7*	*93.0*[c]
Planned Parenthood	103	103	100.0	708	708.0	100.0
Dispensary	214	206	96.3	9,720	9360.4	96.3
Family Agency	54	33	61.1	648	395.9	61.1
Catholic Welfare	69	38	55.1	420	231.4	55.1
Level III	*410*	*312*	*76.1*	*7,716*	*5161.1*	*66.9*[c]
Welfare, adult	232	135	58.2	6,108	3554.9	58.2
Welfare, children	24	24	100.0	432	432.0	100.0
Home Care Service	66	65	98.5	120	118.2	98.5
Social Service, Dispensary	88	88	100.0	1,056	1056.0	100.0

[a] Estimated as in Table 19-5.
[b] Estimated as in Table 20-2.
[c] A smaller proportion of applicants to Level III than to Level II received the core service of the agencies in that level, when the numbers were weighted according to the rate of intake into the agency. (Critical Ratio = 9.3, $P < .001$.)

the Dispensary's high rate of service colored Level II even though that level contained the two more selective counseling services.

In general, these findings suggest that client behavior was more uniform for the characteristics studied here than agency behavior; that is, the more vulnerable and troubled the client, the more likely he was to appear at a Level III agency, but within each level, agency response to the client was variable.

When the services given to the clients were examined, no agency was found to reject a surplus of clients with high trouble scores (Table 21-6). In Table 21-7 the agencies are seen grouped together and the finding that trouble score is unrelated to service given is dramatized. In other words, even though more clients with multiple troubles approached Level III agencies, and even though a greater proportion of clients were refused in Level III, this refusal was unrelated to the trouble score.

Referrals

Slightly more than 20 per cent of all of the clients in the study groups were referred to other agencies (Table 21-4). The one gatekeeper agency, Catholic Charities, not unexpectedly made the highest proportion of referrals, directing 59 per cent of its clients to other services; Catholic Welfare referred 42 per cent of its clients, and the Dispensary's Social Service Department and the Family Agency each referred 32 per cent. No other agency referred as many as 20 per cent of its clients. In every agency, referrals, like core services, were given independently of trouble scores (Table 21-6). This finding appears to conflict with those reported in Parts I and II on the screening and allocating activities of some agencies, especially those specializing in counseling services. Apparently any screening of clients for desirability was unrelated to the presence of problems reflected by the trouble score. A review of the studies in Part I shows that only three agencies appeared to be selecting clients according to the type of problem presented at application. In the Family Agency, one spe-

Table 21-6. PROPORTION OF 182 CLIENTS WITH A TROUBLE SCORE OF 2 OR 3
WHO RECEIVED SERVICE OR REFERRAL FROM NINE AGENCIES

Agency Type	All clients	Total with score 2–3	No.				%			
			Served and Re-ferred	Served	Re-ferred	Not served	Served and Re-ferred	Served	Re-ferred	Not served
Total	**947**	**182**	**27**	**114**	**19**	**22**	**14.8**	**62.6**	**10.4**	**12.1**
Gatekeeper										
Catholic Charities	97	16	2	6	6	2	12.5	37.5	37.5	12.5
Medical specialist										
Planned Parenthood	103	7	0	7	0	0	0	100.0	0	0
Dispensary	214	29	6	23	0	0	20.7	79.3	0	0
Diffuse counsel										
Family Agency	54	6	1	2	3	0	16.7	33.3	50.0	0
Catholic Welfare	69	17	5	5	4	3	29.4	29.4	23.5	17.7
Protective control										
Welfare, adult	232	55	3	29	6	17	5.5	52.7	10.9	30.9
Welfare, children	24	17	0	17	0	0	0.0	100.0	0	0
Home Care Service	66	5	0	5	0	0	0.0	100.0	0	0
Social Service, Dispensary	88	30	10	20	0	0	33.3	66.7	0	0

Table 21-7. OUTCOME OF 947 APPLICATIONS FOR SERVICE AT NINE AGENCIES BY TROUBLE SCORE

| | | Trouble score | | | | | | | |
| | | No. | | | | % | | | |
Outcome	Total	*0*	*1*	*2*	*3*	*0*	*1*	*2*	*3*
All clients	*947*	*307*	*458*	*144*	*38*	*32.4*	*48.4*	*15.2*	*4.0*
Served and referred	114	32	55	23	4	28.1	48.2	20.2	3.5
Served only	628	214	300	90	24	34.1	47.8	14.3	3.8
Referred only	90	27	44	14	5	30.0	48.9	15.6	5.6
Not served	115	34	59	17	5	29.6	51.3	14.8	4.3

cial group of clients, those with transitional problems, had a small but significant advantage over those in the other two categories insofar as either receiving counseling or having arrangements made for them was concerned (see Table 10-4) ; in the Dispensary's Social Service, the client group complaining of transitional problems had a similar advantage (see Table 11-3), and in one of the two psychiatric clinics there was evidence that a larger proportion of patients whose illnesses reflected failure in central life roles was kept in care (Table 7-4).

In view of all these findings it might be concluded that agencies were selecting clients on the basis of the style of their problems, or perhaps on the basis of whether or not they were chronic, rather than on their actual content. In other words, a client who was temporarily unemployed and hence receiving welfare assistance would have a better chance of being counseled than one whose economic career showed a long pattern of failure, and a client who was in sudden acute conflict with her husband would have a better chance of being served than one who had already deserted her husband and children.

A preference for serving the transitional problems may rest on the fact that, by definition, there are crises that are more or less bound to get better by themselves, and it may be that the agencies selecting them for treatment valued successful outcomes above all, although other goals, such as serving the relevant population or inventing new skills for refractory disorders, were open to them.

As the agencies showing selective practices offered casework services, there is a possibility that the moment in time at which the data were collected, which could perhaps be called the end of the Freudian ascendancy, coupled with the particular nature of casework, accounted for this pattern of referral.

When weighted referral rates from the populations approaching Levels II and III were compared (Table 21-9), no difference between the proportions referred was found. When the agencies themselves were compared, they were found not to differ in the proportion of clients referred. In other words,

Table 21-8. PROPORTION OF 947 CLIENTS FROM NINE AGENCIES WHO WERE REFERRED TO OTHER AGENCIES, BY TROUBLE SCORE

Agency Type	All applicants					Referred to another agency				
	Total	No. (Trouble score)		% (Trouble score)		Total	No. (Trouble score)		% (Trouble score)	
		0–1	2–3	0–1	2–3		0–1	2–3	0–1	2–3
Total	947	765	182	80.8	19.2	204	158	46	77.5	22.5
Gatekeeper										
Catholic Charities	97	81	16	83.5	16.5	57	49	8	86.0	14.0
Medical specialist										
Planned Parenthood	103	96	7	93.2	6.8	2	2	0	100.0	0.0
Dispensary	214	185	29	86.4	13.6	31	25	6	80.6	19.4
Diffuse counsel										
Family Agency	54	48	6	88.9	11.1	17	13	4	76.5	23.5
Catholic Welfare	69	52	17	75.4	24.6	29	20	9	69.0	31.0
Protective control										
Welfare, adult	232	177	55	76.3	23.7	29	20	9	69.0	31.0
Welfare, children	24	7	17	29.2	70.8	0	0	0	0	0
Home Care Service	66	61	5	92.4	7.6	11	11	0	100.0	0
Social Service, Dispensary	88	58	30	65.9	34.1	28	18	10	64.3	35.7

Table 21-9. COMPARISON OF PROPORTION OF APPLICANTS APPROACHING EIGHT AGENCIES AT LEVELS II AND III WHO WERE REFERRED TO OTHER AGENCIES

Agency level	Study groups			Annual estimates		
	Total Number	Referred out No.	%	Total[a] Number	Referred out No.[b]	%
Level II	**440**	*79*	*18.0*	*11,496*	*1803.4*	*15.7*[c]
Planned Parenthood	103	2	1.9	708	13.5	1.9
Dispensary	214	31	14.5	9,720	1409.4	14.5
Family Agency	54	17	31.5	648	204.1	31.5
Catholic Welfare	69	29	42.0	420	176.4	42.0
Level III	**410**	*68*	*16.6*	*7,716*	*1119.3*	*14.5*[c]
Welfare, adult	232	29	12.5	6,108	763.5	12.5
Welfare, children	24	0	0.0	432	0.0	0.0
Home Care Service	66	11	16.7	120	20.0	16.7
Social Service, Dispensary	88	28	31.8	1,056	335.8	31.8

[a] Estimated as in Table 19-5.
[b] Estimated as in Table 20-2.
[c] There was no difference in the proportion of applicants referred from the two agency levels. (Critical Ratio = 0.4.)

the *direction* and *absolute size* of client flow reported in Part II appeared to be unrelated to the proportion of clients referred. The agencies at Levels II and III were perhaps directing broad streams of clients out from their services to other parts of the regulative system for reasons connected with their own workings as agencies and not because of the characteristics of the clients themselves.

Summary

This chapter has described the tendencies of clients who have had more than one serious trouble to approach the agencies in the protective controlling group and for those who have had fewer troubles to seek out the counseling and medical specialties. Whether this would still have been the case if specific counseling agencies, such as lawyers, had been represented in Level II, and if controlling agencies whose functions were to protect society rather than the client, such as prisons, had been represented in Level III, cannot be guessed at because of the preliminary quality of these studies. Nevertheless, as the grouping of the agencies was based on logical as well as empirical distinctions, it seems reasonable to predict that the inclusion of the missing types of agencies in future studies would not completely obscure the pattern.

In all, the amount and direction of client flow reported in this chapter seemed to be more related to the type of agency than to the type of client selected for referral. All these findings lead to the tentative conclusion that referral is a property of agencies rather than of clients and can be better understood in terms of social systems rather than in terms of client characteristics.

PLUS ÇA CHANGE ?   22

Although these studies were intended to produce baseline information about the regulative system, some of the findings
may reflect peculiarities of the moment rather than any
fundamental characteristics of a modern industrial society
busy at the work of regulating and integrating its citizens.
(See Appendix A for a concrete example of change in agency
practice.) In the five years between the collection of the data
and the writing of the report there were a number of specific changes of practice, among which a tendency toward a
new pattern of delivery of services could be discerned. In this
chapter, changes that have taken place will be noted first,
then potential changes will be suggested, and, finally, predic-

tions will be made about which elements in the system can be expected to remain stable.

Specific Changes in the System

No evidence was available about changes in the general practice of medicine in the Syracuse area during the five-year period, but presumably it was following the national pattern, moving inexorably away from neighborhoods and toward group practices and higher levels of specialization. At the same time, there was the beginning of a tendency for publicly supported medical care to be located physically closer to its patient groups. The Dispensary, for example, had begun to experiment with the delivery of health care in small decentralized units in central city neighborhoods in an attempt to remove those discomforts, such as long waiting periods, that were believed to have been preventing patients from making the best use of its service. It was also hoped that decentralization would provide the clinic doctors with a closer knowledge of the lives of their patients so that their nonmedical recommendations might be more relevant.

The Planned Parenthood Center had made a parallel move toward its client group by opening a branch clinic in a neighborhood church to attract women who might not have been willing or able to travel to the parent agency; it had also started a research clinic in collaboration with the County Health Department. A recent merger of the City and County Health Departments had, in itself, added impetus to these changes in the delivery of health care.

The Home Care Nursing Program had been able to arrange private medical care for its patients through the important Medicare and Medicaid* programs, both inaugurated during the period. (These new programs were not, in general, an unmitigated blessing; they required much paper work, such as eligibility checking and the reporting of the exact services given, and, because of a concurrent thrust toward profession-

---

* The New York State program of medical aid to families with moderate incomes.

alization, most of it had to be carried out by nurses and social workers. In some cases, this use of professional time inevitably worked to the detriment of the service itself.)

One of the two psychiatric clinics had responded to changes in the goals of psychiatry by moving toward more comprehensive care, incorporating its clinic as the outpatient service of a comprehensive community mental health program operating out of a general hospital.

Nothing is known about changes in the counseling practices of clergymen, or whether their increased involvement in social problems, particularly the civil rights movement, was influencing their relationships with their clients.

Neither of the counseling agencies appeared to have modified their over-all practices during the five-year span, although there was evidence in the social work literature that an interest in serving clients who needed something different from counseling was beginning to emerge.

Shortly before this report was written, the Welfare Department was surveyed by a citizens' committee with the help of expert consultation, and—although its report was primarily concerned with administrative reforms—it did emphasize the need for dispelling from the public mind persistent myths, such as that welfare recipients, for instance, were unwilling to work. The report also interpreted the continued high welfare expenditure by the County as one of the costs of modern industrial life. Following the recommendations of this report, the Welfare Department started to plan for decentralization of its services to various city neighborhoods. Because the Welfare Department, together with the Dispensary, accounted for such a large proportion of client flow, these beginnings of a change toward delivering services nearer to the clients' homes seemed doubly significant; how far this change would eventually be carried, it was impossible to know.

General Changes

There appeared to have been three general changes taking place between the data collection and this final report. First, the particular changes made in the various agencies during the time period could be seen as falling into a pattern of reform, not so much the content of services as the method of their delivery. Concern for the client's view of the service, for his willingness to approach it, and for its relevance to the rest of his life seemed to be growing. Such moves as decentralization of service were intended not only to increase efficiency but also to humanize and civilize services that at times had seemed to treat the client as a chance recipient of a process that existed for quite different reasons. Such a trend must be viewed cautiously, however, because the public temper toward care for society's less competent members has tended in the past to be cyclical, swinging between what Russell (1945) has called disciplinarian and libertarian poles. Whether this was to be a real trend at all, let alone a long-term libertarian one, was in doubt at the time of writing.

A second apparent change was a move both toward and away from local control of local services. Various federal agencies were pouring money into the area during the time period studied, and, although care had been taken to leave local groups nominally in control in most cases, there seemed little question that the balance of control had been tipping toward the federal government.

The temporary effects of these shifts in the source of money were proliferation of the system, with many new services springing up, disequilibrium between the parts of the system, and a loss of domain consensus that led to a number of acrimonious debates. These changes led to a study carried out by the United Council that went so far as to recommend formation of a "super-agency" to coordinate the increasingly complex network of agencies into a coherent system. This marked change in stated policy had not been acted on at the time of writing, but it did reflect a recognition of the breakdown of old patterns and the need for new methods for keeping the system from chaos.

A third change that marked the interim period was the recognition by a number of agencies that the client himself should have some voice in the manner in which he was being served. Because the terms of some of the federal grants the community was receiving required it, there had been a move to include representatives of the client groups on some agency boards, and the United Council had itself set up a committee that included client members. How permanent this pattern would be was problematical at the time of writing because of the complexity of the issues involved, but it was another indication of a trend toward the humanizing of services.

In summary, there seemed to be a movement of the agent toward the client and a civilizing trend in the delivery of services at the same time that the fundamental structure of the consensually operated system appeared to be about to undergo revision. A more centralized bureaucratic structure seemed to be developing, at least in the minds of some of the member agencies. Once again, it was difficult to say how far these ideas would be translated into action.

Chances of Change

INDIVIDUAL AGENCY PRACTICES

The unique characteristics of the individual agencies described in Part I were obviously the most liable to change, and some of the changes that took place after the studies were completed have been described above. If there was indeed an over-all liberalizing and civilizing change in process, the balance between support and control could be expected to shift in some of the more controlling agencies, although others, like the Children's Division of the Welfare Department, might be expected to be little affected.

LOCUS OF THE INTEGRATING AND ALLOCATING FUNCTIONS

The shift of financial control away from local agencies and the increase in the number of services, both of which had already led to a proposal for a superordinate coordinating structure, would inevitably, if continued, lead to a shift in the allocating and integrating function: away from domain consensus alone and toward a permanent centralized structure.

In a sense, such a change was inevitable; consensus must be built by each member of the system in interaction with all the others, and the size of the system alone was beginning to make this impossible. In other words, a traditional, consensual method was giving way to the more rational planning techniques supposedly characteristic of industry and government. This is not to imply that a system can run without consensus about some things at all levels and about many things at some levels, but rather that large systems with complicated divisions of labor cannot run on consensus alone.

AGENCY INTENTION AND CLIENT ACTION

The discrepancies between the numbers of agency referrals and the corresponding numbers of clients' applications at target agencies that were reported in Chapter 17 would be expected to be reduced as the system moved toward a more rational allocating process, and especially if a simultaneous liberalizing change allowed clients more voice in their own destinies. There is no reason why, if each agency gave sufficient energy to understanding the client's intentions, an efficient allocating system could not ensure a much better fit.

GRADIENT OF CLIENT CIRCULATION

The relative isolation of the more controlling agencies from interaction with the rest of the system, described in Chapters 16-18, would have to be slowly modified if a more humane viewpoint toward the most deviant clients became prevalent, and if both client and the agent came into everyday contact with other agencies, particularly medical services. Some Supreme Court decisions of the mid-1960's, such as those finding it illegal to hold certain mentally ill patients in custody against their will and those ensuring that arrested citizens be told of their rights, were pointing to the possibility that the more controlling agencies would be forced into more open policies. Such decisions were themselves, however, a reflection of a change in public mood, and once again, it is difficult to say how persistent that change will be.

Stable Patterns

DIVISION OF LABOR BETWEEN AGENCY LEVELS

Even though the mechanisms of integration of the system seemed to be on the verge of change, the division of labor between the agency levels, which was the major finding of these studies, could be expected to remain. The following is a brief review of these findings with some of the reasons for thinking that they were among the more stable features of the regulative system.

Level I agencies were found to accept clients directly into service without a referral and then either to serve them or to refer them to other agencies. It is not foreseeable that this process can change much because any system must provide conditions for entrance, and some agency must stand at the threshold of the regulative system, linking it to the informal networks of everyday life. Furthermore, the self-selection of caretaking agents by clients, especially those who pay for their services, is part of the fabric of freedom as it is understood in modern American life.

Level II agencies were found to accept clients with moderate amounts of trouble from both Levels I and III and to offer almost all of them a supportive service or a referral to a Level III service. The services within Level II varied from specialized medical care to diffuse counseling of the whole man, but referral among the member agencies was not common. It was concluded that the clients of these agencies were still sufficiently within the network of everyday social control to be able to exercise choices as to whom they would approach for support, and, by the same token, some of them could be refused service or diverted elsewhere by the agency they themselves chose.

Level III agencies received the most disordered clients and exercised the highest level of control over them; their clients had the least choice about who should serve them, and ironically they were less likely to be served than those approaching Level II. Most referrals from Level III were back to Level II, although a small fraction were returned to the gatekeeper agents. Few referrals were made within the level.

It seems unlikely that changes in the administrative arrangements within the regulative system would make much difference to the over-all division of labor, although it might alter the proportion of clients served and referred. It was argued in Chapter 1 that offering both support and control is difficult, and for this reason agents will perhaps continue to specialize in one or the other style of service. At the same time, there will always be a gradient of problems running from mild transitional troubles that do not seriously impede the individual or disrupt his society and for which treatment is totally elective, to the severe, threatening deviations that must, for society's sake if not the client's, be brought under control. For both of these reasons, the tendency to specialize along the support-control axis will probably continue, even though the actual content of care may change.* Whether or not it would be desirable to break up this pattern is a different question from whether or not it is likely to persist, and one that is not asked here.

In contrast to the division of labor between agency levels, that within each level depended not upon the level of control exerted or upon the type of client served but upon the content of the agent's training and skill. That the distinction between a doctor and a lawyer should disappear is, of course, unthinkable, but it is questionable whether several family agencies offering similar services under different religious auspices would persist in a less traditional and more rational system.

INTEGRATIVE MEASURES

It was observed that agents tended to exchange information with others like themselves but to make arrangements for

---

* The newly created comprehensive community mental health centers were an example of a service intended to care for everyone from the most mildly to the most seriously affected, but there was evidence that "everyone" might still exclude the most refractory chronically ill patients (Cumming, 1967).

clients with others unlike themselves. In any society the similar elements, which are potentially competitive and redun-
dant, must integrate themselves in a different way from that
used by dissimilar elements, which are potentially complementary. These two types of integration are part of the solidarity of social life (Durkheim, 1964) and can be expected to
persist.

SITUATIONAL DETERMINANTS OF ACTION

The suggestion made in Part III that agency behavior
seemed more related to the structural character of the whole
regulative system than to the kinds of clients speaks of a tension between individual aspirations and social constraints that
pervades all group life, whether the individuals are single
human beings or corporate entities like social agencies, and
partly accounts for the discrepancy between agency intention
and client action. Concretely, any agency must deal with
those who approach it, but at the same time its members
must adhere to their own values and norms about the humane
treatment of illness and deviance, practice their chosen skills,
satisfy the administrative demands of their superiors, and
maintain a consensus with other agents about what each
should be doing. In such a field of forces, it would not be
surprising if both agent and client were ultimately moved by
considerations other than those arising immediately from the
client's own individual requirements. The discrepancy between the system's demands and the client's requirements
was seen at its most obvious in the Department of Social Welfare where the demands made on the agency by other agents
in the system and by the taxpaying public combined with the
general cultural devaluation of "dependency" to produce a
service in which the client's own situation was clearly of
secondary interest to the structural and legalistic considerations of eligibility.

Elimination of all tension between the individual and the
group can never be expected, but a greater understanding of
the relative weight of agency policy and agency environment
in determining agency action might make for a more rational
planning of the concerns of the whole system.

NORM CREATION

The inference that norms were being developed in those parts of the system where client flow was heaviest—that is, in interaction among the Dispensary, the Welfare Department and the police contains predictions for both stability and change. For example, if social insurance coverage were to increase to the level already reached by most Western European countries, fewer people would have to make personal application for assistance, and many of the eligibility procedures that brought the Welfare Department and the Dispensary into contact with others would subside, and with them the values and sentiments peculiar to the Welfare Department. Services will always have to be integrated around the ill and the old, however, and deviant behavior will always have to be controlled. For this reason, medical and correctional agencies might be expected to have a proportionately greater weight in norm formation in the future. The norms of the policeman, however, seemed unlikely to permeate this type of system because their messenger role gives them more opportunity to learn the norms of others than to teach their own. It is proposed, therefore, that the values, norms, and ideologies of those who provide health services to large numbers of people will tend to permeate the regulative systems of the future even more than they have done in the past, and that this may increase the tendency to look upon all deviance as illness, a process which, although humanizing, is itself not immune from abuse (Szasz, 1963).

Conclusion

This report has described part of one regulative system in one city. It has proposed that certain of the systematic patterns described were inherent features of an advanced division of labor. Other findings have been more ephemeral, but they have recorded a phase in the development of the regulative function in American society in the first half of the twentieth century.

REFERENCES

Cumming, Elaine, 1968. "Community Psychiatry in a Divided Labor" in Joseph Zubin, ed., *Social Psychiatry,* New York, Grune & Stratton.

Durkheim, Emil, 1964. *The Division of Labor in Society,* New York, The Free Press.

Russell, Bertrand, 1945. *A History of Western Philosophy,* New York, Simon and Schuster.

Szasz, Thomas, 1963. *Law, Liberty and Psychiatry,* New York, Macmillan.

APPENDIX A

SOURCES OF ERROR:
STABILITY VERSUS CHANGE

One of the research questions behind the analyses reported here was, "If time were stopped, who would be in contact with whom, about what?" Because this question assumed synchronized data while the data for these studies were collected over a period of months, the comparability must be dealt with.*

Mary Newell, Mary Lou Wilkins, and Patricia Healy collected the retrospective data for this appendix.

* Most of the data were collected in the summer and fall of 1961 and the winter of 1961–62, but in a few cases data from 1960 and 1963 were added, and psychiatric clinic data from as late as 1964 were used.

Over long periods of time referral patterns have been shown to change markedly. Krauwell (1966), for example, has shown that in Holland during the economic depression of the 1930's, half of all alcoholics entering clinics were referred by Welfare Departments while none were sent by employers; in the 1960's, a period of labor shortage, employers tried to persuade workers to enter treatment, and referrals from this source reached 10 per cent while referrals from Welfare Departments fell to 2 per cent.

During the studies reported here, employment conditions did not vary greatly, and changes in the system itself, which were reviewed briefly in Chapter 22, were only beginning to take place. To get some estimate of the order of error introduced by using our data as if they had been collected simultaneously, the activities of two agencies, one of which had experienced marked changes and the other of which had not, were compared at different time intervals. The first, the Family Agency, had undergone changes of policy and staff in the years prior to the study, while the second, the Planned Parenthood Center, had experienced a relatively straight-line career.

Background: Policy Changes and Growth Rates

According to staff members who had had a long association with the Family Agency, it had undergone a period of decline, followed by a rebirth just prior to the study period. In 1956, the agency had been in turmoil and many workers had resigned; by 1958, there were only a handful left. In 1959, a new, energetic director was appointed, and the agency began to expand again; by 1961, it was reaching a new peak of activity.

A retrospective group of applications were collected from the files for the year 1956, when the agency was declining, for comparison with the study year, 1961, when it was expanding. Between the two study periods, the new director had been emphasizing the need for increased professionalization and specialization, and the agency had expanded its casework services and reduced its adoption and placement services.

In a contrasting career, the Syracuse Planned Parenthood Center had maintained a steady course throughout the period. It was impractical to go back to 1956 in this agency, however, because of the way in which the records were kept; therefore, study groups from 1959, 1962, and 1965 were compared.

Table A-1. COMPARISON OF NUMBERS OF APPLICATIONS AT GENERAL INTAKE PER MONTH IN THE STUDY PERIODS TO THE FAMILY AGENCY AND TO THE SYRACUSE PLANNED PARENTHOOD CENTER

Family Agency	Cases per month	% increase
1956	18.2	
1961	45.0[a]	147.3
Planned Parenthood Center		
1959	48.9	
1962	61.2	25.2
1965	74.0	20.9

[a] Excluding unwed mothers who were included under general adult intake in 1961, but not in 1956, and excluding one 1961 "walk-in" client about whom no record was kept.

Table A-1 compares the average numbers of clients and patients recorded as applying each month to the two agencies during the study years. The sharp increase in the number of applicants to the Family Agency reflected its upturn in staff. Over the five-year period, the average annual increase was 30 per cent, while the average annual increase of applicants to the Planned Parenthood Center over the six-year period was only 9 per cent.

Referral Source

If the rest of the regulative system knew of the Family Agency's fluctuations of fortune, their referrals did not reflect this knowledge. As Table A-2 shows, there were no statistically significant differences in the referral rate to the agency from any other single agency or category of agencies. The Planned Parenthood Center experienced a similarly stable pattern of referrals except that in 1965 there was a reduction in referrals from hospital social services, reflecting a change in one Syracuse hospital where an active social service department was closed down.

Table A-2. REFERRAL SOURCE OF PATIENTS AND CLIENTS AT DIFFERENT TIMES, FAMILY AGENCY AND SYRACUSE PLANNED PARENTHOOD CENTER

Referral source	Family Agency		Planned Parenthood		
	1956	1961	1959	1962	1965
All clients and patients	77	45	103	103	103
Without agency referral	36	18	54	55	67
With agency referral	41	27	49	48	36
All referrals	41	28	54	53	37
Medical					
Private physician	5	9	9	10	15
Dispensary			1	1	1
All other clinics			5	3	5
Hospital doctors and nurses			9	3	3
Public health nurses			3	2	1
Planned Parenthood	2		3	6	4
Psychiatric facilities	3	1	1		
Health Department				1	
Counseling					
Clergymen	13	8	3	6	
Legal Aid or lawyer	5	3			
Dispensary Social Service	2			1	
Hospital social service	1		16	13	4
School services	3	1	2		1
Americanization League	1				
Employment					
Employer	2	1	1		
Income maintenance					
Welfare		4		6	3
Housing authority		1	1	1	
Correction					
Children's Court	2				
Judge	2				

Problems Presented

Clients approaching the Family Agency presented somewhat different problems at the two time periods. As Table A-3 shows, a larger proportion of the 1961 applicants to the

Table A-3. PROBLEMS PRESENTED TO THE FAMILY
AGENCY, 1956, 1961

Problem category	No.		%	
	1956	1961	1956	1961
All clients	**77**	**45**	**100.0**	**100.0**
Transition states	*38*	*14*	*49.4*	*31.1*
Child behavior	4	4	5.2	8.9
Adolescent behavior	11	4	14.3	8.9
Adult maladjustment		2		4.4
Marital maladjustment	23	4	29.9	8.9
Role failure	*36*	*29*	*46.8*	*64.4*
Inadequate wives and mothers	7	4	9.1	8.9
Emotionally disturbed children		4		8.9
Evidence of crime	1	2	1.3	4.4
Marital breakdown	26	16	33.8	35.6
Economic inadequacy	2	3	2.6	6.7
Contingencies	*3*	*2*	*3.9*	*4.4*
Child health	2		2.6	
Child placement		1		2.2
Adult health	1		1.3	
Insufficient income		1		2.2

agency were categorized as role failures, and a proportionately smaller number as transition states. The proportion of
contingent problems was unchanged. These differences, however, do not quite reach significance. In the Planned Parenthood Center, for the reasons given in Chapter 5, the
patients' problems could not be classified, but the number of
children, occupation, and color of the patient group were
stable for the three time periods, as Table A-4 shows.

Service Given

LENGTH OF SERVICE

The more selective intake policy of the Family Agency
resulted in a significantly greater proportion of the 1961 than
1956 clients either leaving the agency after no more than one
casework interview or remaining for long-term counseling
(Table A-5). Although the agency was selecting clients for
casework services more carefully, no relationship between the
clients' problems and length of service could be found.

Table A-4. NUMBER OF CHILDREN, OCCUPATION, AND COLOR
OF PLANNED PARENTHOOD PATIENTS, 1959, 1962, 1965

Number of children and occupation	Nonwhite			White		
	1959	1962	1965	1959	1962	1965
All patients	**23**	**19**	**23**	**80**	**84**	**80**
0–3 children	*8*	*5*	*15*	*60*	*51*	*56*
Students				15	5	10
White-collar				11	9	13
Blue-collar	6	3	10	32	35	32
Welfare recipient[a]	2	2	5	2	2	1
4+ children	*15*	*14*	*8*	*20*	*33*	*24*
White-collar	1			2	2	3
Blue-collar	7	11	2	15	25	17
Welfare recipient	7	3	6	3	6	4

[a] Defined as in receipt of welfare over a long period.

Table A-5. LENGTH OF SERVICE, FAMILY AGENCY, 1956, 1961

Number of interviews	Clients attending			
	No.		*%*	
	1956	1961	1956	1961
All clients	*77*	*45*	*100.0*	*100.0*
Intake only	21[a]	18[a]	27.3	40.0
2 interviews	6[a]	6[a]	7.8	13.3
3–4	11	4	14.3	8.9
5–6	10	5	13.0	11.1
7–8	19	3	24.7	6.7
9+	10[a]	9[a]	13.0	20.0

[a] More 1961 than 1956 clients either dropped out after 2 interviews or remained for 9 or more interviews. ($\chi^2 = 7.46$; d.f. $= 2$, $.05 > P > .02$.)

The 1965 study group at the Planned Parenthood Center had not been at risk long enough for comparison, but there was no difference in the agency's holding power during the 1959–62 period, as Table A-6 shows.

INTERAGENCY CONTACTS

The most striking difference shown over the five-year period by the Family Agency was the decrease in the number of contacts made with other agencies for eligibility checking, information exchange, or arrangements (Table A-7). In

Table A-6. CASES REMAINING OPEN FOUR YEARS AFTER
INTAKE, PLANNED PARENTHOOD, 1959, 1962[a]

Color and occupation	Total		% open four years after	
	1959	1962	1959	1962
All patients	**103**	**103**	**42.7**	**35.9**
Nonwhite	*23*	*19*	*65.2*	*68.4*
White-collar	1	0	100.0	0.0
Blue-collar	13	14	69.2	64.3
Welfare recipient	9	5	55.6	80.0
White	*80*	*84*	*36.3*	*28.6*
Students	15	5	26.7	0.0
White-collar	13	11	23.1	27.3
Blue-collar	47	60	44.7	33.3
Welfare recipient	5	8	20.0	12.5

[a] 1965 patients were not at risk long enough to allow a comparison.

1956, 57 contacts with 24 agencies on behalf of 32 of 77 clients were made. In this pattern of interaction, the Family Agency closely resembled the medical social work agency whose core service was the mobilization of outside resources. By 1961, following its shift to a more exclusively casework service, the number of outside contacts made by the agency dropped to nine contacts with five agencies regarding eight clients. These differences are all statistically significant, and they are not concentrated in any one problem category. During this period, the Planned Parenthood Center continued to work without benefit of collaboration with other agencies (Table A-7).

OUT-REFERRAL

Allied to the shift in interagency contacts was the Family Agency's increased numbers of out-referrals to a wider range of agencies (Table A-8). Ten of the 45 1961 clients were referred to six agencies compared to five of the 1956 clients who were referred to four agencies. The difference in the number of clients referred is statistically significant. The reduction in interagency collaboration combined with this increased referral rate reflected the agency's sharpening concept of its casework role.

Table A-7. INTERAGENCY RELATIONSHIPS REGARDING FAMILY AGENCY CLIENTS, 1956, 1961[a] AND PLANNED PARENTHOOD PATIENTS, 1959, 1962

	Information, eligibility, and arrangements			
	Family Agency		*Planned Parenthood*	
Agency contacted	1956	1961	1959	1962
All clients	**77**	**45**	**103**	**103**
Without contacts	45	37	98	101
With contacts	32	8	5	2
All contacts	*57*	*9*	*5*	*2*
Medical				
Private physician	2			
Planned Parenthood, elsewhere	1		4	
T.B. sanitarium	1			
Mental health clinic	3	2		
Private psychiatrist	15			
Counseling				
Clergyman	1			
Legal Aid or lawyer	3	1		
Alcoholism services	1			
School services	6	4		
Family agency elsewhere	3		1	
Hospital social service	1			
Private psychologist		1		
Recreation				
Children's camp	1			
Neighborhood center	1			
Employment				
N.Y.S. Employment Service	1			
Vocational Rehabilitation	1			
Income maintenance				
Social welfare	4			1
Salvation Army	1			
Red Cross	2			
Travelers Aid	1			
Housing Authority				1
Institutions				
Children's Homes	2			
Psychiatric hospital	2			
Correction				
Children's Court	2	1		
Police	1			
Judge	1			

[a] The Family Agency made fewer contacts in 1961 than 1956. ($\chi^2 = 15.42$; d.f. = 1; P < .01.) The Family Agency made contact with fewer agencies in 1961 than 1956. ($\chi^2 = 4.82$, d.f. = 1, .05 > P > .02.) Contacts were made on behalf of fewer clients in 1961 than 1956. ($\chi^2 = 6.25$, d.f. = 1, .02 > P > .01.)

Table A-8. REFERRAL TARGET OF CLIENTS AND PATIENTS AT
DIFFERENT TIMES FROM FAMILY AGENCY AND SYRACUSE
PLANNED PARENTHOOD CENTER

Referral target	Family Agency		Planned Parenthood		
	1956	1961	1959	1962	1965
All clients and patients	*77*	*45*	*103*	*103*	*103*
Not referred	72	35	98	100	95
Referred	5[a]	10[a]	5	3	8
All referrals	*5*	*13*	*5*	*3*	*8*
Medical					
Private physician				1	2
Dispensary			2		3
Planned Parenthood			3	1	3
Psychiatric facility	2	8			
Counseling					
Legal Aid or lawyer	1	1			
School services		1			
Alcoholics Anony-					
mous		1			
Private psychologist				1	
Recreation					
Neighborhood center	1				
Employment					
N.Y.S. Employment					
Office		1			
Income maintenance					
Welfare		1			
Institutions					
Children's shelters	1				

[a] Proportionately more clients were referred in 1961 than 1956. ($x^2 = 5.14$; d.f. = 1; $.05 > P > .02$.)

In 1961, unlike 1956, out-referrals were concentrated
among those who had intake interviews only (9 out of 18,
compared with 2 out of 21), suggesting that the agency's policy of selection of cases was resulting in a more efficient sorting and allocation of clients at intake. This suggestion is made
more plausible by the fact that most of these clients were actively referred rather than steered to other services. Once
again, the Planned Parenthood Center presented a stable picture of a sprinkling of referrals to other medical facilities.

In summary, the Family Agency's changed policy and

practice were reflected in more out-referrals at the point of intake to a greater variety of target agencies and fewer inter-agency collaborations. No similar changes could be found in the more stable Planned Parenthood Center. In view of this finding and because changes in other parts of the system were not explored, the possibility of some distortion in a picture of the regulative system presented as if the agencies had been studied synchronically should be borne in mind. Although it is unlikely that any other agency showed as sharp a change in the two years of the study as the Family Agency did in the five-year span reported on here, it is possible that this could have happened. Furthermore, the over-all effect of changes in agency practice can vary depending on how these practices are linked to other parts of the system. For example, if the Planned Parenthood Center had doubled its contacts, it would still have been an isolated agency, but if the Social Service Department of the Dispensary had doubled its activity, some other agencies would probably have had to make changes to accommodate to the difference.

Although it is impossible to decide how much change is too much for the purpose of structural analyses, the goal of this comparison has been to give an indication of the limits of stability in the system.

REFERENCE

Krauwell, H. J., 1966. "Some Considerations of the Treatment of Alcoholics and Others," Paper prepared for an International Research Seminar on Evaluation of Community Mental Health Programs, Warrenton, Virginia, May 17–20.

APPENDIX B

SOURCES OF ERROR:
INCIDENCE VERSUS PREVALENCE

The people who approach an agency in any given period of time can be called its incidence population, and their numbers will give some indication of the rate at which the problem in which that agency specializes is arising in the population during that period. The people who are already in care can be called the prevalence population, and they represent the amount of disorder of the kind cared for in that agency prevalent at any given time. When a disorder is acute, epidemic, and short-lived, like German measles, the incidence and the prevalence tend to be almost the same because the remission rate is so high that there are not many more people ill with the disease at any given moment than are at that moment becoming ill. When a disorder is chronic and runs a long course, like schizophrenia, the prevalence is many times greater than the incidence because although few people become ill with this disease, a considerable number have it at any given moment. This difference was dramatically evident in the state mental hospitals during the first half of this century when the rate of admission of schizophrenics was low but a large proportion of the residents of the custodial wards of the hospitals were suffering from this long-term, chronic illness.

The studies in this series have been concerned only with incidence populations, the study groups being intercepted as they applied for service. Because of this, there was an unknown amount of discrepancy between the characteristics of the clients already in the care of the various agencies and those approaching them. For most of the study agencies, this difference could not be estimated, but in two agencies it was known to exist: in the Planned Parenthood Center, the group of women who remained in care was different from those who had used the agency for a time and then left (Table 5-4), and it was known that the applicant group at the Welfare Department was not so severely disordered as the group already in care (Moreland Commission, 1963). In order to get a further idea of the relationship between these two kinds of populations, comparisons were made in two agencies—the Dispensary's Social Service and the Mission Shelter—both with a group of clients already in care.

The Dispensary's Social Service

The data from the Social Service Department of the Dispensary were collected by the agency workers themselves, who kept logs of their daily activities (Chapter 11). These logs included information about 48 clients who both visited the agency during the study period and were in care at the time that the observations began. Because these clients had been referred for medically related problems and because they had been in care for variable lengths of time, it was assumed that the group would include more clients with more serious problems than the incidence group of applicants, which contained a large proportion of people requiring such simple arrangements as payment for children's glasses. This assumption turned out to be totally unfounded, as Table B-1 shows. Seven client characteristics were considered, and in no case

Table B-1. COMPARISON OF SELECTED CHARACTERISTICS OF 88 APPLICANTS TO THE SOCIAL SERVICE DEPARTMENT OF THE DISPENSARY WITH THOSE OF 48 CLIENTS ALREADY IN CARE

Characteristics	Total	No. affected		% affected	
		Appli-cants	*In care*	*Appli-cants*	*In care*
All clients	**136**	**88**	**48**	**64.7**	**35.3**
Welfare history	*117*	74	43	63.2	36.8
Mental hospitalization	*36*	22	14	61.1	38.9
Placement of children	*18*	11	7	61.1	38.9
Problem type					
Role failure	*33*	20	13	60.6	39.4
Transition state	*16*	10	6	62.5	37.5
Contingency	*87*	58	29	66.7	33.3
Trouble score 2–3	*46*	30	16	65.2	34.8
Nonmarried	*78*	50	28	64.1	35.9
Over 60 years	*26*	18	8	69.2	30.8

did the proportions with the characteristics differ by more than 5 per cent from that which would have been expected. Because more than three-quarters of the agency's clients were receiving service, it can only be concluded that this agency was dealing with acute, perhaps concrete, problems that could be solved reasonably quickly, and that the impression of the field workers that there was always a group of "old timers" waiting to see "their worker" must have been in error. In view of the small numbers involved, this unexpected finding deserves further study.

The Mission Shelter

It was assumed that the transients applying to the Mission Shelter would be entirely different from the resident or prevalence group. Men coming into the Mission for the night were believed to include both derelicts and working men whose jobs had taken them away from home. The residents, in contrast, were believed to be homeless men who had failed in the outside world but who had made a reasonably permanent adjustment to working in the Mission's factory or on its maintenance crews. Both the field observations and the reports of the staff suggested these differences, but as Table B-2 shows, of the four characteristics compared, two of which, birthplace and the naming of next-of-kin, might reasonably

Table B-2. COMPARISON OF SELECTED CHARACTERISTICS OF 63 APPLICANTS TO THE MISSION SHELTER AND 34 PERMANENT RESIDENTS

Characteristics	Total	No. affected		% affected	
		Appli-cants	Resi-dents	Appli-cants	Resi-dents
All clients	**97**	*63*	*34*	*64.9*	*35.1*
Mental hospitalization	*14*	6	8	42.9	57.1
No next-of-kin	*46*	32	14	69.6	30.4
Born outside New York State	*49*	35	14	71.4	28.6
Age					
Under 40	*22*	17	5	77.3	22.7
40–59	*58*	40	18	69.0	31.0
60–over	*17*	6[a]	11[a]	35.3	64.7

[a] A greater proportion of the Mission Shelter residents than of the applicants were over 60 years of age. ($\chi^2 = 6.4$; d.f. = 1; $.02 > P > .01$.)

be expected to indicate transience, the residents differed only in having a higher proportion of men over 60 years of age among them. None of the differences in the other characteristics, history of mental hospitalization, listing no next-of-kin in the Mission registry, and being born outside New York State, reached statistical significance.

In summary, a Level I service, the Mission Shelter, showed no differences, for the characteristics that could be compared, between the incidence and prevalence groups. The Planned Parenthood Center, a Level II agency, was found to be keeping more Negro than white women in care when occupation was held constant, and therefore it had more Negroes in its prevalence group. In Level III, the Welfare Department was known to have a more seriously disordered prevalence than incidence group, but no differences could be found in the Dispensary's Social Service between the two client groups.

The lack of consistency among all these findings suggests that further study of the rate at which agencies handle clients would throw light on both the general problem of the residual groups that are said to "silt up" in the public agencies and the social concomitants of decisions to keep or eject various kinds of clients. These findings also draw attention to the fact that the division of labor described in this study refers to the treatment only of incoming or incidence population and not of those clients and patients already in care.

REFERENCE

Moreland Commission, 1963. *Public Welfare in the State of New York,* Albany, New York.

NAME INDEX

SUBJECT INDEX

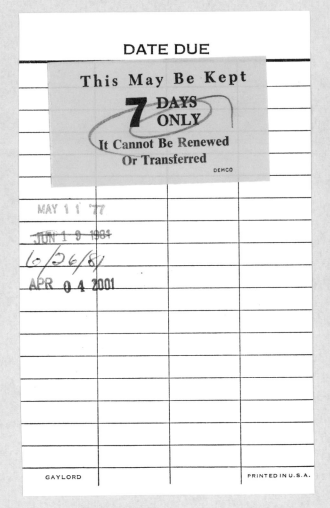